"THE SHAM SQUIRE";

AND

THE INFORMERS

OF

1798.

WITH A VIEW OF THEIR CONTEMPORARIES.

TO WHICH ARE ADDED

Jottings about Ireland Seventy Years ago.

BY

WILLIAM JOHN FITZ-PATRICK, J.P.,

BIOGRAPHER OF BISHOP DOYLE, LORD CLONCURRY, LADY MORGAN, ETC.

"Truth is stranger than fiction".

LONDON:

JOHN CAMDEN HOTTEN, 74 PICCADILLY.

DUBLIN: W. B. KELLY, 8 GRAFTON STREET.

1866.

THE RIGHT HON. THOMAS O'HAGAN,

JUSTICE OF THE COURT OF COMMON PLEAS, AND ONE
HER MAJESTY'S MOST HONOURABLE PRIVY COUNCIL
IN IRELAND.

DEAR JUDGE O'HAGAN,

Contrasts are often pleasant and instructive.
could not make a better one than in dedicating
him who dignifies the judgment seat by the pur
of his justice and the soundness of his law, a bo
demonstrative of the way in which both were :
vestied in bad times by unconstitutional judges.'

It may seem strange, that a man who has alrea
written the lives of sundry Irish worthies, sho
touch, even with stigma, the life of one eminen
unworthy. But we must not forget that Plutar
the Prince of Biographers and Moral Philosophe
in his introduction to the Life of Demetrius Po

* See pages 96, 110-13, 196, etc.

cises, to be followed by and compared with that of Antony the Triumvir—two personages remarkable for their vices, says: "We shall behold and imitate the virtuous with greater attention, if we be not entirely unacquainted with the characters of the vicious and the infamous".

Owing to the recently discovered Fenian Conspiracy, and the attention which it has excited, this work possesses, perhaps, more than ordinary interest; but, lest it should be supposed that I was influenced in my choice of the subject by its aptness to existing circumstances, I am bound to add, that the book was written, and in great part printed, before the Fenian movement obtained notoriety.

With a cordial appreciation of your public and private worth, and thanking you for allowing me to dedicate this book to you,

I beg to remain, dear Judge O'Hagan,

Yours very faithfully,

WILLIAM JOHN FITZ-PATRICK.

Kilmacud Manor, Stillorgan,
Nov. 1st, 1865.

PREFACE.

A PAMPHLET which forms but a small part of the present work appeared in 1859. It excited considerable attention, and has been, for some years, quite out of print. Early in the present year, several letters and leaders appeared in an influential print, desiring particulars of Francis Higgins, and the fate of his bequests. This induced me to resume my exploration of the eventful period in question, and the results of that research are now offered to the public.

The *Irish Times* of January the 11th, 1865, in a third leading article on the subject, says:

" A scarce pamphlet has been kindly forwarded to us, compiled by Mr. Fitzpatrick, the biographer of Lady Morgan, Bishop Doyle, etc. The subject is the Francis Higgins, who bequeathed £1,000 to be vested in land for the liberation of poor prisoners in the Four Courts Marshalsea, Dublin. The work contains copies of informations taken from the records of the courts of law, passages from long-forgotten histories, extracts from the newspapers and satirical poetry which startled Dublin eighty years ago, and clauses from the authenticated will of Francis Higgins. The picture drawn, and truthfully drawn, of the society of Dublin at that period, is anything but edifying. Riots, tumults, abduction of heiresses, the abuse of the forms of justice for the perpetration of wrong, corruption openly employed by the government of the day, the passionate resistance and cowardly submission of parliament,—these are the prominent features of the picture. But throughout the whole appears the terrible figure of Francis Higgins, whose history would furnish materials for twenty sensation novels. We stand amazed at discovering that one man, apparently endowed with no great talent, should have acted as he did with impunity even in that wild time, and been appointed to dispense the justice he had outraged".

The rest of the article urges that a royal commission should be appointed to inquire into the condition and revenues of the charities bequeathed by Higgins, Webb, and others, and expresses a hope that parliament will at once take the matter in hand.

The original object, however, of the pamphlet which has suggested the present work—was to remove a misapprehension which pervaded almost the entire reviewing press of Great Britain and Ireland.

For sixty-one years the name of the person who received the Government reward of £1,000 for the betrayal of Lord Edward Fitzgerald remained an impenetrable mystery, although historians have devoted much time and labour in seeking to discover it. Among other revelations, recently published in the Cornwallis Papers, we find that "Francis Higgins, proprietor of the *Freeman's Journal*", was the person who gave all the information which led to the arrest and death of the Patriot Chief. In the following pages, however, it will appear that Higgins was not the actual Betrayer, but the employer of the Betrayer, a much respected "gentleman", who, although in receipt for forty-five years of a Pension—the price of Lord Edward's blood—was not suspected of the treachery.

The *Athenæum*, after justly reprobating some of the duplicity practised in 1798, observed:

" The second item was scarcely less disgusting. The *Freeman's Journal* was a patriotic print, and advocated the popular cause, and its proprietor earned blood-money by hunting down the unfortunate Lord Edward Fitzgerald !"

" Truth is stranger than fiction", however; and the *Freeman's Journal*, when owned by Higgins, was not only the open and notorious organ of the then corrupt government, but the most violent assailant of the popular party in Ireland.

The *Times*, noticing the United Irishmen, said:

" They believed themselves to be embarked in a noble cause, and were cheered on the path that led to martyrdom by the spirit-stirring effusions of a press which felt their wrongs, shared their sentiments, and deplored their misfortunes. Alas! the press that encouraged was no more free from the influence of government than the advocate who defended them. Francis Higgins, proprietor of the *Freeman's Journal*, was the person who procured all the intelligence about Lord Edward Fitzgerald. When we reflect that the *Freeman's Journal* was a favourite organ of the United Irishmen,* that in that capacity it must have received

* The organ of the United Irishmen was the *Press*; and Higgins, who then published a tri-weekly paper, came out every Tuesday, Thursday, and Saturday, with his " thundering" denunciations of the "*disaffected*" prints of the " turbulent traitors" and " malign incendiaries", who conspired with " French agents" to seduce Higgins's ." countrymen" into treasonable plots against the "*able, wise, and clement*" government of the day. Here is the opening of a Higgins leader:—
" It is with the most heartfelt regret that we find the *lenity* which has been extended to the abettors of treason and rebellion has had no permanent effect, and that the temporary obedience to the laws which it produced has proceeded more from fear and inability to do mischief than from a *sense of gratitude.* . . .
. . . Those wretched remains of United Irishmen, worked on by the *arts of incendiaries* and French agents. . . . The *violence and outrages* of these deluded wretches can have but a

much secret and dangerous information, and that all this information was already bargained for and sold to the Irish government before it was given, we can appreciate at once the refinement of its policy, and the snares and pitfalls among which the path of an Irish conspirator is laid".

The misapprehension under which the para-graphs of the *Times* and *Athenæum* were written, found a prompt echo in the *Mail, Nation, Post,* and other influential Irish journals. The *Nation* gave it to be understood that Higgins, having become a secret traitor to his party, published "next morning thundering articles against the scoundrels who betrayed the illustrious Patriot"; and in a subsequent article added: "What fouler treachery was ever practised than the subornation of the journals and the writers in whom the people placed a mistaken confidence, whereby the unsuspecting victims were made to cram a mine for their own destruction!"

These statements excited a considerable sensation. The Irish provincial press reiterated them, and locally fanned the flame. The *Meath People*, in an article headed, "Who does the government work?" after alluding to Higgins, said: "Shame, shame for ever on the recreant who had patriotism on his pen point, and treason to the country in his heart!" I felt that this statement, if unrefuted, would soon find its way into the permanent page of Irish and European history.

Having ascertained, on inquiry, the groundlessness

very short-lived existence, as, *fortunately*, we have in this country *troops sufficient to crush* any renewed effort at rebellion. Major Sirr discovered a brace of loaded pistols, some powder, *and a pike* of the *revolutionary description*, such as were used by *the rebels in their* atrocities. By this day's search another *treasonable conspiracy* has been happily developed".

of the charge of duplicity imputed to the *Freeman's Journal* in 1798; and believing that those more legitimately concerned were cognizant to the same extent, I looked forward, for many days, to some editorial statement which would have the effect of dispelling the erroneous impression. But I found, that so confidently had this charge of duplicity against the *Freeman* been rung, that its present editors had themselves begun to regard it as not wholly unfounded. A short letter from me, explanatory of the real facts, was therefore gladly accepted by the conductor of the *Freeman's Journal*, who introduced it in the following words, less by an observation too complimentary to me:—

"We publish to-day a most interesting letter from William John Fitz-Patrick. The sad fate of the gallant Lord Edward excited peculiar and permanent interest in the minds of all who prized chivalry and patriotism; and when the Cornwallis papers disclosed the name of the government agent who had tracked the noble chief to his doom, a host of reviewers, ignorant of the history of the time, and anxious only to cast a slur on the patriots of a by-gone century, wrote beautiful romances about the betrayer of Lord Edward. The reviewers, without exception, have represented Higgins as the confidant of the United Irishmen—as a 'patriotic' journalist, who sustained the popular party with his pen, and sold them for Castle gold. Mr. Fitzpatrick dissipates the romance by showing who and what Higgins was—that he was the public and undisguised agent of the English government—that his journal, instead of being 'patriotic', or even friendly to the United Irishmen, was the constant vehicle of the most virulent assaults upon their character and motives—that he was the ally and *friend of the* notorious John Scott—*that, as a journalist, he was the* panegyrist of the notorious Sirr,

and his colleague, Swan—and that he never mentioned
the name of an Irish patriot—of Lord Edward, O'Connor, Teeling, or their friends—without some such insulting prefix as ' traitor', ' wretch', ' conspirator', ' in-
cendiary', while the government that stimulated the revolt, in order to carry the Union, is lauded as ' able',
' wise', ' humane', and ' lenient'! These events are
now more than half a century old ; but, though nearly
two generations have passed away since Higgins received his blood-money, it is, as justly remarked by
Mr. Fitzpatrick, gratifying to have direct evidence that
the many high-minded and honourable men who were,
from time to time, suspected for treachery to their
chief, were innocent of his blood".

Having, in the letter thus referred to by the
Freeman, glanced rapidly at a few of the more startling incidents in the life of the once famous, but
long forgotten " Sham Squire", which elicited expressions of surprise, and even of incredulity, I
conceived that I was called upon to give his history more in detail, and with a larger array of
authorities than I had previously leisure or space to
bring forward. From the original object of this
book I have in the present edition wandered, by
pressing into the mosaic many curious *morceaux*
illustrative of the history of the time, while in the
appendix will be found some interesting memora-
bilia, which could not, without injury to artistic
effect, appear in the text.

Kilmacud Manor, Stillorgan,
    February 20th, 1865.

THE SHAM SQUIRE.

CHAPTER I.

Early Struggles and Stratagems of the Sham Squire.—How to catch an Heiress.—Judge Robinson.—John Philpot Curran.—The Black Dog Prison. — Honesty not always the best policy!—Uprise of the Sham Squire.—Lord Chief Justice Clonmel.—Irish Administrations of Lord Temple and the Duke of Rutland.

IN the year of our Lord 1756, a bare-legged boy with cunning eyes might be seen carrying pewter quarts in Fishamble Street,* Dublin, then a popular locality, owing to the continual ridottos, concerts, and feats of magic, which made the old Music Hall an object of attraction. This bare-legged boy became the subsequently notorious Justice Higgins, or as he was more frequently styled, the Sham Squire. Fishamble Street, as the scene of his *debut*, is mentioned in a file of the *Dublin Evening Post* for 1789; and this account we find corroborated by a traditional anecdote which Mr. R—— of Dublin has communicated, on the authority of his late grandmother, who often told him how she remembered her father, a provision merchant in Fishamble Street, employing Higgins, then a bare-footed lad, to sweep the flags in front of his door.

* *Dublin Evening Post,* No. 1789.

Our adventurer was the only survivor of a large family of brothers and sisters, the children of humble people named Patrick and Mary Higgins, who died about the year 1760, and were interred* in Kilbarrack churchyard, near Howth. They are said to have migrated from Downpatrick, and we learn from the same authority that their real name was M'Quignan.† He himself was born in a cellar in Dublin, and while yet of tender years, became successively " errand boy, shoeblack, and waiter in a porter house".

The number of times which Higgins used his broom, or shouldered pewter pots, would be uninteresting to enumerate, and unprofitable to record. Passing over a few years occupied in this manner, we shall reintroduce Mr. Higgins to the reader, discharging his duties as a " hackney writing clerk" in the office of Daniel Bourne, attorney-at-law, Patrick's Close, Dublin.‡ He was born a Roman Catholic, but he had now read his recantation, as appears from the *Official Register of Conversions* preserved in the Record Tower, Dublin Castle.§ Nevertheless, he failed to rise in the social scale. Having become a perfect master of scrivenery, a strong temptation smote him to turn his talent for caligraphy to some more substantial account

* Will of Francis Higgins, Prerogative Court, Dublin.
† *Dublin Evening Post*, No. 1837.
‡ *Dublin Evening Post*, No. 1765.
§ The same book, which seems unknown to most Irish historical and biographical writers, contains the names of Barry Yelverton, afterwards Lord Avonmore, Leonard MacNally, and several other men of mark. Thanks to the energy of Sir Bernard Burke, the courteous and efficient custodian of the Records, many valuable MSS., of which the existence was *previously almost* unknown, are constantly turning up, to the *great pleasure* and profit of historical students.

than £16 per annum, the general salary of hackney writing clerks in those days.* Higgins had great ambition, but without money and connexion he was powerless. Accordingly, to gain these ends, we find him in 1766 forging with his cunning brain and ready hand a series of legal instruments purporting to show that he was not only a man of large landed property, but in the enjoyment of an office of some importance under the government. Trusting to his tact for complete success, Higgins, full of daring, sought Father Shortall, and on his knees hypocritically declared himself a convert to the Roman Catholic Church. The iron pressure of the Penal Code had not then received its first relaxation; Catholics were daily conforming to the Establishment; Father Shortall regarded Mr. Higgins's case as a very interesting and touching one, and he affectionately received the convert squire into the heaving bosom of the suffering Church of Ireland. "And now, holy father", said the neophyte, "I must implore of you to keep my conversion secret. My parent has got a property of £3,000 a-year, and if this matter transpires I shall be disinherited". The good pastor assured him that he would be as silent as the grave; he gave him his blessing, and Higgins retired, hugging himself in his dexterity, and offering mental congratulations on the prospect that began to open to his future success. When this religous intercourse had continued for some time, Higgins told his spiritual adviser that the ease of his soul was such as induced him humbly to hope that the Almighty had accepted the sincerity of his repentance. "If anything be now wanting to my

* *Faulkner's Dublin Journal*, January 24th, 1767.

complete happiness", he added, "it is an amiable wife of the true religion, whose bright example will serve to keep my frail resolutions firm; as to the amount of fortune, it is an object of little or no consideration, for, as you are aware, my means will be ample".[*] His engaging manner won the heart of Father Shortall, who resolved and avowed to befriend him as far as in his power lay. Duped by the hypocrisy of our adventurer, the unsuspecting priest introduced him to the family of an eminent Catholic merchant named Archer, who resided in Thomas Street.

To strengthen his footing, Higgins ordered some goods from Mr. Archer, and requested that they might be sent to 76 Stephen's Green, the house of his uncle, the then celebrated Counsellor Harward. Mr. Archer treated his visitor with the respect due to the nephew and, as it seemed, the heir presumptive of that eminent lawyer. The approach to deformity of Higgins's person had made Miss Archer shrink from his attentions; but her parents, who rejoiced at the prospect of an alliance so apparently advantageous, sternly overruled their daughter's reluctance. The intimacy gradually grew. Higgins accompanied Mr. Archer and his daughter on a country excursion; seated in a noddy they returned to town through Stephen's Green, and in passing Mr. Harward's house, Higgins in a loud tone expressed a hope to some person at the door that his uncle's health continued to convalesce.[†] When too late Mr. Archer discovered that no possible relationship existed between his hopeful son-in-law and the old counsellor.

[*] *Sketches of Irish Political Characters.* By Henry Mac Dougall, *M.A., T.C.D.* Lond. 1799, p. 182.
[†] *Tradition* communicated by the late Very Rev. Monsig. Yore.

It is also traditionally stated by Mr. R——, of Dublin, that Higgins turned to profitable account an intimacy which he had formed with the servants of one of the judges. His lordship having gone on circuit, a perfect "high life below stairs" was performed in his absence; and Higgins, to promote the progress of his scheme, succeeded in persuading his friend, the coachman, to drive him to a few places in the judicial carriage.

The imposture was too well planned to fail; but let us allow the heart-broken father to tell the tragic tale in his own words.

"*County of the City* } The examination of William Archer,
of Dublin, to wit. } of Dublin, merchant, who being duly sworn and examined, saith, that on the 9th day of November [1766] last, one Francis Higgins, who this examinant now hears and believes to be a common hackney writing clerk, came to the house of this examinant in company with a clergyman of the Church of Rome,*

* I am indebted to John Cornelius O'Callaghan, Esq., the able author of *The Green Book*, and historian of *The Irish Brigades in the Service of France*, for the following tradition, which he has obligingly taken down from the lips of an octogenarian relative:

"1 Upper Rutland Street,
"January 16th, 1865.

"The circumstance respecting the 'Sham Squire' to which I alluded, was as follows:—The Rev. Mr. Shortall (I believe a Jesuit) became acquainted with Higgins through the medium of religion; the fellow having pretended to become a convert to the Catholic Church, and even so zealous a one, as to confess himself every Saturday to that gentleman, in order to receive the Blessed Sacrament the following day! This having gone on for some time, Mr. Shortall formed a high opinion of Higgins, and spoke of him in such terms to the parents of the young lady he was designing to marry, that they were proportionately influenced in his favour. After the 'fatal marriage' Mr. Shortall was sent to Cork, and was introduced there *to my maternal* grandmother and her sisters, to and was introduced as a man possessing lands in the county of Down, to the amount of £250 per annum, which he, the said Francis Higgins, pretended to this examinant, in order to deceive and cheat him; and also that he was in considerable employ in the revenue; and that he was entitled to a large property on the death of William Harward, Esq., who the said Higgins alleged was his guardian and had adopted him. In a few days after this introduction (during which time he paid his addresses to Miss Maryanne Archer, the daughter of this examinant) he produced a state of a case, all of his own handwriting, saying, that he was entitled to the lands of Ballyveabeg, Islang, Ballahanera, and Dansfort, in the county of Down; and the more effectually to de ceive and cheat this examinant and his daughter, Higgins had at the foot thereof obtained the legal opinion of the said William Harward, Esq., that he was entitled to said lands under a will mentioned to be made in said case. Higgins, in order to deceive this examinant, and to induce him to consent to a marriage with his daughter, agreed to settle £1,500 on her, and informed examinant that if said marriage was not speedily performed, his guardian would force him to take the oath to qualify him to become an attorney, which he could not think of, as he pretended to be of the contrary opinion; and that as to the title deeds of said lands, he could not then come at them, being lodged, as he pretended, with William Harward, Esq. But that if examinant thought proper, he would open a window in William Harward's house, in order to come at said deeds, let what would be the consequences. Examinant was advised not to insist on said measure, and therefore

whom he used to mention how bitterly he regretted having been so imposed upon. The story made such an impression on —— as a child, that, shortly after she came to Dublin, she went to see the ' Sham Squire's' tomb, in Kilbarrack churchyard.

"I am, most sincerely yours,

"JOHN CORNLS. O'CALLAGHAN".

·waived it; and relying on the many assertions and representations of the said Higgins, and of his being a person of consideration and property, and particularly having great confidence in the opinion of so eminent a lawyer as William Harward, this examinant having found on inquiry the same was the handwriting of Harward, agreed to give Higgins £600 as a portion with examinant's daughter, and one half of this examinant's substance at his death, which he believes may amount to *a considerable sum*, and executed writings for the performance of said agreement. And upon said marriage Higgins perfected a deed, and thereby agreed to settle the lands above mentioned on the issue of said marriage, together with £1,500 on examinant's daughter. Soon after the marriage, the examinant being informed of the fraud, he made inquiries into the matters so represented by the said Higgins to facilitate said fraud, and the examinant found that there was not the least colour of truth in any of the pretensions or suggestions so made by Higgins, and that he was not entitled to a foot of land, either in this kingdom or elsewhere, nor of any personal property, nor hath he any employment in the revenue or otherwise. Notwithstanding the repeated assurances of the said Higgins, and the said several pretences to his being a person of fortune or of business, he now appears to be a person of low and indigent circumstances, of infamous life and character,* and that he supported himself by the craft of a cheat and impostor; nor is the said William Harward either guardian or any way related to Higgins, as this examinant is informed and verily believes".

Mr. Harward, whose name has been frequently

* From a contemporary publication, *Irish Political Characters*, p. 180, we learn that when Higgins acted as an attorney's clerk his talents were not confined exclusively to the desk. " His master's pleasures found an attentive minister in Sham, and Sham *found additional* profits in his master's pleasures".

2

mentioned, became a member of the Irish bar in Michaelmas term, 1718, and was the contemporary of Malone, Dennis, Lord Tracton, and Mr. Fitzgibbon, father of Lord Clare, and sat for some years in the Irish Parliament. At the period when Higgins took such strange liberties with his name, Mr. Harward was in an infirm state of health; he died, childless, in 1772.

The biographer of Charlemont mentions Harward as " deservedly celebrated for the acuteness of his understanding, his pleasantry, and his original wit". He would seem, indeed, to have been fonder of Joe Miller than of Blackstone. We find the following anecdote in the recently published life of Edmund Malone:—

" Harward, the Irish lawyer, with the help of a great brogue, a peculiar cough, or long h-e-m, was sometimes happy in a retort. Harward had read a great deal of law, but it was all a confused mass; he had little judgment. Having, however, made one of his best harangues, and stated, as he usually did, a great deal of *doubtful* law, which yet he thought very sound, Lord Chief Justice Clayton, who, though a most ignorant boor, had got the common black-letter of Westminster Hall pretty ready, as soon as Harward had done, exclaimed, ' You do n't suppose, Mr. Harward, that I take this to be law?' ' Indeed, my lord', replied Harward, with his usual shrug and cough, ' I do n't suppose you do !' "

The following is a copy of the true bill found by the grand jury against Higgins:

"County of the City } The jurors for our Lord the King, *of Dublin, to wit.* } upon their oath, say that Francis *Higgins,* of Dublin, yeoman, being a person of evil

name, fame, and dishonest conversation, and a common deceiver and cheat of the liege subjects of our said Lord, and not minding to gain his livelihood by truth and honest labour, but devising to cheat, cozen, and defraud William Archer of his moneys, fortune, and substance, for support of the profligate life of him, the said Francis Higgins, and with intent to obtain Mary-anne Archer in marriage, and to aggrieve, impoverish, and ruin her, and with intent to impoverish the said William Archer, his wife, and all his family, by wicked, false, and deceitful pretences, on the 19th November, in the seventh year of the reign of King George III., and on divers other days and times, with force and arms, at Dublin, in the parish of St. Michael, the more fully to complete and perpetrate the said wicked intentions and contrivances, did fraudulently pretend to the said William Archer that—[here the facts are again recited in detail]. The said F. Higgins, by the same wicked pretences, procured Maryanne Archer to be given in marriage to him, to the great damage of the said William Archer, to the great discomfort, prejudice, injury, and disquiet of mind of the said Maryanne and the rest of the family, to the evil example of all others, and against the peace of our said Lord the King, his crown and dignity".

A person named Francis Higgins really held an appointment in the Custom-House, and our adventurer availed himself of the coincidence in carrying out his imposture. In the *Freeman's Journal* of October 21st, 1766, we read:

"Mr. Francis Higgins, of the Custom-House, to Miss Anne Gore, of St. Stephen's Green, an accomplished young lady with a handsome fortune".

There is a painfully interesting episode connected with *this imposture* which the foregoing documents do not tell, and we give it on the authority of the late venerable divine, the Very Rev. Dr. Yore, who was specially connected with the locality. As soon as the marriage between Higgins and Miss Archer had been solemnized, he brought her to some lodgings at Lucan. The bride, after a short matrimonial experience, found that Higgins was by no means a desirable husband either in a pecuniary or a companionable sense, and having watched her opportunity to escape, she at length fled, with almost maniac wildness, to Dublin. Higgins gave chase, and came in sight just as the poor girl had reached her father's house in Thomas Street. It was the dawn of morning, and her parents had not yet risen; but she screamed piteously at the street door, and Mrs. Archer, in her night dress, got up and opened it. The affrighted girl had no sooner rushed through the threshold than Higgins came violently up, and endeavoured to push the door open. Mrs. Archer resisted. She placed her arms across the ample iron sockets which had been formed for the reception of a large wooden bolt. Higgins applied his strength. Mrs. Archer cried wildly for relief and mercy; but her hopeful son-in-law disregarded the appeal, and continued to force the door with such violence that Mrs. Archer's arm was crushed in two.

Immediately on the informations being sworn, Higgins was committed to prison. We read that on January 9th, 1767, the citizens of Dublin witnessed his procession from Newgate in Cutpurse Row to the Tholsel, or Sessions' House, at Christ Church Place, then known as Skinner's Row.*

The Hon. Christopher Robinson, Second Justice

---

* *Dublin Evening Post, No.* 1829.

of the King's Bench, tried the case. It was unusual in those days to report ordinary law proceedings; and there is no published record of the trial beyond three or four lines. But the case excited so strong a sensation that its leading details are still traditionally preserved among several respectable families. *Faulkner's Journal* of the day records:—" At an adjournment of the Quarter Sessions, held at the Tholsel, January 9th, 1767, Francis Higgins was tried and found guilty of several misdemeanours".* At the commission of oyer and terminer following, we find that Higgins stood his trial for another offence committed subsequent to his conviction and imprisonment in the case of Miss Archer. The leniency of the punishment inflicted on Higgins, which permitted him to roam abroad within a few weeks after having being found guilty of " *several misdemeanours*", will not fail to surprise the humane reader. But a violent hatred of Popery prevailed at that time; and even the Bench of Justice often rejoiced whenever it had the power to give a rebuff to those who had rejected the allurements of Protestantism, and clung with fidelity to the oppressed Church.† With reference to the Archer case, we

* *Faulkner's Dublin Journal*, No. 4144.

† About 1759, Laurence Saul, of Saul's Court, Fishamble Street, a wealthy Catholic distiller, was prosecuted for having harboured a young lady who had sought refuge in his house to avoid being compelled by her friends to conform to the Established Church. The Lord Chancellor, in the course of this trial, declared that the law did not presume an Irish Papist existed in the kingdom ! Saul, writing to Charles O'Conor, says:—" Since there is not the least prospect of such a relaxation of the penal laws as would induce one Roman Catholic to tarry in this place of bondage, who can purchase a settlement in some other land where freedom and *security of property* can be obtained, will you condemn me *for saying that if I cannot* be one of the first, I will not be one of

find that Judge Robinson in his charge to the jury observed, that Higgins could not be heavily punished for attempting false pretences, and flying under false colours in the family of Mr. Archer, inasmuch as if they believed the prisoner at the bar to be the important personage which he represented himself, their own conduct presented a deception and *suppressio veri* in not acquainting the prisoner's pretended guardian and uncle with the matrimonial intentions which unknown to his family he entertained. " Gentlemen", added the judge, " that deception has existed on both sides we have ample evidence. 'T is true this *sham squire* is guilty of great duplicity, but so also are the Archers".[*]

In thus fastening upon Higgins that admirable nickname, which clung to him throughout his subsequent highly inflated career, Judge Robinson unintentionally inflicted a punishment by far more severe than a long term of imprisonment in Newgate or the Black Dog.

Higgins exhibited great self-possession in the dock; and he is said to have had the incredible effrontery to appeal to the jury as men, and ask them

the last to take flight?" Saul then bemoans the hard necessity of quitting for ever friends, relatives, and an ancient patrimony, at a time of life when nature had far advanced in its decline, and his constitution by constant mental exercise was much impaired, to retire to some dreary clime, there to play the schoolboy again, to learn the language, laws, and institutions of the country, to make new friends—in short, to begin the world anew. " But", he adds, " when religion dictates, and prudence points out the only way to preserve posterity from temptation and perdition, I feel this consideration predominating over all others. I am resolved, as soon as possible, to sell out, and to expatriate". Saul retired to France, and died there in 1768—(Gilbert's *Dublin; Memoirs of Charles O'Conor*).

[*] *Tradition* communicated by Mr. Gill, publisher, Dublin.

if there was one amongst them who would not do as
much to possess so fine a girl.*

Judge Robinson had scant reputation as a lawyer,
and was eminently unpopular. When proceeding
to the Armagh assizes, in 1763, he found a gallows
erected, and so constructed across the road that it was
necessary to pass under it. To the "Heart-of-Oak-
Boys" Judge Robinson was indebted for this com-
pliment.† He was called to the Bar in 1737, and
died in Dominick Street, in 1786. Mr. O'Regan, in
his *Memoir of Curran*, describes Judge Robinson as
small and peevish. A member of the Bar named
Hoare sternly resisted the moroseness of the judge;
at last, Robinson charged him with a design to bring
the king's commission into contempt. "No, my
Lord", replied Hoare; "I have read that when a
peasant, during the troubles of Charles I. found the
crown in a bush, he showed it all marks of reverence;
but I will go further, for though I should find the
king's commission even upon a *bramble*, still I
shall respect it". Mr. Charles Phillips tells us
that Judge Robinson had risen to his rank by the
publication of some political pamphlets, only remarkable for their senseless, slavish, and envenomed scur-
rility. This fellow, when poor Curran was strug-
gling with adversity, and straining every nerve in
one of his infant professional exertions, made a most
unfeeling effort to extinguish him. Curran had declared, in combating some opinion of his adversary,
that *he had consulted all his law books*, and could not
find a single case in which the principle contended
for was established. "I suspect, sir", said the
heartless blockhead, "that your law library is rather

* *Dublin Evening Post*, No. 1765.
† *Hardy's Life of Charlemont*, v. i., p. 189.

contracted!"   So brutal a remark applied from the
bench to any young man of ordinary pretensions
would infallibly have crushed him; but when any
pressure was attempted upon Curran, he never failed
to rise with redoubled elasticity. He eyed the judge
for a moment in the most contemptuous silence: "It
is very true, my lord, that I am poor, and the circumstance has certainly rather curtailed my library;
my books are not numerous, but they are select, and
I hope have been perused with proper dispositions.
I have prepared myself for this high profession
rather by the study of a few good books than *by the
composition of a great many bad ones.*   I am not
ashamed of my poverty, but I should of my wealth,
could I stoop to acquire it by servility and corruption.   If I rise not to rank, I shall at least be honest;
and should I ever cease to be so, many an example
shows me that an ill-acquired elevation, by making
me the more conspicuous, would only make me the
more universally and the more notoriously contemptible".

Poor Miss Archer did not long survive her humiliation and misfortune.   She died of a broken
heart, and her parents had not long laid her remains
in the grave, when their own mournfully followed.

Mr. Higgins's companions throughout the period
of his detention in Newgate were not of the most
select description, nor were the manners prevalent
in the place calculated to reform his reckless character.   Wesley having visited the prison, found
such impiety prevailing, that he always looked
back upon it with loathing.   "In 1767", observes
Mr. Gilbert, "Newgate was found to be in a very
bad condition, the walls being ruinous, and a con-
stant communication existing between the male

and female prisoners, owing to there being but one pair of stairs in the building".[*] The gaoler carried on an extensive trade by selling liquors to the inmates at an exorbitant price; and prisoners refusing to comply with his demands were abused, violently· beaten, stripped naked, and dragged to a small subterranean dungeon, with no light save what was admitted through a sewer which ran close by it, carrying off all the ordure of the prison, and rendering the atmosphere almost insupportable. In this noisome oubliette, perversely called "the nunnery"; from being the place where abandoned females were usually lodged, twenty persons were frequently crowded together and plundered. Criminals under sentence of transportation were permitted to mix among the debtors. By bribes and collusion between the gaoler and the constables, legal sentences, in many instances, were not carried out. These practices at length attracted the attention of Parliament. Among other facts which transpired in the resolution of the Irish House of Commons, we find that the gaoler had " unlawfully kept in prison and loaded with irons persons not duly committed by any magistrate, till they had complied with the most exorbitant demands".

Even when in durance Mr. Higgins's cunning did not forsake him. Though far from being a Macheath in personal attractions, he contrived to steal the affections of the Lucy Lockit of the prison, and the happy couple were soon after married.[†] The gaoler was an influential person in his way, and promoted the worldly interest of his son-in-law.

* *History of Dublin*, p. 265–6, v. i.
† *Dublin Evening Post*, No. 1796.

For his "misdemeanours" in the family of Mr. Archer, Higgins was committed to Newgate on January 9th, 1767; but the punishment failed to make much impression on him. In the *Freeman's Journal* for February 28 — the paper of which Higgins subsequently became the influential proprietor—we find the following:—

" At the commission of oyer and terminer, Mark Thomas, a revenue officer, and Francis Higgins, the celebrated adventurer, were convicted of an assault against Mr. Peck. . . . . . Higgins was fined £5, to be imprisoned one year, and to give £1,000 security for his good behaviour for seven years".

The details embodied in an interesting letter, addressed on July 23, 1789, by " An old gray-headed Attorney", to John Magee, editor of the *Dublin Evening Post*, who, through its medium, continued with indomitable perseverance to execrate Higgins when he became an efficient tool of the government, and was absolutely placed on the bench by them, being chronologically in place here, we subjoin the letter:—

" In one of your late papers mention was made that the Sham had taken off the roll the record of his conviction in the case of Miss Archer, but if you wish to produce another record of his conviction, you will find one still remaining, in a case wherein the late John Peck was plaintiff, and the Sham and the late Mark Thomas, a revenue officer, were defendants. Sham being liberated from Newgate on Miss Archer's affair, sought out the celebrated Mark Thomas, who at that time kept a shop in Capel Street for the purpose of registering numbers in the then English lottery at 1*d.* *per number.* Thomas found Sham a man fitting for *his purpose,* and employed him as clerk during the drawing, and afterwards as setter and informer in revenue matters.

"Sham's business was to go to unwary grocers, and sell them bags of tea by way of smuggled goods, and afterwards send Thomas to seize them and to levy the fines by information. One evening, however, Sham and Thomas being inebriated, they went to John Peck's, in Corn Market, to search for run tea. Words arose in consequence : Sham made a violent pass at Peck with his tormentor (an instrument carried by revenue officers) and wounded him severely in the shoulder. Peck indicted them both : they were tried, found guilty, and ordered a year's imprisonment in Newgate, where they remained during the sentence of the court.

"The time of confinement having passed over, they were once more suffered to prowl on the public. Thomas died shortly after, and Sham enlisted himself under the banners of the late Charles Reilly, of Smock Alley, who then kept a public house, with billiard and hazard tables. Reilly considered him an acquisition to prevent riotous persons spoiling the play ; for Sham at that time was not bloated, and was well known to be a perfect master in bruising, having carefully studied that art for two years in Newgate under the noted Jemmy Stack.

"Sham having lived some time at Reilly's, contrived by means of his cunning to put Reilly in the Marshalsea, and at the same time to possess himself of Reilly's wife, his house, and his all. The unfortunate Reilly from his sufferings became frantic and insane, and his wife　*　*　*　died miserably. Sham still holds the house in Smock Alley. It is sometimes let out for a b——l, at other times his worship occupies it as a warehouse for the disposal of hose".*

For this assault on Peck, we learn that Higgins

* *Dublin Evening Post*, No. 1886.

" was publicly led by the common hangman through the streets of Dublin to the Court of King's Bench; and while in durance vile had no other subsistence than bread and water, save what he extorted by his piteous tale, and piteous countenance exhibited through the grated bars of a Newgate air-hole".[*]

The next glimpse we get of Mr. Higgins is in the year 1775, exercising the craft of a hosier at "the Wholesale and Retail Connemara Sock and Stocking Warehouse, Smock Alley",[†] and as a testimony to his importance, elected president of the Guild of Hosiers.[‡] In 1780 we find his services engaged by Mr. David Gibbal, conductor of the *Freeman's Journal*, and one of the proprietary of *Pue's Occurrences*.

The Public Register or Freeman's Journal stood high as a newspaper. In 1770 it became the organ of Grattan, Flood, and other opponents of the corrupt Townshend administration; while in *Hoey's Mercury* the viceroy was defended by Jephson, Marley, and Simcox. In literary ability the *Freeman* of that day has been pronounced, by a competent authority, as " incomparably superior to its Dublin contemporaries, and had the merit of being, with the exception of the *Censor*, the first Irish newspaper which published original and independent political essays".[§] Dr. Jebb, and the subsequently famous Judge Johnson, contributed papers to the *Freeman* at this period. Until 1782 it was printed at St. Audeon's Arch; but at the close of that year Gibbal transferred it to Crane Lane.

In the journals of the Irish House of Commons we find an order issued, bearing date April 7, 1784,

---

[*] *Dublin Evening Post*, No. 1779.   [†] *Ibid.*, No. 1791.
[‡] *Ibid.*, No. 1775.   [§] Gilbert's Dublin, vol. i. p. 294.

" That leave be given to bring in a bill to secure the liberty of the press, by preventing abuses arising from the publication of seditious, false, and slanderous libels. *Ordered*—That Francis Higgins, one of the conductors of the *Freeman's Journal*, do attend this House to-morrow morning".* The terms in which Mr. Higgins was reproved are not recorded.

A short discussion on the subject may be found in the Irish Parliamentary Debates. The Right Hon. John Foster impugned the conduct of the *Freeman's Journal*, and General Luttrel, afterwards Lord Carhampton, defended it.†

On April 8th following, Mr. Foster brought in a bill to secure the liberty of the press, by preventing the publication of slanderous libels. The provisions of the bill were, that henceforth the name of the proprietor of every newspaper should be registered upon oath at the Stamp Office, and that the printer enter into a recognizance of £500 to answer all civil suits which might be instituted against him for publications. Mr. Foster severely censured " those papers that undertake slander for hire, and calumny for reward"; Sir Hercules Rowley saw no necessity for the bill; " he knew of no traitorous, scandalous, or malicious libels but one, viz., the title of the bill itself, which was an infamous libel on the Irish nation". On April 12th the subject was again debated. Mr. Grattan declared that there was one paper which daily teemed with exhortations and incitements to assassination; parliament was called upon to interfere, not by imposing any new penalty, nor by compelling printers to have their publications licensed, but merely to oblige them to put

* *Commons' Journals*, vol. xl., pp. 267-268.
† *Irish Parl. Debates*, vol. iii., p. 147.

their names to their newspapers. The Attorney General observed that these violent publications had great effect on the popular mind. A conspiracy had recently been discovered for murdering no less than seven members of that House. " The conditions were that the assassins should, upon performance of the business, receive £100; and, in the meantime, they were actually furnished with money, pistols, ammunition, and bayonets. They were urged to use the latter weapon, because it would neither miss fire nor make a noise". The bill, in an amended form, passed both Houses, and received the royal assent on May 14th following.

We must now go back a little. While engaged in Mr. Burne's office as an attorney's clerk, in 1766, Higgins had contrived to acquire no inconsiderable knowledge of law; and as his ambition now pointed to the profession of solicitor, for which, having renounced " Popery",* he was eligible, a short course of study sufficed to qualify him. Higgins made several attempts to grasp the privileges and gown of an attorney; but the antecedents of his life were so damnatory, that opposition was offered by high legal authorities to his efforts. But Higgins was not a man on whom rebuffs made any impression, and we learn that so indomitable was his perseverance in endeavouring to obtain admittance as an attorney of the Court of Exchequer, that Chief Baron Foster† pro-

---

* "Attorneys were sworn not to take a Catholic apprentice. I have heard that there were instances of judges swearing in their own servants as attorneys"—MS. Letter.
Until 1793 Roman Catholics were inadmissable as attorneys.

† Anthony Foster, Chief Baron of the Exchequer; called to the Bar in 1732; died 1778. He was father of the Right Hon. *John Foster*, last Speaker of the Irish House of Commons, and *first Lord Oriel.*

nounced it "impudence", and threatened a committal to Newgate if again repeated.*

The importance of having a friend in court was, ere long pleasantly exemplified. John Scott, afterwards Earl of Clonmel, had in the days of his obscurity known the Sham Squire Mr. Scott, as we are reminded by Sir Jonah Barrington,† Charles Phillips,‡ and Walter Cox,§ was a person of very humble origin, but of some tact and talent. In 1765 he became a member of the Irish Bar.‖ In 1769 we find Lord Chancellor Lifford recommending him to the patronage of Lord Townshend, then viceroy of Ireland. "The Marquis", observes one who knew Scott well, "had expressed his wishes for the assistance of some young gentleman of the bar, on whose talents and fidelity he might rely in the severe parliamentary campaigns". Scott was accordingly returned for Mullingar. "The opposition", adds Hardy, "was formidable, being composed of the most leading families in the country, joined to great talents, and led on by Flood, whose oratorical powers were then at their height. Against this lofty combination did Mr. Scott oppose himself with a promptitude and resolution almost unexampled. No menace from without, no invective within, no question, however popular, no retort, however applauded, no weight or vehemence of eloquence, no delicate satire, for a moment deterred this young, vigorous, and ardent assailant. On he moved, without much incumbrance of argument certainly, but all the light artillery and total war of jests were peculiarly his own".¶

* *Dublin Evening Post*, No. 1828.   † *Personal Sketches*, p. 314.
‡ *Curran and his Cotemporaries*, p. 35,
§ *Irish Magazine* for 1810, p.
‖ Wilson's *Dublin Directories.*
¶ *Hardy's Life of Charlemont*, v. i., p. 269.

The eager manner in which the government adopted and patronised Mr. Scott showed the straits to which they had been reduced for some parliamentary fugleman. Mr. Scott's antecedents had been foreign to his new duties. Originally in the ranks of the people, a zealous disciple of Lucas, the companion of patriots, and even while in college a staunch opponent of the government, Mr. Scott was, in principle and practice, more than democratic. When introduced to Lord Townshend by Lord Chancellor Lifford, he observed with some humour, not unmixed with regret, " My lord, you have spoiled a good patriot !"[*] A few months subsequent to his return for Mullingar, we find Mr. Scott created a king's counsel; in 1772, counsel to the Revenue Board; in 1774, solicitor-general; in 1774, privy councillor and attorney-general. During the administration of Lord Northington, he became prime sergeant; and in that of the Duke of Rutland, chief justice of the King's Bench, with a peerage.[†]

Politically speaking, Lord Clonmel was a bad Irishman and a worse logician. " When he failed to convince", writes Mr. Phillips, "he generally succeeded in diverting; and if he did not, by the gravity of his reasoning, dignify the majority to which, when in parliament, he sedulously attached himself, he, at all events, covered their retreat with an exhaustless quiver of alternate sarcasm and ridicule. Added to this, he had a perseverance not to be fatigued, and a personal intrepidity altogether invincible. When he could not overcome, he swaggered; and when he could not bully, he fought". On the bench, too, he was often very overbearing,

* Grattan's Memoirs, v. ii., p. 141.
† Archdall's Lodge's Irish Peerage, v. vii., pp. 242-3.

and for having subjected a barrister named Hackett to some discourtesy, which, at a meeting of the bar, was reprobated and resented as a personal offence, Lord Clonmel was obliged to apologize in the public papers. He had many social virtues, however, and Mr. Hardy informs us that in convivial hours his *bonhommie* and pleasantry were remarkable. " To his great honour be it recorded", adds the biographer of Charlemont, ". he never forgot an obligation ; and as his sagacity and knowledge of mankind must have been preëminent, so his gratitude to persons who had assisted him in the mediocrity of his fortune was unquestionable, and marked by real generosity and munificence".

With Francis Higgins, whom he had known in that darkly clouded period which preceded the dawn of his good fortune, Lord Clonmel ever afterwards kept up a friendly intercourse.* It is traditionally asserted that Higgins had been of some use to Mr. Scott, not only in early life, but during his subsequent connection with the Irish government. Higgins having been peremptorily refused admission to the craft of solicitors by Chief Baron Foster, Mr. Scott, when Attorney-General, kindly undertook to introduce him to Lord Annaly,† Chief Justice of the King's Bench, and the request so influentially urged was immediately granted.‡

The name of Francis Higgins, as an attorney-at-law, appears for the first time in the *Dublin Direc-*

* *Dublin Evening Post* file for 1789, *passim.*
† Letter of an " Old Gray-headed Attorney", *D. E. Post*, No. 1791. See also No. 1786.
‡ John Gore having served the government with fidelity, as member for Jamestown, was appointed, in 1764, Chief Justice of the King's Bench. Gore was created Baron Annaly in 1766, but, *dying without issue* in 1783, the title became extinct.

3

tory for 1781.   His then residence is given as Ross
Lane.   From 1784 to 1787 he is styled Deputy
Coroner of Dublin.*   We further learn that his practice as solicitor throughout those years was exclusively confined to the court in which Lord Clonmel
presided as chief justice.

Notwithstanding our adventurer's legal avocations
and professional business, which, owing to his natural aptitude and pleasant cordiality of manner, were
daily increasing, he contrived, nevertheless, to contribute, regularly, political squibs to the *Freeman's
Journal.*   His pecuniary means increased, and he
sometimes lent money on good security.   The proprietor of the *Freeman's Journal,* then somewhat
embarrassed, requested an accommodation.   With
some apparent good nature Higgins at once granted
the request; but after a little time he asked his employer to pay back the money; the proprietor seemed
surprised, and begged that a longer period of accommodation might be extended.   The Sham Squire
declined; the journalist expostulated; but Mr. Higgins was inexorable, and without more ado levied
an execution on the *Freeman's Journal* †

Mr. Higgins, having now acquired the sole control, literary and pecuniary, of the paper, became a
person of some importance in the public eye, and of
boundless consequence in his own.   His wealth and
influence, swagger and effrontery, increased; but it
keenly chagrined him to find that, the more important he became, the more inveterately he was pursued by the nickname of the Sham Squire.

" Till the Volunteers have, in some degree, sub-
sided, your government can only subsist by expe-

* *Wilson's Dublin Directories.*
† *Tradition* preserved in the office of the Freeman's Journal.

dients, painful as such an idea must be to your feelings",[*] writes Mr., afterwards Lord, Grenville, brother to the Lord Lieutenant of Ireland. The Irish Government of these days was eminently weak and venal; and Mr. Higgins at once prostituted to its purposes the once virtuous journal, of which he had now become the master.

Lord Temple retired from the government, and was succeeded by the Duke of Rutland. Mr. Connolly, and other large landed proprietors, who had formerly supported government, took, in 1786 and following years, a decided part against his Grace's administration. They denounced various bills as unconstitutional jobs, introduced solely for the purpose of ministerial patronage. But the grand attack of the opposition was on the Pension List. Mr. Grattan gave great offence to the Treasury Bench, by causing the whole list to be read aloud by the clerk, and exclaiming: " If I should vote that pensions are not a grievance, I should vote an impudent, an insolent, and a public lie". The Duke of Rutland fell into great unpopularity with the populace, and narrowly escaped personal outrage at the theatre. Meanwhile the discontent which prevailed in the city, extended to the country parts, and found noisy exponents in the " Right Boys" and the " Defenders".

Yet the Duke possessed qualities and characteristics which made him not unpopular with the gentry and middle classes. It was supposed that he had sown his wild oats in England; but, as events proved, he had still some bushels to scatter broadcast in the green fields of Erin. His mission in Ireland seemed to aim at extending luxury and ex-

* *Court and Cabinets of George III.*, by the Duke of Buckingham and Chandos. Vol. i. p. 87.

travagance, conviviality and unbridled pleasure.
He had great affability, and was free from the
haughty deportment which marked his predecessor's
intercourse with the Irish people. Moreover, he
showered knighthoods around with a lavish hand;
and it is told of him that, having one evening in
his cups knighted a jolly innkeeper at Kilbeggan
named Cuffe, of which he repented in the calm re-
action of the following day, he sent for the landlord,
and told him that as the whole affair was a joke,
the sooner it was forgotten the better. "I should
be well plazed to obleedge your Ex-cèl-lency", he
replied, "but I unfortunately mentioned the matter to Leedy Cuffe, and she would part wid her life
afore she 'd give it up".[*] In the Duke of Rutland's
energetic attempt to attain popularity, he found in
his beautiful and accomplished wife a zealous ally.
She made the Circular Road, now a comparatively
deserted highway, the Rotten Row of Dublin.[†]

* This incident occurred on the property of the Lamberts of
Beauparc, in whose family the story is preserved.
† For several years afterwards this pleasant innovation continued. The late Lord Cloncurry, in his *Personal Recollections*
(2nd ed., p. 187), writes:—" It was the custom, on Sundays, for
all the great folk to rendezvous, in the afternoon, upon the
North Circular Road, just as, in latter times, the fashionables of
London did in Hyde Park; and upon that magnificent drive, I
have ferquently seen three or four coaches-and-six, and eight or
ten coaches-and-four, passing slowly to and fro in a long procession of other carriages, and between a double column of
well-mounted horsemen.   Of course the populace were there,
too, and saluted with friendly greetings, always cordially and
kindly acknowledged, the lords and gentlemen of the country
party, who were neither few in number nor insignificant in station. . . . . The evenings of those Sunday mornings were
commonly passed by the same parties in promenading at the
Rotundo. I have frequently seen there, of a Sunday evening, a
third of the members of the two houses of parliament".
Moore mentions in his Memoirs (i. 10), that about the year

If, says a contemporary song—

"If you wish to see her grace,
The Circular Road it is the place".

There this beautiful woman, with her six spanking ponies, sparkling postillions, and gorgeously attired out-riders, was daily to be seen smiling and bowing. She was considered the handsomest woman in Ireland with one exception—Mrs. Dillon, wife of a Roman Catholic woollen draper, residing at No. 5 Francis Street. We are informed by Mr. O'Reilly, in his *Reminiscences of an Emigrant Milesian*, that one day the Liberty was thrown into a state of unwonted excitation by the appearance of her grace and out-riders in front of Mrs. Dillon's door. She entered the shop, but Mrs. Dillon was not behind the counter. "Shall I call her?" inquired an agitated shopman. "No", said the Duchess, "I shall go to her myself", saying which she entered the parlour, and received a graceful bow from the lady of the house. "There is no exaggeration in the description", said the Duchess, as she peered into the dove-like eyes of Mrs. Dillon,

---

1790 a curious toy called "a quiz" became fashionable with the class of pedestrians to whom Lord Cloncurry alludes. "To such a ridiculous degree", he writes, "did the fancy for this toy pervade at that time all ranks and ages, that in the public gardens and in the streets, numbers of persons, of both sexes, were playing it, up and down as they walked along". The subsequent Duke of Wellington, when in Ireland in 1797, was much given to playing with this toy; and Lord Plunkett said, that while serving on a committee with him he never for a moment ceased the puerile indulgence. The early life of "the Iron Duke", if honestly told, would exhibit him deficient in ballast. Having had some warm words with a Frenchman in Dublin, he wrested from his hand a cane which was not returned. The Frenchman brought an action for the robbery of the cane, and Wellesley was absolutely tried in the *Sessions House*, Dublin, for the offence. He was *acquitted of the robbery, but found guilty of the assault.*

"you *are* the handsomest woman in the three kingdoms".

The Duchess had many devoted admirers who loved to flatter her with extravagantly fulsome compliments. The late "Counsellor" Walsh in his *Ireland Fifty Years Ago*, mentions that Colonel St. Ledger having seen the Duchess wash her mouth and fingers one day after dinner, he snatched up the glass and literally drained the contents. "St. Ledger", said the Duke, "you are in luck; her Grace washes her feet to-night, and you shall have another goblet after supper".

The attractions of his wife failed to make this young viceroy as domestic as could be desired. On his way home from the theatre one evening he was induced to visit the residence of Peg Plunket. He forgot that a guard of honour attended him, and on glancing from the window next morning, his embarrassment may be conceived at recognizing a troop of mounted dragoons with drawn sabres in front of the house. Curran used to tell that a noisy god at Crow Street theatre archly inquired of Miss Plunket, on the occasion of a command night, "Peg, who was your visitor the other evening?" In a tone of mock rebuke she wittily retorted, "MANNERS, fellow".

A career so dissipated was not likely to last long. Charles Manners, Duke of Rutland, died in the government of Ireland from the effects of a fever induced by intemperance, and the imposing pageantry which marked the funeral procession was consistent with the splendour of his memorable regime.

He who writes the history of the Rutland vice-royalty should consult the files of the Sham Squire's journal. *Higgins* was its organ and eulogist; but, setting aside political considerations, the Duke possessed tendencies which specially recommended him to the cordial appreciation of Francis Higgins. The services of Shamado did not pass unrewarded. During the Rutland viceroyalty he received the office of under sheriff for the county of Dublin,* one in those days of considerable emolument. Mr. Higgins had a busy time of it. Presiding in court with all the assumption of a judge, he not only tried all the forty-shilling causes, but much larger questions, under the writ of *Scire Facias*. He executed the writs which had been issued by the superior courts, superintended the gibbeting of criminals, and throughout the popular tumults, which locally raged at this time, he no doubt frequently figured at the head of his *posse comitatus*, or sheriff's guard.

Nefarious practices had long degraded the office of sheriff, but in 1823 they received a decided check by the parliamentary inquiry into the conduct of Mr. Sheriff Thorpe. The partiality with which sheriffs habitually packed juries for particular cases, was then unveiled; and it transpired that they pledged themselves, before their election, to take a decided part in politics against every Catholic. " Catholics", observed Mr. O'Connell, " would rather submit to great wrongs than attempt a trial in Dublin". Competent witnesses were examined at the same time; and the *Edinburgh Review*, noticing their evidence, said that, " No one could fail to be equally surprised and disgusted with the abominable course of profligacy and corruption which is there exhibited". That the Sham Squire was no better than his predecessors and successors we have reason to believe.

Mr. Higgins became every day a richer man.

* *Wilson's Dublin Directory* for 1787, p. 112.

From the publication of the government proclamations alone he derived a considerable income. When we know that the sum paid in 1788 to Mr. Higgins for proclamations, was £1,600, according to the parliamentary return, it is not surprising that the popular organs of the day should have complained that "Signor Shamado" received from the government annually, more than a commissioner of his majesty's revenue.*

CHAPTER II.

Peculation.—The Press subsidised and debauched.—Lord Buckingham.—Judges revel at the board of the Sham Squire.—A Pandemonium unveiled.—Lord Avonmore.—A great struggle.—The Regency.—Peerages sold.—John Magee.—Lord Carhampton.—Mrs. Lewellyn.—Squibs and Lampoons.—The Old Four Courts in Dublin.—Dr. Houlton—The Duke of Wellington on bribing the Irish Press.

THE viceroy's leisure in the last century was heavily taxed by unceasing applications from Lord Clonmel and his unpopular colleagues, to authorise and sign proclamations on every imaginable infraction of the law. Mr. Griffith, on January 23, 1787, complained in his place in parliament that the " newspapers seemed under some very improper influence. In one paper the country was described as one scene of riot and confusion; in another, all is peace. By the proclamations that are published in them, and which are kept in for years, in order to make the fortunes of some individuals, the kingdom is scandalised and disgraced through all the nations of the world where our newspapers are read. The

* *Dublin Evening Post,* No. 1765.

proclamations are a libel on the country. Was any offender ever taken up in consequence of such publications? And are they not rather a hint to offenders to change their situation and appearance? He did hope, from what a right hon. gentleman had said last year, that this abuse would have been redressed, but ministers have not deigned to give any answer on the subject".[*] On February 2nd following, Mr. Corry animadverted to the same effect. Foreigners would mistake the character of our people, and look upon us as a savage nation; hence the low price of land in Ireland and the difficulty of raising money. He denounced the bills furnished by newspapers as a gross attempt to waste the public money. Hussey Burgh declared that more proclamations were to be found in the *Dublin Gazette*, in the time of profound peace, long before the Right Boys created a disturbance, than in the *London Gazette* during the rebellion! Mr. Wolfe observed that government absolutely abetted the Right Boys; they had inserted Captain Right's manifesto in the middle of a government proclamation, and so sent it round the kingdom much more effectually than Captain Right ever could have done, and that without any expense to the captain.

Mr. Forbes "thought it hard that the payment of the *Freeman's Journal* should be disputed; for he was sure that the proprietor was a very generous man. An inn-keeper in the town he represented, regularly received that paper. On his inquiring what he paid for it, and who sent it, the inn-keeper replied that he did not know. A *Mr. F. H.*, some worthy gentleman, God bless him, had sent it to

* *Irish Parl. Register*, vol. vii. p. 87-8.

him, and never troubled him for payment or anything else!"*

Thus it would appear that F. H. considered himself so overpaid by the peculating government of
that day, that he might well afford to push his paper
into an enormous gratuitous circulation.

The Duke of Rutland was succeeded as Lord
Lieutenant by the Marquis of Buckingham, who, as
Lord Temple, had already held the viceregal reins.
Of this chief governor Mr. Grattan observes: " He
opposed many good measures, promoted many bad
men, increased the expenses of Ireland in a manner
wanton and profligate, and vented his wrath upon
the country".† Such being the case, it is not surprising that Lord Bulkley, in a letter to his Excellency, dated June 14, 1788, should remark: " I
saw your brother, Marquis, who told me that he
heard with the greatest concern that your popularity
in Ireland was falling apace, and that the candles
were out".‡ By way of counterbalance Higgins
swung the censer with more than ordinary energy.
According to the *Post*, a cheque from the treasury
for £1030 was graciously presented to the Sham
Squire at this period, " for puffing the character and
politics of Lord Buckingham".§

The daring and dastardly experiment of bribing
the press was then of recent introduction in Ireland.
A letter from Mr. Eden, afterwards Lord Auckland,
addressed to Lord North, and dated " Phœnix Park,
August 27, 1781", says:—

" We have hitherto, by the force of good words, and

* *Irish Parl. Register*, vol. vii. pp. 88-88-89.
† *Memoirs of Henry Grattan*, vol. iii. p. 146
‡ *Court and Cabinets of Geo. III.*, vol. i. p. 396, London, 1853.
§ *Dublin Evening Post*, Nos. 1806—1808.

with some degree of private expense, preserved an ascendancy over the press, not hitherto known here, and it is of an importance equal to ten thousand times its cost, but we are without the means of continuing it".*

But Higgins had too much natural taste for the "art and mystery" of legal lore, as well as for bills of costs, to forego the emoluments of an attorney-at-law for the editorial desk, however lucrative. We find him figuring as solicitor for prisoners in several cases which excited much noise at this time—instance the "Trial of Robert Keon, gentleman, for the murder of George Nugent Reynolds, Esq."† Retaining the absolute control of the *Freeman's Journal*, Higgins, in order that he might be able to devote more time to his profession, engaged Doctor

* Correspondence of Right Honble. J. C. Beresford, i. p. 170. Mr. Eden was Chief Secretary for Ireland from 1780 until 1782; created, 1789, Baron Auckland; died, 1814. Modern statesmen seem to hold conflicting opinions as to the expediency of subsidising newspapers for political ends. The memorable trial of Birch *versus* Lord Clarendon, in 1850, revealed that hard cash had been given to the editor of the *World* for writing down the Young Ireland Party. Cavour, on the other hand, who was for many years before his death the daily butt of journalistic abuse, disdained the purchase of the press. "One day", writes his secretary, M. Artom, "somebody tried to show him the advantage of founding a semi-official journal, which should have the province of defending the policy of the Government. He replied, 'if you want to bring the best and soundest ideas into discredit, put them into officious or official form. If you have a good cause to defend, you will easily find writers who, without being paid, will defend it with more warmth and talent than paid journalists'".

† Dublin, 1788. 163 pages. Reported by George J. Browne. "The verdict was not given till after midnight. The hall had previously been cleared by order of the court, but a few, among whom was my father, then a student of Trinity College, concealed themselves under the tables, so that they might learn the result *immediately* on its being delivered".—MS. Letter *of Dr. T.*

Houlton as his sub-editor, and George Joseph Browne, barrister, but originally a player*, and C. Brennan, formerly a fierce democratic writer in the *Dublin Evening Post*,† as contributors. In a short time the *Freeman's Journal* became an important and influential organ of the Irish Government. The Sham Squire's society is said to have been courted by high authorities in the Law and the State. In the great liberal organ of the day it is alleged that "Judges are the companions of his festive hours"—that "Judges revel at his Board, and are his associates".‡ But the most startling feature in this epoch of the Sham Squire's life, is the allegation repeatedly made by the *Dublin Evening Post*, that Higgins, at the very period of which we write, was the proprietor of, or secret partner in, a gambling house of the worst possible description in Crane Lane. In prose and verse, this public nuisance received energetic denunciation.

> "Where is the muse that lashed the Roman crimes?
> Where now is Pope with all his poignant rhymes?
> Where 's Churchill now, to aim the searching dart,
> Or show the foulness of a villain's heart?
> Where is the muse to tune the piercing lay
> And paint the hideous monster to the day?
> Alas! all gone! let every virtue weep:
> Shamado lives, and Justice lies asleep.
> How shall I wake her—will not all the cries
> Of midnight revels, that ascend the skies,
> The sounding dice box, and the shrieking [———]
> The groans of all the miserable poor:
> Undone and plunder'd by this outcast man,
> Will not these wake her?"——— etc., etc.

The satiric bard proceeds to describe Shamado raising the unhallowed fabric in Crane Lane:—

* *Dublin Evening Post*, No. 1793.
† *Ibid.*, No. 1794.   ‡ *Ibid.*, No. 1756.

" Henceforth, he cried, no watchman shall presume
To check the pleasures of each festive room ;
Henceforth, I say, let no policeman dare,
No sheriff, alderman, or e'en lord mayor,
No constable, or untaught bailiff rude,
With hideous visage, on these realms intrude.
He said, and striking with a golden wand,
The doors obey the impulse of his hand ;
The portals back upon their hinges flew,
And many a hazard-table rose to view.
On every table did a dice-box stand,
Waiting impatient for the gamester's hand,
Full many a couch prepar'd for soft delight,
And a few lamps gleam'd out a glimmering light".*

But we have quoted sufficient as a specimen. In
a subsequent number of the *Dublin Evening Post*
the editor asks :—

" Will not a day of retribution come for all this ac-
cumulation of villainy and enormity at which the blood
runs cold ? Oh! that we had a Fitzgibbon Judge.
Then would not longer the Newgate felon, the murderer
of wretched parents, the betrayer of virgin innocence,
the pestiferous defiler of the marriage couch, *Sham* his
fate, and defy the laws of God and man".†

In the Directory for 1788 is recorded Mr. Higgins's removal from the obscurity of Ross Lane to
72 Stephen's Green, South, one of the fine old Huguenot houses, of which Grattan occupied one.
From the above date, we find his professional practice extended from the King's Bench to the Common
Pleas, besides acting at the Tholsel or Sessions'
Court—the very edifice in whose dock he stood a
fettered malefactor a few years before. Chief Baron
Yelverton, afterwards Lord Avonmore, presided in
the Exchequer, and discountenanced the impudent

* *Dublin Evening Post*, No. 1743.   † Ibid., No. 1767.

pretensions of the Sham Squire to practise in that court. Yelverton, as one of the illustrious patriots of 1782, had not much claims to the favourable consideration of the Sham Squire. He was accordingly lampooned by him. On May 3rd, 1789, we read:

"Counsel rose on behalf of Mr. Higgins, who had been ordered to attend, to answer for certain scandalous paragraphs reflecting on that court.

"Chief Baron Yelverton said, 'If you had not mentioned that affair, the court would not have condescended to recollect its insignificance, but would have passed it by, as it has done every other paragraph, whether of praise or censure, which has appeared in that paper, with the most supreme contempt. Let the fellow return to his master's employment. Let him exalt favourite characters, if there be any mean enough to take pleasure in his adulation : let him continue to spit his venom against everything that is praiseworthy, honourable, or dignified in human nature : but let him not presume to meddle with the courts of justice, lest, forgetting his baseness and insignificance, they should at some time deign to inflict a merited punishment'".*

Yelverton's opinion of the Sham Squire's insignificance was not endorsed by Inspector-General Amyas Griffith, who, in his tracts published this year, after returning thanks to the "established Bishops of Dublin, Cashel, Cloyne, and Kildare," and other personages who had patronized him, acknowledges his obligation to Sham Squire, Esq.†

To render the career of Francis Higgins more distinct, we may, perhaps, be permitted to make a slight historical digression.

A most important and embarrassing struggle between England and Ireland took place in 1789, in

* *Dublin Evening Post*, No. 1757.
† *Advertisement to Miscellaneous Tracts.*

reference to the regency which George the Third's mental aberration had made necessary. The Prince of Wales at this period professed not unpopular politics, and favoured the Catholic claims. Mr. Pitt, apprehensive that the regency might prove fatal to his ambition and to his cabinet, powerfully resisted the heir-apparent's right to the prerogative of his father, and declared on 11th Dec., 1788, that " the Prince of Wales had no better right to administer the government during his father's incapacity than any other subject of the realm".* An address to his Royal Highness from the Irish Parliament requested that he would " take upon himself the government of Ireland during the continuation of the king's indisposition, and no longer, and under the title of Prince Regent of Ireland, in the name, and on behalf of his Majesty, to exercise, according to the laws and constitution of that kingdom, all regal powers, jurisdiction, and prerogatives to the crown and government thereof belonging". Ireland called upon the prince, in virtue of the federative compact, to assume at once the sceptre of authority; but Mr. Pitt's followers furiously struggled against it. Grattan headed the independent party in the Commons. Mr. Pelham, afterwards Lord Chichester, after speaking of what he styles " the tricks and intrigues of Mr. Pitt's faction", says, " I have not time to express how strongly the prince is affected by the confidence and attachment of the Irish Parliament. I have only time to say in his own words, ' Tell Grattan that I am a most determined Irishman'". The Duke of Portland, writing to Mr. Grattan on the 21st February, 1789, says: " I beg most sincerely to congratulate you on the decisive

* *The Prospect Before Us.* 1788, p. 4.

effect of your distinguished exertions. Your own country is sensible and worthy of the part you have taken in defence and protection of her constitution. The prince thinks himself no less obliged to you; and whenever this deluded country, becomes capable of distinguishing her true friends, she will contribute her quota of applause and gratitude".*

"The probability of his Majesty's recovery", writes Sir Jonah Barrington, "had a powerful influence on placemen and official connections. The viceroy took a decisive part against the prince, and made bold and hazardous attempts upon the rights of the Irish Parliament". The recently published Buckingham correspondence† confirms Sir Jonah's statement. Every day a bulletin announcing the monarch's convalescence reached the viceroy. The good news was orally circulated among his supporters. Mr. Fitzgibbon was promised the seals and a peerage if he succeeded for Mr. Pitt. Each member of the Opposition was menaced, that he should be made the "*victim of his vote*". Lures were held out to the wavering—threats hurled at the independent.

This extraordinary threat elicited that spirited

---

* *Life and Times of Henry Grattan*, by his son, vol. iii., pp. 373-4.

† *Memoirs of the Courts and Cabinets of George III., from Original Family Documents*, by the Duke of Buckingham and Chandos, 1853. The noble editor of these valuable state papers admits that "the Parliament of Ireland preserved the unquestionable right of deciding the Regency in their own way. The position of Lord Buckingham", he adds, "had become peculiarly embarrassing. What course should be taken in the event of such an address being carried? The predicament was so strange, and involved constitutional considerations of such importance, as to *give the most serious* disquietude to the Administration".—Vol. *ii. p. 101.*

protest familiarly known as "the Round Robin", to which the Duke of Leinster, Lords Charlemont, Shannon, Granard, Ross, Moira, and a host of other influential men, affixed their signatures. The document dwelt on the recent threat of making individuals "the victim of their vote", and stigmatised it "as a reprobation of their constitutional conduct, and an attack upon public principle and the independence of Parliament; that any administration taking or persevering in such steps was not entitled to their confidence, and should not receive their support".

The address to the regent having passed both the Lords and Commons, it was presented to Lord Buckingham for transmission; but the viceroy declined to have anything to say to it, and thus parliament was reduced to the necessity of forwarding the address by the hands of delegates. Previous to their departure the following resolution was carried by 115 to 83:—"That his Excellency's answer to both Houses of Parliament, requesting him to transmit their address to his Royal Highness, is ill advised, contains an unwarrantable and unconstitutional censure on the proceedings of both Houses, and attempts to question the undoubted rights and privileges of the Lords spiritual and temporal, and of the Commons of Ireland". The viceroy, as a last resource, endeavoured to multiply his partizans by the most venal means. Mr. Fitzgibbon gave it to be understood that half a million of money had been placed in his hands for corrupt purposes; and as the first law officer of the crown made this disgusting avowal, he casually confessed that one address of thanks to Lord Townshend, a few years before, had cost the nation £500,000!*

* *The corrupt policy and proceedings of the Townshend administration received effective exposure in a publication called Baratariana.*—See Appendix.

4

Grattan, who was an eye-witness of all these disreputable proceedings, observed at a later period:
" The threat was put into its fullest execution; the
canvass of the minister was everywhere—in the
House of Commons, in the lobby, in the street, at
the door of the parliamentary undertakers, rapped
at and worn by the little caitiffs of government, who
offered amnesty to some, honours to others, and corruption to all; and where the word of the viceroy
was doubted, they offered their own. Accordingly,
we find a number of parliamentary provisions were
created, and divers peerages sold, with such effect,
that the same parliament who had voted the chief
governor a criminal, did immediately after give that
very governor implicit support".*   " They began",
said Curran, " with the sale of the honour of the
peerage—the open and avowed sale for money of
the peerage to any man who was rich and shameless
enough to be the purchaser. It depraved the Commons, it profaned the sanctity of the Lords, it poi-
soned the sources of legislature and the fountains of
justice, it annihilated the very idea of public honour
or public integrity!" Curran did not speak thus
strongly from any cankering feeling of wounded
pride at slights received from the government.
Describing the events of 1798, his biographer tells
us: " To Mr. Curran it was communicated that his
support of the government would be rewarded with
a judge's place, and with the eventual prospect of a
peerage; but, fortunately for his fame, he had too
much respect for his duties and his character to sa-
crifice them to personal advancement".†

Grattan, Curran, and Ponsonby offered to prove,

* *Life and Times of Henry Grattan,* v. iii., p. 338.
† *Life of Curran,* by his Son, v. i., p. 240.

on evidence, the startling charges to which we have
referred; but the government, knowing that it had
been guilty of an impeachable offence, shrunk from
the inquiry. The peerages of Kilmaine, Cloncurry,
and Glentworth were, beyond doubt, sold for hard
cash in 1789, and the proceeds laid out for the purchase of members in the House of Commons.

Mr. Wright, in his history of Ireland, pronounces
Mr. Johnson's to be the ablest speech on the government side during this struggle. He quotes it in full;
but the effect is spoiled by Mr. Johnson's confession
to Thomas Moore in 1831, that he had always supported Grattan's policy until the regency question,
when he ratted, and at once became the recipient of
state favours. "In fact", added the ex-judge John
son, "we were all jobbers at that time".[*]

The struggle between the viceroy and the parliament was a sadly exciting one. Political profligacy stalked, naked and unblushing, through the
Senate and the Castle. Vows, resolutions, rules, reputations, and faith were daily broken. Meanwhile,
the royal physicians opined that the king would
soon be restored to health. "Your object", says the
secretary of state, in a letter to the viceroy on Feb.
19th, 1789, "your object will be to use every possible endeavour, by all means in your power, de-
bating every question, dividing upon every question, moving adjournment upon adjournment, and
every other mode that can be suggested, to gain
time!"[†] Sheridan's politically penetrating eye saw
through the ruse. "I am perfectly aware", he writes
in a private letter to the prince, "of the arts that
will be practised, and the advantages which some

* *Diary of Thomas Moore*, vi., p. 55.
† *Buckingham Correspondence*, v. ii., p. 117.

people will attempt to gain by time".* These expe-
dients, coupled with the energetic efforts daily made
by a venal press and minister, at last triumphed;
and the king was now, to quote the words of Lord
Grenville in writing to the viceroy, " actually well!"
The struggle was therefore at an end, but not the
results of that struggle.   The master of the rolls, the
treasurer, the clerk of permits, the postmaster-ge-
neral, the secretary at war, the comptroller of stamps,
and many other public servants of importance, were
summarily expelled from office.   The Duke of
Leinster, one of the most respected officers of 'the
crown, received a supersedeas, together with Lord
Shannon.   The influential family of Ponsonby, long
the unwavering supporters of government, but who
on this occasion joined the legislature in asserting
its constitutional independence, were also cashiered.
But the promotions and appointments vastly exceeded the dismissals.   Of the former, which included a long string of creations in the peerage,
there were forty—of the latter fifteen only.   Em-
ployments that had long remained dormant were
revived, useless places invented, sinecures created,
salaries increased; while such offices as the board
of stamps and accounts, hitherto filled by one, became a joint concern.   The weighmastership of
Cork was divided into three parts, the duties of
which were discharged by deputies, while the prin-
cipals, who pocketed the gross amount, held seats in
parliament.   In 1790 one hundred and ten placemen sat in the House of Commons!   On February
11th in that year, Mr. Forbes declared that the
pensions had been recently increased upwards of
£100,000.   In 1789 an additional perpetuity of

* *Life of Sheridan by Thomas Moore,* chap. xiii.

£2,800 was saddled on the country. The viceroy, however glad of his victory, had not much reason, one would think, to be proud of the means whereby that victory was attained. But an examination of his correspondence shows the utter unscrupulosity of his heart. Writing to Lord Bulkley he observes: " In the space of six weeks, I have secured to the crown a decided and steady majority, created in the teeth of the Duke of Leinster, Lord Shannon, Lord Granard, Ponsonby, Conolly, O'Neill, united to all the republicanism, the faction, and the discontent of the House of Commons; and having thrown this aristocracy at the feet of the king, I have taught to the British and Irish Government a lesson which ought never to be forgotten; and I have the pride to recollect, that the whole of it is fairly to be ascribed to the steady decision with which the storm was met, and to the zeal, vigour, and industry of some of the steadiest friends that ever man was blessed with".

Amongst " the steadiest friends" by whom the viceroy was " blessed", the Sham Squire deserves mention. He worked the engine of the press with unflagging vigour, and by means of a forced circulation he succeeded to some extent in inoculating the public mind with the virus of his politics. It was Lord Buckingham's policy to feed the flame of Shamado's pride and ambition; and we are assured by John Magee, that so essential to the stability of the Irish government were the services of this once fettered malefactor, that on frequent occasions he was admitted to share the hospitalities and confidence of the viceroy's closet.

The first allusion to Francis Higgins, which the leading organ of the popular party in the last century contains, is an article on March 8th, 1789.

wherein the Sham Squire is spoken of as "Frank Paragraph, the Stephen's Green Attorney", who on the previous night, having been escorted up the backstairs of the Castle by Major Hobart,* received the Marquis of Buckingham's hospitality and confidence. The article concluded by expressing a hope that Frank, whether as an attorney, as proprietor of a prostitute print, or as the companion of a viceroy, should not in the day of his happy exultation forget his original insignificance.

Mr. John Magee was the then proprietor of the *Dublin Evening Post.* Sir Jonah Barrington tells us that although eccentric he was a most acute observer, a smart writer, and a ready wit. Politically honest and outspoken, often to indiscretion, he enjoyed the confidence and love of the popular party in Ireland. By the government he was feared and hated; and on more occasions than one he was consigned to a dungeon. Magee exercised considerable influence on the public events of his time, and he may be not inapplicably styled the Irish Cobbett of the eighteenth century.

Against the Sham Squire Magee had no personal enmity; and previous to 1789 there is no allusion to him direct or indirect in the *Post;* but Mr. Higgins's importance having in that year swelled to an unprecedented extent, as the accredited organ of the Castle, Magee felt urged by a sense of public duty to declare uncompromising war against the fortunate adventurer. Probably Magee's labours had good effect in checking the further promotion of Higgins.

Magee first wielded the lash of irony; but finding

* *Major Hobart,* afterwards Lord Buckinghamshire, was the *diplomatic chief secretary* for Ireland at this period.

that this failed to tell with sufficient effect, he thereupon applied the loaded bludgeon of denunciation.
Several poetic diatribes appeared in the *Post* at this
period; but they are too voluminous to quote in full.
One, in which the Sham Squire is found soliloquis-
ing, goes on to say:

> "You know my power; at my dread command
> B—wds, pimps, and bullies, all obedient stand:
> Nay, well you know, at my terrific nod
> The *Freeman* lifts aloft the venal rod:
> Or if you still deny my sovereign awe,
> I 'll spread the petty-fogging nets of law".

Higgins's antecedents are glanced at:

> "You know my art can many a form assume.
> Sometimes I seem a hosier at a loom;
> Then at the changing of my magic wand
> Before your face a wealthy Squire I stand,
> With a *Sham* title to seduce the fair,
> And murder wretched fathers by despair".

As soon as the struggle respecting the Regency
question had ceased, the viceroy is said to have
acknowledged Higgins's fidelity by recommending
him to Lord Lifford* as a fit and proper person
to grace the magisterial bench!
We resume the Sham Squire's soliloquy:—

> "And if Old Nick continues true, no bar shall
> Prevent me from becoming Four Courts marshal.
> Behold me still in the pursuit of gain,
> My golden wand becomes a golden chain.

* Before Lord Lifford accepted the seals, then estimated as
worth £12,000 per annum, they had been offered to Judges
Smyth, Aston, and Sewell, of the English Bench, and declined.
He was the son of William Hewit, a draper in Coventry, and
began life as an attorney's clerk. See *Irish Polit. Characters*—
London, 1799, p. 58; also *Sleator's Dublin* Chronicle, 1788-9,
pp. 240, 550, 1256. Lord Lifford's personalty was £150,000.

See how I loll in my judicial chair,
The fees of office piled up at my rear;
A smuggl'd turkey or illegal hare.
Those I commit, who have no bribe to give,—
Rogues that have nothing don't deserve to live.
Then nimbly on the turning of a straw,
I seem to be a pillar of the law;
See even nobles at my tables wait.

* * * * *

But think not that (like idiots in your plays)
My friendship any saves but him who pays;
Or that the foolish thought of gratitude
Upon my callous conscience can intrude;
And yet I say, not Buckingham himself
Could pardon one, unless I touch the pelf;
There 's not a robber hanged, or pilferer whipt,
Till at my word he 's halter'd or he 's stript".*

By the 5 George the Second (c. 18, s. 2) no
attorney can become a justice of the peace while in
practice as an attorney; but in the case of the Sham
Squire all difficulties were smoothed. Some of the
most influential political personages of the time tra-
velled out of the way in order to mark their approval
of Mr. Higgins's elevation. The letter to which
we have already referred, signed " An Old Gray-
headed Attorney", and published on July 23rd,
1789, records that Francis Higgins had the honour of
being first " introduced as a justice of his Majesty's
peace for the county of Dublin, to the bench assembled at Kilmainham, by the good, the virtuous, the humane Earl Carhampton; that peer
who so truly, nobly, and gallantly added to the
blushing honour of a before-unsullied fame, by
rescuing from a gibbet the chaste Mrs. Lewellyn.
Mr. Higgins was also there, and there accompanied by that enlightened senator, independent

* *Dublin Evening Post*, No. 1742.

placeman, and sound lawyer, Sir Frederick Flood, Bart".*

Lord Carhampton, who regarded Higgins with such a fatherly eye of patronage and protection, has received scant courtesy from the historians of his time, Hardy alone excepted. As Colonel Luttrel he first attained notoriety at the Middlesex Election, where he acted as unconstitutional a part as he afterwards did in Ireland in his military capacity. Mr. Scott on this occasion publicly declared that Luttrel "was vile and infamous". Luttrel did not resent the insult, and his spirit was called in question. "He was a clever bravo", writes Mr. Grattan, "ready to give an insult, and perhaps capable of bearing one".† "There is in this young man's conduct", wrote Junius to Lord North, "a strain of prostitution, which for its singularity I cannot but admire. He has discovered a new line in the human character. He has disgraced even the name of Luttrel". Unpopular to loathing in England, and hooted from its shores, Luttrel came to try his fortune in Ireland, where, having openly joined the Beresford party in their system of coercion, he daily sank lower and lower in popular estimation. Lord Carhampton's utter contempt of public reputation was evidenced in every act. Flippant and offensive in his speech, arrogant, haughty, and overbearing in his manner, steadily opposing on a per-

* Frederick Flood, Esq., K.C., M.P. for Wexford, received his baronetcy (which is now extinct) on June 3, 1780. He was a commissioner of the Stamp Office. For a notice of Sir F. Flood see *A Review of the Principal Characters of the Irish House of Commons* by Falkland (i.e., John Robert Scott, B.D.) Lond. 1795, p. 50; also Barrington's *Personal Sketches,* i. 207.

† *Grattan's Memoirs,* v. iii., p. 167.

verse principle, generous sentiments and public opinion, Lord Carhampton soon acquired an unenviable character and fame. But even had his lordship the purity of a Grattan or a Fox, he might have vainly attempted to cast off an hereditary stigma of unpopularity which had been originally fastened on his family by Luttrel, the betrayer of King James.

The picketings, free quarters, half-hangings, floggings, and pitch-cappings, which at length fanned the flame of disaffection into open rebellion, were understood to be mainly directed by Lord Carhampton. In 1797 the Rev. Mr. Berwick, under whose windows men had been flogged, and in some instances left for dead, having humanely procured proper surgical treatment for some of the sufferers, was sent for by Lord Carhampton, who told him " that he had heard he was interfering with what was going on; that it was shameful for him! and that if he persevered he would send him in four days on board the tender !"* Thirteen hundred of the king's subjects had been already transported by Lord Carhampton without trial or sentence.†

Under the auspices of this peer, who at last attained the dignity of commander-in-chief, the army were permitted to riot in the most demoralising license. Cottages were burnt, peasants shot, their wives and daughters violated.‡ General Sir Ralph Abercrombie viewed the state of the army with disgust, and declared that they had become " formidable to all but the enemy". As a commander, Lord

* Grattan's *Memoirs*, v. iv. p. 334.
† Plowden's *History of Ireland*. v. ii. p. 372.
‡ *Speech* of Lord Moira, Nov. 22, 1797. See also Speeches of *Lord Dunsany*, Sir L. Parsons, and Mr. Vandeleur.

Carhampton was ruthless and capricious. The Lord
Lieutenant on several occasions interfered, but Lord
Carhampton as often refused to obey the viceroy".[*]

In the letter of " A Gray-headed Attorney", from
which we have taken an extract, Lord Carhampton's
name is mentioned in conjunction with that of a
woman named Lewellyn, who seventy years ago enjoyed an infamous notoriety in Dublin. A young
girl named Mary Neal, having been decoyed into a
house by Mrs. Lewellyn, met with some ill usage
for which Lord Carhampton got the credit. Against
Mrs. Lewellyn, as mistress of this house, the father
of the girl lodged informations. But in order to
avert the prosecution, a friend of Mrs. Lewellyn,
named Edgeworth, trumped up a counter-charge to
the effect that Neal, his wife, and daughter, had
robbed a girl, and thus got warrants against them.
" She had interest enough with the gaoler", writes
Hamilton Rowan, " to procure a constable who, in
the middle of the night, took the Neals to Newgate
and locked them up in separate cells". Mrs. Neal it
seems was *enceinte*, and in the morning, on opening
the cell, she, and an infant of whom she had been
delivered, were found dead.[†]   Neal was tried for
the alleged robbery, but the case fell to the ground.
Meanwhile, Mary Neal remained dangerously ill at
a public hospital, where, adds Mr. Rowan, "she was
protected from the examinations and interrogations
of some persons of high rank, which did them no
credit, in order to intimidate her, and make her
acknowledge that she was one of those depraved
young creatures who infest the streets, and thus to
defend Lewellyn on her trial". Mrs. Lewellyn was

[*] Barrington's *Rise and Fall of the Irish Nation*, p. 261.
[†] *Autobiography of A. Hamilton Rowan*, p. 95.

tried for complicity in the violation, and received sentence of death. Edgeworth was convicted of subornation of perjury, and ordered to stand three times in the pillory, and to be imprisoned for one year. Both culprits were shortly after pardoned and liberated by the viceroy! Several pamphlets appeared on the subject. Hamilton Rowan wrote "An Investigation of the Sufferings of John, Anne, and Mary Neal"; another writer published "The Cries of Blood and Injured Innocence, or the Protection of Vice and Persecution of Virtue", etc., addressed "to his Excellency the Marquis of B——". Dr. Boyton also entered the lists and was called out by Lord Carhampton. Rowan espoused the cause of Mary Neal with almost Quixotic fervour. He challenged to mortal combat every man who dared to asperse her fame. He accompanied her to the Castle, and presented a petition to the Lord Lieutenant, praying that as Lewellyn's "claim to mercy was founded on the principle of Mary Neal being soiled with guilt which her soul abhorred, such a communication of the evidence might be made as she may defend herself against". The viceroy, however, declined to grant the prayer; and the statue of Justice over the Castle gate was thereupon supposed to say:

"Since Justice is now but a pageant of state,
Remove me, I pray you, from this Castle gate.
Since the rape of an infant, and blackest of crimes,
Are objects of mercy in these blessed times,
On the front of new prison, or hell let me dwell in,
For a pardon is granted to Madame Lewellyn".

John Magee declared that the Sham Squire's influence in high quarters had been exerted to the uttermost in effecting the liberation of Mrs. Lewellyn *and her obliging friend Edgeworth. The Post of the day, in* a parody on the Rev. Dr. Burrowes'

slang song, " The Night afore Larry was stretched",
tells us that

> " Oh ! de night afore Edgwort was tried,
> De council dey met in despair,
>   George Jos—he was there, and beside,
> Was a doctor, a lord, and a play'r.*
> Justice Sham den silence proclaim'd,
> De bullies dey all of them harken'd:
>   Poor Edgwort, siz he, will be framed,
>   His daylights perhaps will be darkened,
>   Unless we can lend him a hand".†

Several stanzas to the same effect are given. At
length—some further squibs intervening—a valentine from Maria Lewellyn to the Sham Squire appeared.

> " With gratitude to you, my friend,
> Who saved me from a shameful end,
>   My heart does overflow;
> 'T was you my liberty restor'd,
> 'T was you that influenced my lord,
>   To you my life I owe.‡

A facetious report received circulation that Mrs.
Lewellyn was about to be allied in marriage to Mr.
Higgins; whereupon Magee's poet exclaimed in
pompous mock heroic:

> " Irradiate Phœbus, ruling god of light,
> Let not thy coursers chase away this night
> Thy beams effulgent and resplendent hide,
> Nor interrupt Francisco and his bride.
> This night, escap'd from gaol and gaol's alarms,
> The chaste Lewellyn fills his circling arms !"§

Mrs. Lewellyn was not the only frail member of
her family. Her sister, who kept a house of in-

* Counsellor George Joseph Browne and Dr. Houlton, assist-
ant editors of the *Freeman's Journal;* Lord Carhampton, and
Richard Daly, lessee of Crow Street theatre.
† *Dublin Evening Post,* No. 1757.
‡ *Ibid.,* No. 1762. § *Ibid.,* No. 1768.

famous notoriety,* fell from one crime to another,
until at last, in 1765, it was deemed necessary to
make a public example of her, and the wretched
woman was burned alive in Stephen's Green !

But, perhaps, the wittiest poetic satire on the Sham
Squire which appeared in the *Post*, is an ingenious
parody, extending to fourteen stanzas, on a then
popular slang song.   Pandemonium, Belzebub, and
a select circle of infernal satellites, developing a
series of diabolical plans, are described.   In the ninth
verse Shamado is introduced :—

" From Erebus' depths rose each elf, who glow'd with infernal
   desire,
But their prince judged it fit that himself should alone hold
   confab with the Squire".

The eleventh stanza is pithy :—

" 'T is well, said Shamado, great Sire ! your law has been always
   my pleasure;
I conceive what your highness desires—'t is my duty to second
   the measure.
The deeper I plunge for your sake, the higher I raise my condition;
Then who would his fealty break—to a prince who thus feeds
   his ambition,
            And gratifies every desire ?

Through life I 've acknowledged thy aid, and as constantly tasted
   thy bounty,
From the Newgate solicitor's trade till a sub-sheriff plac'd in
   the county.
Shall I halt in the midst of my sins, or sink fainting and tremb-
   ling before 'em.
When my honour thick-spreading begins—when, in fine—I am
   one of the quorum,
            And may in the senate be placed ?"†

* Female immorality seems to have been regularly punished
in the last century. In the *Freeman's Journal* of Dec. 6, 1766,
we read :—" Alice Rice was pilloried at the Tholsel, pursuant to
her sentence, for keeping a house of ill fame in Essex Street".
† *Dublin Evening Post,* No. 1744.

In May, 1789, Justice Higgins gave a grand entertainment to his patrons and supporters in Stephen's Green. All Dublin spoke of it; the papers of the day record it. Magee ridiculed the Sham Squire's pretensions. He called upon Fitzgibbon, the new chancellor, to reform the magistracy, and for a statement advanced in the following passage Magee was prosecuted by Higgins; but of this anon. "Can it be denied—nay, is it not known to every individual in this city—that the proprietor of a flagitious gambling house—the groom-porter of a table which is nightly crowded with all that is vile, base, or blasphemous in a great capital, that the owner and protector of this house is a justice of peace for the county Dublin?"[*]

Mr. Higgins had no longer any necessity to bribe the judge's coachman to drive him through the streets in the judicial carriage. The Sham Squire had now a gorgeous chariot of his own. In the *Post* of June 4th, 1789, we find a description of it, *i.e.* a dark chocolate ground, enlivened by a neat border of pale patent yellow; the arms emblazoned in a capacious mantle on each pannel. In front, behind, and under the coachman's footboard, the crest is handsomely engraved on every buckle of the silver plated harness.[†] In this shining equipage, with as puffed a demeanour as Lord Clonmel or Sergeant Toler, Mr. Higgins constantly drove to the courts. We read, "Mr. Higgins appeared in his place yesterday at the courts. He was set down in his own carriage, immediately after that of the attorney-general".[‡] And in a subsequent number, it is reproachfully remarked that Higgins sits on the

* *Dublin Evening Post*, No. 1759.　† Ibid., No. 1770.
‡ *Ibid.*, No. 1767.

same bench with Sergeant Toler, arrayed in chains
of gold, and dispensing justice.* The ostentatious
manner of the Sham, and above all, his impudent
swagger, excited a general feeling of disgust. He
openly " boasted his influence at the seat of power,
and bragged that the police magistrates† lived on
terms of the closest intimacy with him".‡

On Sunday, June 16th, 1789, the celebrated
pulpit orator, Walter Blake Kirwan, afterwards
Dean of Killala, and originally a Roman Catholic
priest, preached an eloquent sermon on morality in
Saint Andrew's Church, and, according to the *Post*
of the day, took occasion, in the course of his
homily, to lash the proprietors of the flagitious
gambling house in Crane Lane.§ Higgins denied
that he was the proprietor of it; but the *Post* per-
sisted in declaring that if not the avowed owner, he
was the secret participator in its profits. This vile
pandemonium was said to yield £400 a-year to Mr.
Higgins.‖ In vain were the authorities implored,
year after year, to suppress it. At length the following curious "card", as a last resource, was published:

"The Freemen and Freeholders of the Parish of
Saint Andrew's take liberty to demand from Alderman
Warren, their representative in Parliament, and president at the Police Board, why some measures are not
taken by him, to immediately and effectually suppress
that nursery of vice—that receptacle for vagrants—that
hell of Dublin—the gambling house in Crane Lane.
The alderman has been so repeatedly applied to on the
subject, that it is high time that Freeholders who know
and respect themselves, should not longer be trifled

* *Dublin Evening Post*, No. 1779.   † *Ibid.*, No. 1782.
‡ *Ibid.*, No. 1760.   § *Ibid.*, No 1777.   ‖ *Ibid.*, No. 1782.

with. Reports are now current, and circulated with a confidence that render inattention somewhat more than censurable. A magistrate and a city representative ought to be above suspicion. The Freeholders are aware that infamous house is not in their district, yet they know how their representative ought to act whether as a man or a magistrate. His future conduct shall alone determine their votes and influence".*

Weeks rolled over, and still nothing was done. At length a correspondent, who signed himself "An Attorney", threw out the following astute inuendo: "Alderman Nat, and Level Low, are in gratitude bound not to disturb the gambling-house in Crane Lane, as the Sham is very indulgent to them by not calling in two judgments which he has on their lands".†

The sumptuousness of Mr. Francis Higgins's entertainments continued to be the town talk. Judges, as we are assured by Magee, revelled at his board.‡ The police magistrates basked in the sunshine of his smile;§ but it is at least gratifying to learn that there were some high legal functionaries who indignantly scouted the Sham Squire's pretensions. Magee observes, " To the honour of Lord Fitzgibbon (Clare), be it recorded that he never dined with Higgins on his public days, or suffered his worship to appear at any table which his presence dignified".‖

Higgins, meanwhile, surrounded by a swarm of toadies and expectants for place, with a loose gown wrapped like a toga around him, would sometimes swagger through the hall of the old Four Courts. He is traditionally described as having been one of

* *Dublin Evening Post,* No. 1756.   † *Ibid.,* No. 1789.
‡ *Ibid., No. 1756.*   § *Ibid.,* No. 1776.   ‖ *Ibid., No. 1798.*

5

the ugliest men in existence, and the following contemporary portrait, though somewhat exaggerated, serves to confirm that account:

> " Through the long hall an universal hum
> Proclaims, at length, the mighty man is come.
> Clothed in a morning gown of many a hue,
> With one sleeve ragged and the other new,
> While filthy eructations daub his chin
> With the remaining dregs of last night's gin;
> With bloated cheek and little swinish eye,
> And every feature formed to hide a lie,
> While every nasty vice, enthroned within,
> Breaks out in blotches o'er his freckled skin".

The bard, after describing Enmity, Treachery, Duplicity, and other disreputable qualities, adds:

> " And artful, cunning, simpering the while,
> Conceals them all in one unmeaning smile.
> *   *   *   *   *   *   *
> He comes, and round him the admiring throng
> Catch at the honey dropping from his tongue;
> Now promises—excuses round him fly;
> Now hopes are born—and hopes as quickly die;
> Now he from b——ds his daily rent receives,
> And sells indemnity to rogues and thieves".*

The hall of the Four Courts, through which Francis Higgins was wont to stalk, is not the stately vestibule now known by that name in Dublin. The old Four Courts stood adjacent to Christ Church; its hall, crowned by an octangular cupola, was long and narrow, and entered by a door leading from the lane known as " Hell". The chancellor, on entering, was always preceded by his mace-bearer and tipstaffs, who were accustomed to call out " High Court of Chancery", upon which the judges rose, and remained standing until the chancellor had taken his seat.†

* *Dublin Evening Post*, No. 1746.
† *Gilbert's Dublin*, v. i. pp. 136 7.

Daniel O'Connell had some reminiscences of the old Four Courts and prison. The gaoler, it will be remembered, was the Sham Squire's father-in-law.

"As we drove along Skinner's Row, O'Connell pointed out the ruins of the old Four Courts, and showed me where the old gaol had stood. 'Father Lube', said he, 'informed me of a curious escape of a robber from that gaol. The rogue was rich, and gave the gaoler £120 to let him out. The gaoler then prepared for the prisoner's escape in the following manner: he announced that the fellow had a spotted fever, and the rogue shammed sick so successfully that no one suspected any cheat. Meanwhile, the gaoler procured a fresh corpse, and smuggled it into the prisoner's bed; while the pseudo-invalid was let out one fine dark night. The corpse, which passed for that of the robber, was decently interred, and the trick remained undiscovered till revealed by the gaoler's daughter, long after his death. Father Lube told me', added O'Connell, 'that the face of the corpse was dappled with paint, to imitate the discolourment of a spotted fever' ".[*]

To reduce the overcharged importance of the Sham Squire, Magee published, in June, 1787, an outline of his escapade in the family of Mr. Archer. On June 30, a note appeared from the " reverend gentlemen of Rosemary Lane", stating they had no official or other knowledge of an imposture alleged to have been committed twenty-three years previously on the late Mr. Archer by Mr. Higgins, and adding, that during Mr. Higgins's residence in Smock Alley, his conduct had been always marked with propriety and benevolence. " This sprig of Rosemary", observed the *Post*, " may serve to revive the

[*] *Personal Recollections of O'Connell*, by W. J. O'Neil Daunt, v. i. p. 110.

fainting innocence of the immaculate convert of
Saint Francis". But in the following number a
different aspect is given to the matter, thus: "We
have it from authority that the advertisement from
the reverend gentlemen of Rosemary Lane chapel is
a sham; for confirmation of which we refer the in-
quirer to any of the reverend gentlemen of said
chapel".* How far this may be in accordance with
the truth it is not easy to determine.

Mr. Higgins was not without some redeeming
qualities. He regularly attended divine service in
the Protestant church of Saint Andrew, and he
occasionally dispensed sums in charity. But for all
this he received little thanks and less credit. In a
trenchant poem levelled at Higgins, numbering some
fifty lines, and alleged to be from the pen of Hussey
Burgh, we find:

> "The cunning culprit understands the times,
> Stakes private bounty against public crimes,
> And conscious of the means he took to rise,
> He buys a credit with the spoils of vice".†

The Sham Squire's duties were onerous and
various. He not only presided, as we are told, with
the subsequent Lord Norbury, at Kilmainham,‡
but often occupied the bench of the Lord Mayor's
court, and there investigated and confirmed the
claims of persons to the rights and privileges of
freemen.§

Mr. Higgins had, ere long, nearly the entire of
the newspaper press of Dublin in his influence;‖ to
quote Magee's words, they were all " bowing down

---

* *Dublin Evening Post*, No. 1782.　　† *Ibid.*, No. 1794.
‡ *Ibid.*, No. 1779.　　　　　　　　　§ *Ibid.*, No. 1789.
‖ *Ibid.*, No. 1796.

to Baal",[*] or as Magee's poet described the circumstance:

> " Now, hireling scribes, exert the venal pen,
> And in concerto shield this best of men".

And again:

> "Nay e'en Shamado is himself on fire,
> And humdrum Houlton tunes his wooden lyre;
> But virtue their resentment cannot dread,
> And truth, tho' trampled on, will raise her head".[†]

Dr. Houlton, the Sham Squire's sub-editor, whose name frequently appears in the local squibs of the day, is noticed in *Boaden's Life of Mrs. Jordan*, as " a weak man with an Edinburgh degree in physic, who wrote for a morning paper, and contributed a prologue so absurd that it has been banished from the play".[‡] From *Raymond's Life of Dermody* we learn that Houlton humanely befriended the unfortunate poet. The doctor lost nothing by his connexion with Higgins. The same work informs us that he received " a medical appointment under the Irish Government", and that his house in Dublin was as showy as his style, having been put through a process of decoration by Daly's head scene painter.[||] The *Literary Calendar of Living Authors*, published in 1816, mentions that Houlton was a native of England, " practised in Ireland with some success", brought out some musical pieces on the Dublin stage, wrote poems for newspapers, and songs for Vauxhall; and through the patronage of Hook brought out at Drury Lane Theatre, in 1800, his opera called *Wilmore Castle*, which having

* *Dublin Evening Post*, No. 1796.   † *Ibid*, No. 1748.
‡ *Boaden's Life of Mrs. Jordan*, p. 62, v. ii.
|| *Raymond's Life of Dermody*, v. i. p. 26, et seq.

been damned, he retorted in a pamphlet entitled *A Review of the Musical Drama of the Theatre Royal, Drury Lane, tending to develop a system of private influence injurious to the public.* 8vo. 1801".

Houlton as a poetaster was useful on the Sham Squire's journal, which freely employed satirical poetry in assailing reputations.

In 1789 the bill furnished by Higgins to the Treasury amounted to £2,000; but the viceroy, we are told, cut it down to £1,000.*

* *Dublin Evening Post,* No. 1761. This payment may have been on account of proclamations inserted as advertisements; but the Duke of Wellington's correspondence, when Irish Secretary, makes no disguise that all money paid on such grounds was for purposes of corruption. This arrangement was partially relinquished from the death of Pitt; but in 1809, on the restoration of the old Tory regime, we find a Dublin journalist petitioning for a renewal. Sir A. Wellesley, addressing Sir Charles Saxton, the under secretary, alluded to " the measures which I had in contemplation in respect to newspapers in Ireland. *It is quite impossible to leave them entirely to themselves;* and we have probably carried our reforms in respect to publishing proclamations as far as they will go, excepting only that we might strike off from the list of those permitted to publish proclamations in the newspapers, both in town and country, which have the least extensive circulation, and which depend, I believe, entirely upon the money received on account of proclamations. *I am one of those, however, who think that it will be very dangerous to allow the press in Ireland to take care of itself, particularly as it has so long been in leading strings.* I would, therefore, recommend that in proportion as you will diminish the profits of the better kind of newspapers, ... on account of proclamations, *you shall increase the sum they are allowed to charge on account of advertisements and other publications.* It is absolutely necessary, however, to keep the charge *within the sum of ten thousand pounds per annum,* voted by parliament, which probably may easily be done when some newspapers will cease to publish proclamations, and the whole will receive a reduced sum on that account, even though *an increase* should be made *on account of advertisements* to the accounts *of some. It will also be* very necessary that *the account of this money should be of a description* always to be produced before parliament.—*Ever yours, etc.,*   ARTHUR WELLESLEY".

CHAPTER III.

Lord Clonmel and the Fiats.—Richard Daly.—Persecution
of Magee.—A Strong Bar.—Caldbeck, Duigenan, and Egan.
—The Volunteers to the rescue.—Hamilton Rowan.—An
artist arrested for caricaturing the Sham Squire.—More
squibs.—The Gambling Hell.—Inefficiency of the Police.—
Magisterial delinquencies exposed.—Watchmen and Watches.
—Mr. Gonne's Chronometer.—Juggling Judges.—Outrages
in the face of day —Ladies unable to walk the streets.—
Sedan chairs.—Unholy compacts.

MAGEE continued in his efforts to take down the
Sham Squire's pride and swagger. Squib after squib
exploded:—

> "There lives a Squire near Stephen's Green,
>   Crockledum he, crockledum ho,
> And in Newgate once was seen,
>   Bolted down quite low.
> And though he now is a Just-Ass,*
> There was a day when he heard mass,
> Being converted by a lass,
>   There to *cross* and go.
> On stocking-making he can jaw,
>   Clockety heel, tippety toe;
> Now an attorney is at law,
>   Six and eightpence, ho!†

These squibs Mr. Higgins regarded as so many
"infernal machines", and he resolved to show his
own power, and to be revenged at the same time.
Lord Chief Justice Clonmel was known to entertain
a strong prejudice against the press, especially such
newspapers as adversely criticized the administration.
In the authorised report of the parliamentary debates on April 8, 1784, his views on the subject are
forcibly but curtly conveyed, viz.: *"The Prime
Sergeant expressed his thorough detestation of news-*

* Until 1793, Catholics were excluded from the magisterial
bench.
† *Dublin Evening Post*, No. 1796.

papers and public assassins of character".[*] We have already seen that Lord Clonmel, long after his elevation to the bench and peerage, maintained friendly relations with Higgins, in memory of auld lang syne. His lordship's house, observes a correspondent, stood on the west side of Harcourt Street, near the corner of Montague Street. He possessed also very extensive pleasure grounds on the east side of Harcourt Street, stretching behind the entire south side of Stephen's Green. A subterraneous passage under[†] Harcourt Street opened communication with those grounds, which joined the garden at the rere of Francis Higgins's mansion in Stephen's Green; and there is a tradition to the effect, that some of the chief's inquisitive neighbours often used to see him making his way through the pleasure grounds for the purpose of conferring with the Sham Squire.[‡]

Higgins is said to have directed Lord Clonmel's attention to Magee's lampoons, in many of which the chief himself figured subordinately. His lordship expressed indignation at liberties so unwarrantable, and seems to have encouraged the Sham Squire to follow up a plan of legal retribution, which the active brain of Higgins had been for some time concocting.

In the various onslaughts which Magee made upon the Sham Squire, some passing prods were bestowed on Richard Daly, the lessee of Crow Street theatre, on Charles Brennan, a writer for the *Freeman's Journal*, as well as on a certain member of the female sex, with all of whom Higgins was believed to be on terms of close intimacy. In June,

* *Irish Parl. Debates*, vol. iii., p. 155.
† *MS. Letter of Dr. T——, 20th August, 1859.*
‡ *Tradition* communicated by M—— S——, Esq.

1789, four fiats, marked with the exorbitant sum of £7,800, were issued against Magee by Lord Clonmel in the King's Bench, at the suit of Francis Higgins and the three other persons to whom we alluded. The *Evening Post* of June 30, 1789, announces that " Magee lies on the couch of sickness in the midst of a dungeon's gloom", and publishes a long appeal from Magee to Lord Clonmel, which closes with the following paragraph:—

" I again demand at your hands, John Scott, Baron Earlsfort,* a trial by peers, by my fellows, free and independent Irishmen. Thou hast dragged a citizen by thy officers thrice through the streets of this capital as a felon. Thou hast confined before trial, and hast deprived a free subject of his franchise, that franchise for which his fathers bled on the walls of Derry, the banks of the Boyne, and the plains of Aughrim.

" John Scott, Baron Earlsfort, I again demand from thee, thou delegate of my Sovereign Lord the King, a trial by jury".

On July 3rd, 1789, the trial of John Magee, at the suit of Francis Higgins, was heard before Chief Justice Clonmel. The Sham Squire, notwithstanding his reliance on the partiality of the judge and jury, found it advisable to retain a powerful bar, which included the Prime Sergeant, Mr. Caldbeck, K.C.;†

---

* Mr. Scott was created Baron Earlsfort in 1784, a Viscount in 1789, and Earl of Clonmel in 1789.

† Caldbeck seems to have been as small as Tom Moore, and a great wit. His great grandson, Mr. Wm. Francis Caldbeck, has given us the following traditional anecdote of him:—" But you little vagabond", said the opposite counsel one day, " if you don't be cautious I 'll put you in my pocket". " Then I can tell you, my fine *fellow*", *retorted* Caldbeck, " whenever you do, you 'll *have more law in your* pocket than ever you had in your head" .

John Toler, afterwards Lord Norbury;* Sergeant
Duquerry,† Recorder Burston,‡ Dr. Pat Duigenan,§
John, nicknamed "Bully" Egan,‖ George J. Browne,
(Higgins's collaborator), with Messrs. Ponsonby,
Curran, Johnston, and Hon. S. Butler. That the
last three persons should have accepted briefs in the

* For a notice of Lord Norbury see Appendix.

† Sergeant Duquerry, a forensic orator of great power, "died
at the top first", like Swift, Plunket, Magee, Scott, Moore, and
many a stately oak. For several years before his death, Duquerry groped in utter idiotcy.

‡ Bereaford Burston will be remembered as the early friend
of Moore. See *Memoirs of Moore*, v. i. p. 79.

§ Dr. Patrick Duigenan, originally a Catholic of low degree,
having "conformed" and continued year after year to oppose the
Catholic claims, with a virulence and violence now almost incredible, was appointed by the Archbishops of Armagh and
Dublin, to preside as their judge in the Ecclesiastical Courts.
He was twice married, and each time to a Catholic. He died in
1816.

‖ John Egan's proficiency in vulgar wit and rough invective
is traditionally notorious. If a somewhat unregulated indulgence
in this tendency obtained for him many enemies in early life, he
had the satisfaction of finally making all Ireland his debtor, by
his truly independent conduct at the period of the Union.
Trampling down the metaphorical sophistries of the government
spokesman, "he galloped", writes Sir Jonah Barrington, "like a
dray-horse, over all his opponents, plunging and kicking, and
overthrowing all before him". Tempting proposals were made
to him if he would support the Union. He was offered to be
made Baron of the Exchequer, with £3,500 a-year; but Egan,
although far from being rich, spurned the venal offer, and died
soon after in comparative want.

We are tempted to append two not uncharacteristic anecdotes
of John Egan, which are now published for the first time. Egan
resided at Kilmacud House, and was fond of bathing at the
Blackrock. One morning, having violently flung his enormous
carcase into the water, he came in collision with some other
person who was performing a similar lavement. "Sir", screamed
a mouth out of the water, "I presume you are not aware against
whom you have so rudely jostled". "I didn't care if you were
Old Nick", replied Egan, floundering about like a great sea
monster. "You are a bear, sir", continued the mouth, "and I
am the Archbishop of Dublin". "Well", retorted Egan, not in
the least abashed, "in order to prevent the recurrence of such

case, seems singular, considering their democratic
bias. Curran's name is the history of his life; Mr.
Johnston's is nearly forgotten; but we may remind the
reader that although a judge, he libelled the Hardwicke administration, was tried for the offence,
retired from the bench, and shortly before his death
published a treasonable pamphlet. The Hon. Simon
Butler became in 1792 a leading member of the
Society of United Irishmen, was fined £500, and condemned to a protracted imprisonment in Newgate.
No good report of the trial, Higgins v. Magee, is
accessible. We endeavoured to give the Sham Squire
the benefit of his own report, but the file of the
Freeman for 1789 does not exist in Dublin, so far
as we know, not even in the office of that journal.
A very impartial report may be found in the *Cork
Evening Post* of the day, from which we gather that
Higgins proved the infamous gambling house in
Crane Lane to belong to a Miss J. Darley. This
evidence, however, did not alter Magee's opinion,
and he continued to insist that the Sham Squire was
a secret participator in its spoils.

Poor Magee had not much chance against a bar
so powerful and a judge so hostile. Strictly speaking, he had no counsel retained; but we find that
"for the traverser there appeared as *amici curiæ*,
Mr. Lysaght, and Mr. A. Browne of Trinity College".
The latter gentleman, member for the University of
Dublin, and subsequently Prime Sergeant of Ireland

accidents, I would simply recommend you to get your mitr
painted on your back".

Egan drank hard; and some clients, anxious to secure his pr
fessional services, made a stipulation with him, that no wine w
to be drank previous to the defence. Egan agreed, but casui
cally evaded the *engagement*, by eating large quantities of br
soaked in wine.

made a very able statement on the law of fiats. As
a lawyer, Browne was far superior to Lord Clonmel,
whose indecently rapid promotion by the government was owing solely to his parliamentary services.
In the following session of parliament Mr. Browne,
in conjunction with Mr., afterwards Chancellor, Ponsonby, brought forward a masterly exposure of the
most unconstitutional conduct adopted by Lord
Clonmel at the instance of Francis Higgins. This
exposure with its salutary results shall be noticed
at the fitting period; but meanwhile we will introduce here a few of the salient points in Mr. Browne's
able statement on the law of fiats.

He expressed his amazement that a nation so astute in guarding through her statute book every
avenue to oppression, should have passed unnoticed
and left unguarded this broad road to tyranny. He
was amazed how it could suffer a plaintiff to require
bail to the amount of perhaps £20,000, where very
probably the damages afterwards found by a jury, if
any, might not be twenty pence. Having shown that
fiats, in Lord Clonmel's acceptation of the term, were
utterly unknown to the common law, he added, " I
am not sure whether, if Francis Higgins abused his
adversary's council for two years together, they
would be able to swear to two-penny worth of
damages; and therefore, when any man swears so
positively, either he is particularly vulnerable, and
more liable to damage than other men, or he is a
bold swearer, and the judge ought not to listen to
him". Mr. Browne cited Blackstone, Baines, Gilbert, and a vast array of high legal authorities, to
show the unconstitutional act of Lord Clonmel, in
issuing fiats against Magee to the amount of £7,800.
It appears that even in the case of assault and bat-

tery, moderate fiats had been refused by the bench.
Having, with great erudition discharged an important argument to show that special bail in this and
similar actions was not requirable, Mr. Browne proceeded to prove that, even allowing it to be requirable,
the present amount could not be justified by reason
or precedent. The bail could only with propriety
amount to such a sum as would be sufficient to en-
sure an appearance. To imagine that Mr. Magee
would abscond and abandon his only means of earning a livelihood, was simply ridiculous.

Mr. Browne censured the manner in which Lord
Clonmel prejudiced the case—" telling the jury before the trial began what the damages were, which
in the opinion of the judge they ought to give",—
and Mr. Browne adduced high legal authorities in
proof of the error committed by Lord Clonmel.

He then contrasted some of the few cases on record in which fiats were issued, with the cause then
under discussion. Sir William Drake, a member of
parliament, was charged with being a traitor. The
words against him were of the most scandalous
nature. His life and property were at stake: he
brought his action, and on application special bail
from defendant was refused. Another case was that
of Duke Schomberg, a peer high in favour of his
king and country. He was accused by a miscreant
named Murray with having cheated the sovereign
and the army. Can any words be conceived more
shocking when applied to such a man? Chief Justice Holt, as great a friend to the Revolution and to
the liberties of the country as ever sat on a judicial
bench, felt the same indignation, but he could not
prejudice the cause. He was ready to punish the
man if convicted, but he did not consider him con-

victed beforehánd. He ordered Murray to find
bail—two sureties in £25 each, and the man in
£100! In the last generation fifty pounds for a
duke—in the present, £7,800 for an adventurer and
a player![*]

At the close of the prosecution against Magee at
the suit of Francis Higgins, it was made the subject
of bitter complaint by the prisoner that he had been
refused the privilege of challenging his jurors, and
the benefit of the *Habeas Corpus Act*.[†]

The Lord Chief Justice having summed up and
charged, the jury retired, but returned in half an
hour to ask the bench whether they might not find
the traverser guilty of printing and publishing, without holding him responsible for the libel. His lordship replied that the jury had nothing to do with
the law in this case, and that it was only the fact of
publishing they had to consider. The jury then
desired a copy of the record, but the request was
refused. Having retired a second time, the jury at
length brought in their verdict, " Guilty of printing
and publishing". Lord Earlsfort declined to accept
the verdict.

One of the jurors replied that the difficulty they
found in giving a different verdict was, that they
could not reconcile it to their consciences to find a
man guilty under a criminal charge, who had not
been permitted to confront his accusers or his jurors,
or to listen to the accusations against him, that he
might be prepared for his defence. Therefore, as
the jury had only seen the accusations on one side,
without the defence of the accused, they could not

---

[*] Browne's arguments in the King's Bench on the subject of
admitting John Magee to common bail. Dublin, Gilbert, 1790.
[†] *Dublin Evening Post*, No. 1784.

feel themselves warranted in pronouncing a man guilty under a charge of criminal intentions.

Lord Earlsfort replied that the very reason why they ought not to hesitate, was the one they used in support of their scruples, namely, " the traversers making no defence to the charge against him". He desired that the jury might again retire. A juror said that they had already given the matter full consideration, but the Chief Justice interrupted him, and the jury were ordered to return to their room.

Counsellor Browne, M.P. for the College, addressed a few words to the bench, but was stopped short by his lordship, who declared that he had already given the matter full consideration, and had made up his mind. The jury having again deliberated, returned with a verdict of guilty.[*]

This prosecution did not muzzle Magee. In the very number of his journal which contains a report of the trial reference is made to " the marquis, who, with that condescending goodness that agitates his heart when he can be of any use to Mr. F. Higgins, his familiar friend, and he who in former days contributed not less to the festivity of his board, than generously catered for his pleasure", etc. And in *Magee's Evening Packet*, Shamado is again reminded of the awkward fact " that he has been at a public trial convicted of crimes which the cordial squeeze of his friend Jack Ketch alone can expiate".[†]

. The trial of Daly *versus* Magee soon followed. Dr. Pat Duigenan, " Bully Egan", with Messrs. Duquerry, Smith, Burston, Butler, Brown, Fleming,

* *Dublin Evening Post*, No. 1784.
† *Magee's Evening Packet*, No. 621.

Ball, Curran, and Green were retained for the prosecution.

Mr. Kennedy, treasurer to the Theatre Royal, Crow Street, was examined as a witness for Mr. Daly. We extract a few passages:—

" Were you ever witness to any riots in the theatre ? Very often. The people used to cry out from the gallery 'a clap for Magee, the man of Ireland—a groan for the Sham ! a groan for the Dasher, [Daly] out with the lights, out with the lights !" I have frequently, at the risk of my life, attempted to stop those riots".

It further appeared that men used sometimes to come into the galleries with bludgeons and pistols. Mr Dawson, a person whom Mr. Daly was in the habit of sending to London, with a view to the engagement of actors, was next examined. It transpired that Daly, in consequence of his unpopularity, found a difficulty in obtaining performers.

" Is Mr. Higgins proprietor of any paper? A. I do not know. Q. Is he proprietor of the *Freeman's Journal?* A. I have heard so. Q. Have you read the *Freeman's Journal?* A. Sometimes. Q. Has there not been the same constant series of recriminations between Mr. Higgins and Mr. Magee ? A. I have seen dashes on each side. Q. Is there not a very particular intimacy between Mr. Daly and Mr. Higgins ? A. Have I a right, my lord, to answer that question ?

" Court—No, I must object to that question. I think it wrong to endeavour to involve this case in any party or prejudice, etc.

" Counsel for the defendant—Do you believe yourself that there was any particular intimacy between Mr. Daly and Mr. Higgins ? Sir, I know of no particular intimacy any more than between you and the many gentlemen who are round you.

" Court—You have answered very properly and clearly.

" Q. There is a friendship between them ?   A. The same sort of friendship which subsists between man and man".[*]

There certainly was no stint of hard words between the rival editors. Magee insinuated that Ryder, the former lessee, had been tricked out or the patent by a manœuvre of the Sham Squire's, and that Higgins and Daly conjointly held the license.[†] But of any deliberate act of dishonesty, Daly was, we believe, incapable, although lax enough in other respects.

George Ponsonby conducted the defence. He ridiculed Daly's claims to damages; and added that for the torrent of abuse which had been thrown out against Magee in the *Freeman* no redress was sought. Mr. Higgins had ridiculed Astley with impunity in the *Freeman's Journal;* and for pursuing the same course towards Daly, eight thousand pounds damages were claimed against Magee.

Damages were laid at £8,000; but the jury considered that £200, with 6d. costs, was ample compensation for the wounded feelings of Mr. Daly.

The *Evening Post* steadily declared that the uproar in the galleries of the theatre was due rather to Higgins and Daly, than to Magee. In July, 1789, we are told that two men named Valentine and Thomas Higgins, wool-scribblers, were " very active in several public-houses in and about the Liberty, endeavouring to persuade working people to accept tickets for the theatre, with express directions to

---

[*] *Trial of John Magee for libel on R. Daly.* Dublin, 1790, pp. 30, 31.
[†] *Dublin Evening Post,* No. 1794.

6

raise plaudits for Daly and Higgins, and to groan Magee".*

A few evenings after, an immense troop of " Liberty Boys" in the Higgins' interest proceeded to Crow Street Theatre, marshalled by a limb of the law named Lindsay.†

"The general order is, knock down every man who groans for the Sham Squire or the Dasher; and you have the guards at your back to take every man into custody who resists you. On Tuesday night this party, highly whiskeyfied, forced their way to the front row of the gallery, struck and insulted several of the audience there, and wounded the delicacy of the rest of the house by riotous vociferation and obscenity. Last night several people were knocked down by them; and some of the very persons who were seduced from the Liberty to the theatre, on their refusal to join in the purpose, were charged to the custody of constables for disrespectful language to the said Lindsay, and others were pursued as far as Anglesea Street, for the same cause".‡

On Magee's trial, the prosecuting counsel produced the manuscript of an attack upon the Sham Squire in Magee's handwriting. Magee, who was at first somewhat surprised at the unexpected production of his autograph, soon discovered by what means these papers got out of his hands. Brennan,§ who had been a writer for the *Post* until 1788, when he joined the *Freeman*, conveyed to the Sham Squire several of Magee's private papers, to which, when retained in the office of the *Post* at a salary of £100 a year, he had easy access.‖ Brennan certainly

* *Dublin Evening Post*, No. 1787—1788.
† *Ibid.*, No. 1785.   ‡ *Ibid.*, No. 1788.   § *Ibid.*, No. 1794.
‖ *Brennan figures in the book of Secret Service Money Expenditure as a recipient, though not to a large extent.*

swore to Magee's handwriting on the trial. On the evening that the *Post* advanced the above statement, "Brennan came to Magee's house concealed in a sedan chair, and armed with a large oak bludgeon, and after rapping at the door and being answered by a maid servant, he inquired for Mr. Magee with the design of assassinating him, had he been in the way; but being told he was not at home, Brennan rushed into the shop, and with the bludgeon, broke open and utterly demolished several locked glass cases, together with the sashwork and glass of these interior glazed doors, as well as the windows facing the street. Brennan, in making his escape, was observed by a man named M'Namara, who attempted to seize him; but Brennan knocked him down by three blows of the bludgeon, and then kicked him unmercifully".[*]

Brennan was committed to Newgate by Alderman Carleton; but next day was set at liberty on the bail of two of Daly's officials.[†] This rather intemperate gentleman, however, had not been an hour at large when he proceeded to Magee's house in College Green, armed with a sword, but happily did not succeed in finding the object of his search.[‡]

A word about the "Liberty boys" who, as Magee records, came forward as the paid partizans of Higgins, opens another suggestive glimpse of the state of society in Dublin at the period of which we write. Between these men and the butchers of Ormond Market, both noted for turbulent prowess, a feud long subsisted. On this stronghold the Liberty boys frequently made descents; a formidable battle raged, often for days, during which time the bridges across the Liffey from Essex Bridge

[*] *Dublin Evening Post*, No. 1796. [†] *Ibid.*, No. 1726. [‡] *Ibid.*, 1792.

to " Bloody Bridge" were taken and retaken. Upwards of a thousand men were usually engaged;
business was paralyzed; traffic suspended; every
shop closed; the executive looked on inert; Lord
Mayor Emerson was appealed to, but with a nervous
shrug declined to interfere. The butchers, armed
with huge knives and cleavers, did awful havoc; the
quays were strewed with the maimed and mangled.
But the professional slaughterers were not always
victorious. On one of the many occasions when
these battles raged, the butchers, who displayed a
banner inscribed " Guild of the B. V. Mary", were
repulsed by the Liberty boys near Francis Street,
and driven down Michael's Hill with loss. The Liberty boys drank to the dregs their bloody cup of
victory. Exasperated by the " *houghing*" with
which the butchers had disabled for life many of
their opponents, the " Liberty boys" rushed into the
stalls and slaughter-houses, captured the butchers,
hooked them up by the chin in lieu of their meat,
and then left the unfortunate men wriggling " alone
in their glory." The Liberty boys were mostly
weavers, the representatives of French artizans who,
after the massacre of St. Bartholomew, emigrated to
Ireland. The late Mr. Brophy, state dentist in
Dublin, to whom the students of local history are indebted for many curious traditional data, told us that
in the life-time of his mother a French *patois* was
spoken in the Liberty quite as much as English.*

* Dublin, in these days, possessed a Huguenot church and
burial ground. A curious manuscript memoir, in the autograph
of one of the Huguenot ministers, may be seen in a closet attached to Marsh's Library, Dublin. Among the influential
French who emigrated to Ireland on the revocation of the Edict
of Nantes, may be mentioned Le Poer Trenche (ancestor of
Lord Clancarty), the LaTouches, Saurins, Vignolles, LaBartes,
DuBedate, Montmorencys, Perrins, etc.

The author of *Ireland Sixty Years Ago* furnishes
stirring details of the encounters to which we refer;
but he failed to suggest, as we have ventured to do,
the origin of the feud.

" No army, however mighty", said the first Napoleon, addressing St. Cyr, " could resist the songs of
Paris". The Ormond boys, impelled by a similar
policy, followed up their knife stabs with not less
pointed lines. In one song the following elegant
distich occurred:

> And we won't leave a weaver alive on the Coombe,
> But we'll rip up his tripe bag and burn his loom.
> Ri rigidi di do dee.

One of the last battles between the " Liberty" and
Ormond boys took place on May 11, 1790.

Meanwhile it became every day more apparent
that the Sham Squire was a dangerous man to touch.
On July 23rd we learn that Mr. James Wright, of
Mary's Abbey, was arrested for publishing a caricature likeness of Justice Higgins.* A copy of this
picture, representing the Sham Squire standing
under a gallows, is now in the possession of Dr.
W——— of Dublin. Underneath is written " Bel-
phegor, or the Devil turned Esquire", with the following citation from Psalms: " Yet do I remember
the time past: I muse upon my works, yea, I exercise myself in the works of wickedness". Nailed
to the gibbet is an open copy of the " Infernal
Journal", containing articles headed " A Panegyric
on the Marquis of Misery"—" Prize Swearing"—
" Dr. Dove"—" *A Defence of Informers*", (a prophetic hit)—" Sangrado"—" Theatre Royal: Ways
and Means; to conclude with the Marker's Ghost"—
" New Books: Houltoniana, or mode of Rearing

* *Dublin Evening Post*, No. 1792.

Carrier Pigeons"*—"Bludgeoneer's Pocket Companion".-—"Marquis de la Fiat".

The appearance of Higgins, as presented in this print, is blotched, bloated, and repulsive, not unsuggestive of the portraits of Jemmy O'Brien. A cable knotted into a pendent bow, appears beneath his chin. Surmounting the picture, as it also did the bench where Higgins sometimes administered the justice he had outraged, is " Fiat justitia".

With a sort of barbed harpoon Magee goaded " the Sham" and his friends. In addition to the *Post*, he attacked him in *Magee's Weekly Packet*. The number for Saturday, October 17, 1789, contains another caricature likeness of the Sham Squire, in a woodcut, entitled " The Sham in Lavender". He is made to say " I'm no Sham—I'm a Protestant Justice—I'll Newgate the Dog". At his feet his colleague, Brennan, is recognized in the shape of a cur dog. Behind him stands Mrs. Lewellyn in the short petticoats, high-heeled shoes, large hat, and voluminous ringlets of the day. Under his feet is a letter, addressed " Mrs. Lewellyn, Cell, Newgate—Free—Carhampton"; while the viceroy, Lord Buckingham, complacently presiding, is made to address Higgins as " Frank".

Verses, painfully personal, accompanied the picture, of which the following will suffice as a sample:

> " He that put you in lavender must wish you well,
> You've got by nature, Sham, a fatal smell ;
> A dread effluvia, which some comic bard
> To the burning of bones on the strand once compared".

Conceived in a more legitimate vein of sarcasm was another piece:

---

* *In these days a good deal of lottery stock jobbing took place through the agency of carrier pigeons.*

"In a poem, I think, called ' The Author', you 'll find
Two lines, my dear Sham, which occurr'd to my mind,
When the *Packet* I saw, and your worship saw there,
And your worship so like to yourself did appear;
They were written by Churchill, and tho' they displease,
You must own they are apt, and the lines, Sham, are these:
' Grown old in villainy, and dead to grace,
Hell in his heart, and Tyburn in his face'".*

At a meeting of the Dublin Volunteers on July
10th, 1789, it was resolved: " That, as citizens and
men, armed in defence of our liberties and properties, we cannot remain unconcerned spectators of any
breach of that constitution which is the glory of the
empire.   That the violation of the fundamental
laws of these kingdoms occasioned the melancholy
catastrophe of 1648; that the violation of these laws
brought on the glorious Revolution of 1688; that
we look upon the trial by jury, with all the privileges
annexed to it, to be a most essential part of those
laws; that we highly approve of the firm conduct of
our worthy fellow-citizen, on a late transaction, in
support of those gifts".

Archibald Hamilton Rowan, then a highly influential personage, addressed a public letter to
Magee, saying: " It is with regret I have beheld
you deprived of the inalienable rights of every
British subject on your late trial.   I have no doubt
but that such arbitrary conduct as marked the judge
who presided on that day, will be severely punished,
and that you, sir, will not be so wanting to your
fellow-subjects, as not to bring it before the proper
tribunal.   This being the cause of every man, it
ought to be supported from the common purse, and
not be an injury to your private circumstances.   If
any subscription for that purpose should be accepted

* *Magee's Evening Packet*, Oct. 17, 1789.

by you, I request you will set down my name for twenty-five guineas".

It is a notable instance of Magee's independence of character, that he declined to accept one farthing of the public subscription which had just been inaugurated, with such promise of success, in his honour. This spirited determination was the more remarkable as his pecuniary losses, in consequence of the oppressive treatment to which he was subjected, proved most severe, as we shall presently see.

In Mr. Sheridan's arguments, before the judges of the King's Bench, to admit John Magee to common bail for lampooning the Sham Squire's colleague, it is stated:—

"Magee has made an affidavit in which he swears that a writ issued in last Trinity Term to the sheriffs, marked for £4,000, under authority of a fiat granted by the Lord Chief Justice, and founded on an affidavit; that upon such writ he was arrested in June last; that in consequence of a number of vexatious suits and prosecutions against him, and from the reiterated abuse he has received in the *Freeman's Journal*, he is extremely injured in his credit, insomuch that though he has used every effort in his power, he cannot now procure one bail in this cause for the amount of the sum marked at the foot of said writ, or of any larger amount than £500, and saith he verily believes that the plaintiff had not suffered damage in this cause to any amount whatever".*

* This scarce pamphlet was printed and published in London —a circumstance illustrative of the wide sensation which Lord Clonmel's arbitrary conduct excited. Mr. Sheridan having brought forward a host of high law autnorities to show the illegality of holding to special bail a man charged with defamation, proceeded to exhibit the ludicrous weakness of the affidavit upon *which Lord Clonmel* issued a fiat for £4,000. Daly's claims *against Magee* for damages were based upon a mock heroic poem

These denunciations would doubtless have been stronger were it possible for the patriot mind of John Magee to have taken a prophetic view of the events of '98, and witnessed, like Asmodeus, certain dark doings which the vulgar eye failed to penetrate.

The subterranean passage and the winding path through Lord Clonmel's pleasure ground facilitated the intercourse between him and Shamado, which, as we gather from tradition and contemporary statement, was briskly kept up. Higgins's journal was the organ of Lord Clonmel's party, and in a letter addressed to the latter, published in *Magee's Evening Packet*,* we are told:

"It is made no secret, my lord, that these ingenious sophistications and learned commentaries which appeared in the Higgins journal, in that decent business, had the honour of your lordship's inspection and correction in MS., before they were committed to the press".

The visits of the influential and proverbially convivial chief must have been hailed with no ordinary pleasure and welcome. Sir Jonah Barrington, who lived next door to him in Harcourt Street, writes, "His skill was unrivalled, and his success proverbial. He was full of anecdotes, though not the most refined; these in private society he not only told, but *acted;* and when he perceived that he had made a very good exhibition he immediately withdrew, that he might leave the most lively impression of his

in which Daly was supposed to figure under the title of Roscius, and Higgins under that of Francisco. Daly having recited this absurd poem in his affidavit, added that he had children "among whom are four growing up daughters, who in their future prospects may receive considerable injury"; and Daly wound up by swearing that he had suffered damages to the amount of £,4000 by —— the injuries which his family, or himself might hereafter suffer!

* No. 621.

pleasantry behind him. His boldness was his first
introduction—his policy his ultimate preferment.
Courageous, vulgar, humorous, artificial, he knew
the world well, and he profited by that knowledge.
He cultivated the powerful; he bullied the timid;
he fought the brave; he flattered the vain; he duped
the credulous; and he amused the convivial. He
frequently, in his prosperity, acknowledged favours
he had received when he was obscure, and *occasionally* requited them. Half liked, half reprobated,
he was too high to be despised, and too low to be
respected. His language was coarse, and his principles arbitrary; but his passions were his slaves, and
his cunning was his instrument. In public and in
private he was the same character; and, though a
most fortunate man and a successful courtier, he had
scarcely a sincere friend or a *disinterested* adherent".

" *Arcades ambo*—brothers both", was applicable
in more than one sense to the Chief Justice and the
Sham Squire. "I sat beside Higgins at a lord
mayor's banquet in 1796", observed the late John
Patten ; " sixty years after I well remember how
strongly his qualities as a *bon raconteur* impressed
me".

Mr. Higgins plumed himself on being a little
Curran, and cultivated intimacies with kindred hu-
morists, amongst whom we are surprised to find
Father Arthur O'Leary, one of the persons named
advantageously by Higgins in his will.* O'Leary
was one of those memorable Monks of the Screw who
used to set in a roar Curran's table at " the Priory".†

* Last will of Francis Higgins, preserved in the Prerogative
Court, Dublin.
† A few of O'Leary's jokes have been preserved. " I wish
you were St. Peter", said Curran. " Why ?" responded the

" The Sham", who loved to ape the manners of those above him, also called his country seat at Kilmacud " the Priory";* and we believe it was to him that Dick Hetherington,† in accepting an invitation to dinner, wrote:—

> " Though to my ankles I'll be in the mud,
> I hope to be with you at Kilmacud".‡

Though in open defiance of the laws, the gambling hell in Crane Lane was still suffered to exist, under the very shadow of the Castle, and within three minutes' walk of the board of police. Whether Higgins were really a secret partner in its profits, as confidently alleged, we shall not now discuss, although contemporary record and tradition both favour the allegation. Mr. Higgins is entitled to the benefit of his denial; but no matter who may or may not have been connected with this pandemonium, it is at least evident that the executive had no right to survey placidly for one day, much less for fifteen years, an institution so destructive to the morals, health, wealth, and happiness of the people. These matters may be worthy of note, as curiously illustrative of Dublin at the time of which we write.

Mr. Francis Higgins was no novice in the art and mystery of the gambling table. A scarce

---

Friar. " Because you could let me into Heaven". " It would be better that I had the key of the other place", replied O'Leary, " for then I could let you out". For illustrations of O'Leary's humour see *Recollections of John O'Keeffe*, v. i. p. 245 ; *Reminiscences of Michael Kelly*, vol. i. p. 301 ; Barrington's *Personal Sketches*, vol. ii. pp. 131-137; and the *Memoirs of O'Leary*, by Rev. Dr. England.

* Statement of T—— F——, Esq., J.P., formerly of the Priory, Kilmacud. In 1859 the house was pulled down.

† Richard Hetherington will be remembered as the correspondent of Curran—(See *Memoirs of Curran, passim*).

‡ *Communicated* by the late M. Brett, Esq.

publication, printed in 1799, from the pen of
Henry MacDougall, M.A., and entitled *Sketches of
Irish Political Characters*, mentions " the Sham's
admission to the profession of attorney, in which his
practice is too notorious to require statement", and
adds : " His next step to wealth was in the establishment of a hazard table, which soon attracted a number of sharps, scamps, and flashmen; and they as
soon attracted the attention of the Sham, ever on
the watch to promote his own interest. The sharp
was useful to cheat the unwary of their money,
and keep it in circulation at his table. The scamp
plundered on the road, visited the *Corner House*, and
if taken up by the officers of justice, he seldom
failed, for acquaintance' sake, to employ the owner
in his capacity of solicitor. The flashman introduced him (Higgins) to the convenient matron,
whom he seldom failed to lay under contribution—
the price of protecting her in her profession". We
further learn that the city magistrates were all afraid
to interfere with Mr. Higgins and his delinquencies,
lest a slanderous paragraph or lampoon from the
arsenal of his press should overtake them.

Ten years previous to the publication of the foregoing, the vigilant moralist, Magee, laboured to
arouse the magistracy to a sense of their duty. " For
fifteen years", we are told, " there has existed, under
the eye of magistracy, in the very centre of the me-
tropolis, *at the corner of Crane Lane*, in Essex
Street, a notorious school of nocturnal study in the
doctrine of chances; a school which affords to men
of the town an ample source of ways and means in
the pluckings of those unfledged green-horns who
can be inveigled into the trap; which furnishes to
the deluded apprentice a ready mart for the acquisi-

tion of experience, and the disposal of any loose cash that can be purloined from his master's till; which affords to the working artizan a weekly asylum for the reception of that stipend which honest industry should allot to the purchase of food for a wife and children; and which affords to the spendthrift shopkeeper a ready transfer office to make over the property of his creditors to the plunder of knaves and sharpers".[*]

Two months after we find addressed to the authorities a further appeal, occupying several columns, and to the same effect.[†]

But the board of police was, in fact, eminently imbecile. Among a long series of resolutions adopted in August, 1789, by the gifted men who formed the Whig Club, we find: " The present extravagant, ineffectual, and unconstitutional police of the city of Dublin has been adopted, continued, and patronised by the influence of the present ministers of Ireland. All proceedings in parliament to remove the grievance, or censure the abuse, have been resisted and defeated by the same influence. The expediency of combating by corruption a constitutional majority in parliament has been publicly avowed, and the principle so avowed has been carried into execution".

At last a committee was granted to inquire into the police, whose extravagance and inefficiency had now rendered them notoriously contemptible. They had long wallowed in indolent luxuriousness on the public money. Among their items of expense were: " For two inkstands for the police, £5 5s. 6d.; three penknives, £2 2s. 3d.; gilt-edged paper, £100;

* *Dublin Evening Post*, No. 1782.
† *Ibid.*, No. 1801.

Chambers' Dictionary, £11 7s. 6d.". Among their books was *Beccaria on Crime*, with a commentary from Voltaire.*

A curious chapter might be written on the short-comings of the Dublin police and magistracy, not only during the last, but even throughout a portion of the present century. If not too digressive, a glance at those shortcomings may amuse the reader.

"During the existence of the Volunteers", observes the late Counsellor Walsh, a conservative writer of much accuracy, "gentlemen of that body for a time arranged among themselves to traverse the streets at night, to protect the peaceably disposed inhabitants, and men of the first rank in the king-dom thus voluntarily discharged the duties of watch-men. But the occupation assorted badly with the fiery spirits on whom it devolved, and the streets were soon again abandoned to their so-called legi-timate guardians. In the day-time the streets were always wholly unprotected. The first appointment even of a permanent night-watch was in 1723, when an act was passed under which the different parishes were required to appoint 'honest men and *good Protestants'* to be night-watches. The utter inefficiency of the system must have been felt; and various improvements were from time to time at-tempted in it, every four or five years producing a new police act—with how little success every one can judge, who remembers the tattered somnambu-lists who represented the 'good Protestant watch-men' a few years ago. Several attempts had also been made to establish an efficient civic magistracy, but with such small benefit that, until a compara-*tively recent* period, a large portion of the magis-

* *Grattan's Memoirs*, v. iii. p. 456.

terial duties within the city were performed by
county magistrates, who had no legal authority
whatever to act in them.   An office was kept in the
neighbourhood of Thomas Street by two gentlemen
in the commission for the county, who made a
yearly income by the fees; and the order to fire on
the mob who murdered Lord Kilwarden, so late as
1803, was given by Mr. Bell, a magistrate of
the county and not the city of Dublin.   Another
well-known member of the bench was Mr. Drury,
who halted in his gait, and was called the ' lame
justice' ".   On the occasion mentioned by Mr. Walsh,
Drury retired for safety to the garret of his house in
the Coombe, from whence, as Curran remarked, ' he
played with considerable effect on the rioters with a
large double-barrelled telescope.

It is to be regretted, however, that irregularity
and imbecility are not the worst charges to be
brought against the justices of Dublin, even so late
as fifty years ago.   Frank Thorpe Porter, Esq., late
police magistrate of Dublin, has preserved official
tradition of some of his more fallible predecessors.
Mr. Gonne having lost a valuable watch which he
had long regarded as irretrievable, was urged by
a private hint to remain at the outer door of the
police office, and when the magistrate came out, to ask
him, " What hour is it now exactly, your worship?"
The " beak" took out a watch, and answered the
question.   Its appearance at once elicited from
Gonne the longest oath ever heard before a justice.
" By ——", he exclaimed, " that watch is mine !"

" Gonne obtained his watch", adds Mr. Porter,
" and was with great difficulty prevented from
bringing the transaction under the notice of the
government.   The system by which the worthy

justice managed occasionally to possess himself of a valuable watch, or some other costly article, consisted in having two or three drawers wherein to keep the property found with highwaymen or thieves. If the prosecutor identified the delinquent, he was then shown the right drawer; but if he could not swear to the depredator's person, the wrong drawer was opened. The magistrate to whom this narrative refers was dismissed in a short time for attempting to embezzle fifty pounds".*

Before the establishment of the petty sessions system in Ireland, magistrates in the safe seclusion of their closets were often betrayed into grossly disreputable acts. A parliamentary inquiry, in 1823, into the conduct of Sheriff Thorpe, exposed, in passing, much magisterial delinquency.

Mr. Beecher said, " It was no uncommon thing, when a friend had incurred a penalty, to remit the fine, and to levy a penalty strictly against another merely because he was an object of dislike". Major Warburton proved that a female had been sent to America by a magistrate without any legal proceeding whatever. Major Wilcox established the fact that some justices of the peace were engaged in illicit distillation, and that they took presents and bribes, and bail when other magistrates refused; that they took cross-examinations where informations had been already taken by other magistrates. " They issued warrants against the complaining party in the first instance, at the suggestion of the party complained against". It further appeared that some magistrates took fees in money, and not unfrequently rendered official services in considera-

---

* Some notice of the embezzlements accomplished by Baron Power and Sir Jonah Barrington, both judges on the Irish bench, will be found in the appendix.

tion of having their turf drawn home, or their potatoes planted. The Rev. M. Collins, afterwards
bishop of Cloyne, proved that magistrates corruptly
received presents of corn, cattle, potatoes, and even
money. "If the person of whom the complaint
was made ranked as a gentleman, the magistracy
often decline interfering, because it would lead to
personal results". Mr. O'Driscoll alleged that there
were several magistrates trading on their office;
they "sell justice, and administer it favourably to
the party who pays them best". "It is a convenient thing", said O'Connell, "for a man to have
the commission of the peace, for he can make those
he dislikes fear him, and he can favour his friends".
These venal practices had transpired subsequent to
a judicial form which had professed to revise the
magistracy! But the "revision" had been shaped
rather in obedience to sectarian prejudice than on
legitimate grounds. O'Connell showed that "most
excellent men had been deprived of their office
without any cause. It was particularly severe upon
the Catholic magistrates. In the county Cork,
eighteen out of twenty-one Catholics were struck
out". In Mr. Daunt's *Conversations of O'Connell*,
the details are given of a certain justice who
threatened to flog and hang the sons of a widow to
whom his worship owed £2,000, unless she pledged
herself to cancel the bond!*

With magistrates like these, and with powerless police such as we described, it is no wonder

* For full details, see vol. ii. p. 131. In one of O'Connell's
public letters, he made touching reference to the fact, that he
had known peasant girls sometimes driven to surrender what
ought to be dearer than life, as part of an unholy compact with
magistrates who had threatened the life or liberty of a father
or brother!

that a walk in the streets of Dublin should be encompassed with peril. Stephen's Green, the residence of the Sham Squire, was specially infested with footpads, who robbed in a manner peculiar to themselves.

"So late as 1812", says the author of *Ireland Sixty Years Ago*, "there were only twenty-six small oil lamps to light the immense square of Stephen's Green, which were therefore one hundred and seventy feet from one another. The footpads congregated in a dark entry, on the shady side of the street, if the moon shone; if not, the dim and dismal light of the lamps was little obstruction. A cord was provided with a loop at the end of it. The loop was laid on the pavement, and the thieves watched the approach of a passenger. If he put his foot in the loop it was immediately chucked. The man fell prostrate, and was dragged rapidly up the entry to some cellar or waste yard, where he was robbed and sometimes murdered. The stun received by the fall usually prevented the victim from ever recognizing the robbers. We knew a gentleman who had been thus robbed, and when he recovered found himself in an alley at the end of a lane off Bride Street, nearly naked, and severely contused and lacerated by being dragged over the rough pavement".[*]

[*] Almost equally daring outrages on the liberty of the subject were nightly practised, with the connivance of the law, by "crimp sergeants", who by brutal force, and sometimes by fraud, secured the unwary for foreign enlistment. Attractive women were employed to seduce persons into conversation preparatory to the crimp sergeant's seizing them in the king's name. Startling details of these outrages, which were often marked by bloodshed, will be found in the Dublin newspapers of 1793 and 1794, passim. See also the *Irish Masonic Magazine* for 1794 (pp. 94, 190, 284, 383, 482, 570).

When men fared thus, it may readily be supposed that ladies could not walk the streets without risk to their lives or virtue. " It is deemed a reproach", says an author, writing in 1775, " for a gentle-woman to be seen walking in the streets. I was advised by my bankers to lodge in Capel Street, near Essex Bridge, being in less danger of being robbed, two chairmen* not being deemed sufficient protection".†

Twenty years later found no improvement. The *Anthologia Hibernica* for December, 1794, p. 476, furnishes new proofs of the inefficiency of the police. Robbery and bloodshed " within a few yards of the guard house in Fleet Street" is described.

It does not always follow that idleness is the mother of mischief, for we find that combination among the workmen of Dublin also attained a for-midable pitch at this time. The *Dublin Chronicle* of January the 28th, 1792, contains the following paragraph:

" On the several mornings of the 17th, 18th, 19th, and 20th inst., a number of armed persons, journeymen tailors, assembled in a riotous manner about the house of Mr. Millea, Ross Lane, Mr. Leet, Merchant's Quay, Mr. Walsh, Castle Street, Mr. Ward, Cope Street, and the houses of several other master tailors, and cut, maimed, and abused several journeymen tailors who were peaceably going to their respective places of employ-ment; one of said men, named Michael Hanlon, was killed

* Sedan bearers, familiarly styled " Christian Ponies". There is a well known story in Dublin of a Connaughtman, who, when entering a sedan chair, found that the bottom had, by some accident, fallen out of it, but, nevertheless, he made no demur, and walked to his destination in the chair. On getting out he remarked to the men who assumed to convey him, " Only for the honour of the thing I might as well have walked".

† *Philosophical Survey*, p. 46.

on the spot, in Cope Street; two have had their hands cut off; several others have been cut and bruised in such a manner as to be now lying dangerously ill; and some journeymen are missing, who, it is reported, have been murdered and thrown into the river".

CHAPTER IV.

Magee's vengeance on Lord Clonmel.—Lord Clare.—The gods of Crow Street.—Renewed effort to muzzle Magee.—Letters de Cachet in Ireland.—Seizures.—George Ponsonby and Arthur Browne.—Lord Clonmel crushed.—His dying confession.—Deserted by the Sham Squire.—More turpitude.

The spirit of John Magee was indomitable. An interval of liberty between his conviction and sentence from Lord Clonmel was now at his disposal, and he certainly employed it in a singular way. Profoundly indifferent to all personal consequences, he most imprudently resolved to spend a considerable sum of money in wreaking his vengeance on Lord Clonmel. This eccentric scheme he sought to carry out in an indirect and, as he felt assured, a perfectly legal manner. Having found himself owner of £14,000, Magee settled £10,000 upon his family, and with a chuckle declared that the balance it was his intention, "with the blessing of God, to spend upon Lord Clonmel".* The unpopular chief of the King's Bench resided in a handsome villa near the Black Rock, now known as Temple Hill, but then styled Neptune.† On the splendid parterres and pleasure grounds which luxuriantly environed it, Lord Clonmel had spent several thousand pounds;

* Personal Recollections of Lord Cloncurry (1849, p. 58).
† "Neptune, the elegant seat of Lord Clonmel"—Seward's Topographia Hibernia, Dub. 1795.

while in the direction of the improvements many
an anxious and a precious hour had been consumed.
The wild and uncultivated district of Dunleary
without, only served to make the contrast more
striking. But alas! this exquisite oasis the vindictive proprietor of the *Post* resolved to lay waste.
As an important preliminary step he purchased
from Lady Osborne a large tract of ground immediately adjoining Lord Clonmel's villa, and forthwith dubbed it Fiat Hill.* Magee. speedily announced, but with some mental reservation, that in
honour of the birth-day of the Prince of Wales he
would give, at Dunleary, a grand *Bra Pleasura*, to
which he solicited the company of all his friends,
private and political, known and unknown, washed
and unwashed. Various field sports, with plenty of
Silvester Costigan's whiskey, were promised as an inducement. " At one o'clock", to quote the original
advertisement, " the Ball will be kicked on Fiat
Hill. Dinner on the tented field at three o'clock.
Table d'hote for ladies and gentlemen. Cudgel playing at five, with cool umpires to prevent ill temper
and preserve good humour".†

The late Lord Cloncurry's robust memory has
furnished us with the following graphic sketch of
the singular scene which took place upon this occasion. " I recollect attending", writes his lordship,
" and the fête certainly was a strange one. Several
thousand people, including the entire disposable
mob of Dublin, of both sexes, assembled as the guests
at an early hour, and proceeded to enjoy themselves
in tents and booths erected for the occasion. A
variety of sports was arranged for their amusement,

* *Dublin Evening Post,* No. 1798.
† *Dublin Evening Post,* No. 1798.

such as climbing poles for prizes, running races in sacks, grinning through horse-collars, and soforth, until at length, when the crowd had attained its maximum density, towards the afternoon, the grand scene of the day was produced. A number of active pigs, with their tails shaved and soaped, were let loose, and it was announced that each pig was to become the property of any one who could catch and hold it by the slippery member. A scene impossible to describe immediately took place: the pigs, frightened and hemmed in by the crowd in all other directions, rushed through the hedge which then separated the grounds of Temple Hill from the open fields; forthwith all their pursuers followed in a body, and, continuing their chase over the shrubberies and parterres, soon revenged John Magee upon the noble owner".

Another pen, more powerful but not more accurate than Lord Cloncurry's, tells us that "Lord Clonmel retreated like a harpooned leviathan—the barb was in his back, and Magee held the cordage. He made the life of his enemy a burden to him. Wherever he went, he was lampooned by a ballad singer, or laughed at by the populace. Nor was Magee's arsenal composed exclusively of paper ammunition. He rented a field bordering his lordship's highly-improved and decorated demesne. He advertised, month after month, that on such a day he would exhibit in this field a *grand Olympic pig hunt;* that the people, out of gratitude for their patronage of his newspaper, should be gratuitous spectators of this revived *classical* amusement; and that he was determined to make so amazing a provision of *whiskey* and porter, that if any man went home *thirsty it* should be his own fault. The plan completely succeeded.   Hundreds and thousands assembled; every man did justice to his entertainer's hospitality: and his lordship's magnificent demesne, uprooted and desolate, next day exhibited nothing but the ruins of *the Olympic pig hunt*".*   So far Mr. Phillips.†   The Court of King's Bench had not yet opened for term, and Lord Clonmel was tranquilly rusticating at Temple Hill. Pallid with consternation, he rang an alarum bell, and ordered his post-chaise, with four of the fleetest horses in his stable, to the door. The chief justice bounded into the chariot with an energy almost incompatible with his years; the postillions plied their whips; the chaise rattled amid clouds of dust down Fiat Hill; the mob with deafening yells followed close behind. Lord Clonmel, almost speechless with terror, repaired to the castle, sought the viceroy, swore " *by the Eternal*"‡ that all the country south of Dublin was in a state of insurrection; implored his Excellency to summon the privy council, and to apply at once for extraordinary powers, including the suspension of the Habeas Corpus Act.§

The appeal of the chief justice prevailed, and on September 3rd, 1789, we find Magee dragged from his home by a strong body of the weak and inefficient police of Dublin, and consigned to Newgate.‖   He was previously, however, brought be-

* *Curran and his Contemporaries,* by Charles Phillips, p. 87.
† Sir Jonah Barrington describes the scene to much the same effect, with this addition—that Magee introduced " asses dressed up with wigs and scarlet robes, and dancing dogs in gowns and wigs as barristers".
‡ A favourite exclamation of Lord Clonmel's. Vide *Rowan's Autobiography,* p. 208.
§ Reminiscence communicated by the late Rev. Dr. O'Hanlon.
‖ *Dublin Evening Post,* No. 1809.

fore Sir Samuel Bradstreet, Recorder of Dublin, on
the charge of having announced that " there would
be thirty thousand men at Dunleary". The judge required personal bail to the amount of £5,000, and
two sureties in £2,500 each, for five years,* a demand
not so easy for a printer in a moment to meet. Such
mandates as these, amounting in some instances to
perpetual imprisonment, soon brought but too fatally
the administration of justice into contempt.

No unnecessary harshness seems to have been
shown to Magee during his incarceration. Unlike
the case of Lord Cloncurry, he was permitted the
use of pen, ink, and paper—a concession as accep-
table to him as it was creditable to the government.
He constantly wrote letters for the *Post* signed with
his name, and bearing the somewhat inflammatory
date of " Newgate, 22nd October, fiftieth day of my
confinement"—varied of course according as time
progressed—and he was not diffident in adversely
criticising the policy of the viceroy, as well as some
leading members of the privy council, including
Lord Clonmel. " The man who vilifies established
authority", says Junius, " is sure to find an audience".
Magee was no exception to the rule. He became
an intense popular favourite; and the galleries of
Crow Street theatre used nightly to resound with
" a cheer for Magee, the man for Ireland!" and " a
groan for the Sham!"†

Magee's letters made frequent reference to the
sufferings to which the government had subjected
him. Thus in No. 1789 he tells us, " I have been
four times fiated, and dragged through the streets
like a felon—three times into dungeons!" But

* *Dublin Evening Post*, No. 1814.
† *Trial of Magee for Libel* on R. Daly, p. 30.

having on October 29th received a notification from government declaratory of its willingness to accept the sum of £4,000 as bail "to keep the peace for five years towards Lord Clonmel", Magee bade adieu to prison, and, accompanied by Hamilton Rowan, attended the court and gave the required surety. " Mr. Magee, on being discharged, walked to his own house in College Green, greeted by the loud congratulations of the people".[*]

Poor Magee's spell of liberty seems to have been of lamentably, and we may add, of most capriciously short duration, if the evidence of his own organ can be accepted as conclusive. The sweets of liberty were once more exchanged for the bitters of " durance vile". In the *Dublin Evening Post* of November 12, 1789, we read—" Magee was brought up from the Lock-up House, where he had been confined since Tuesday last upon fiats granted by Lord Clonmel at the suit of Messrs. Higgins, Daly, Brennan, and Miss ——, to the amount of £7,800. Mr. Magee moved for a new trial in the matter of the alleged libel against Higgins. But the chief justice refused the motion, and informed the sheriff that Magee was now a convict, and should be conducted to Newgate forthwith".[†] The struggle was characterised as one of might against right. In October, 1789, the attorney-general is said to have admitted in open court that the prosecution of Magee was " *a government business*".[‡]

Arguments having been, on Nov. 19, heard in arrest of judgment on Magee, the chief justice adjourned the sentence to next term, and admitted

* *Dublin Evening Post*, No. 1833.
† *Ibid*, No. 1839.
‡ *Ibid*, 1834.

him to bail on the comparatively moderate recognizance of £500. Magee was therefore discharged, but it would almost seem as if the law authorities, with Lord Clonmel at their head, had been only playing off some malign practical joke upon him; for we read that no sooner had Magee "reached High Street after receiving his discharge than he was taken into custody by the sheriffs on different fiats amounting to £7,800!"*

The very name of fiats had now become almost as terrible as lettres de cachet: but in the Irish Parliament of 1790 they received their death blow; and Lord Clonmel himself may be said to have perished in their *debris*.

Of this unconstitutional agent Magee remarked: " If the amount of the sum for which bail must be found is to be measured and ascertained only by the conscience of the *affidavit-man*, then indeed any profligate character may lodge in Newgate the Duke of Leinster or Mr. Conolly, for sums which even they would not find it possible to procure bail". On January 28th, 1790, Magee was once more committed to prison.

Owing largely to the unflagging denunciations of Magee, the Police Board in September, 1789, attempted some vigorous reform, and at last nocturnal gambling houses were menaced with extinction. Magee, even in the gloom of his dungeon, exulted over the threatened downfall. The Gambler's soliloquy went on to say :—

> Yes! this a fatal, dreadful revolution!
> A change repugnant to the dear delights
> Of night-enveloped guilt, of midnight fraud,
> And rapine long secure; of dexterous art

* *Dublin Evening Post*, 1844.

To plunge unthinking innocence in woe,
And riot in the spoils of beggar'd youth!
Sad revolution! Hence come lethargy.
Come inactivity, and worse than all,
Come simple honesty! The dice no more
Shall sound their melody, nor perj'ry's list
Swell at the nod of dark collusive practice!
Gaols lie unpeopled, and rest gibbets bare,
And Newgate's front board take a holiday!
Crane Lane, thou spot to Pandemonium dear,
Where many a swarthy son of Chrisal's race
My galligaskin lined", etc.*

Alderman Carleton made four seizures. "And yet", said the *Post*, "as fast as their implements are seized, their tables demolished, and their gangs dispersed, the very next night new arrangements and new operations are on foot. Who but the protected proprietor of this infamous den—who but a ruffian who can preserve his plunder in security, and set law and gospel at defiance, would dare at such audacious perseverance?"†

Meanwhile Mr. Higgins's ready pen continued to rage with fury against all whose views did not exactly chime with those held by his employers. A contemporary journal says: "Squire Higgins, whose protected system of virulent and unremitting slander crows in triumph over the community, does not scruple to avow his indifference to anything which prosecution can do, guarded as he is by the intimate friendship and implicit confidence of the bench. He openly avows his disregard of Mr. Grattan's prosecution for a libel now pending against him, and says that he shall be supported by the Castle".‡ Mr. Higgins having libelled a respectable official in the revenue, legal proceedings were instituted; but one of the government lawyers refused, in

* *Dublin Evening Post*, No. 1813. † *Ibid.*, 1827. ‡ *Ibid.*, No. 1825.

December, 1788, to move, although feed in the cause.

Poor Magee's cup of bitterness was at last filled to the brim, by a proceeding which. is best described in his own letter to Lord Chancellor Clare.   There is a singular mixture of tragedy and farce in the energetic efforts which were now openly made to extinguish him.

"Newgate, Oct. 1.

"MY LORD, I have now been confined in this prison of the felon, housebreaker, and murderer, twenty-nine days—twenty-one of which time mostly to my bed.   Judge, on my rising yesterday, to be served with a notice to appear to-morrow at the House of Lords, on a charge of lunacy, and that by some interested persons, who without even the shadow of relationship, have secured my property, and that to a very great amount, and refused by these very people even ten guineas to procure common necessaries in a prison.   Bail I cannot produce; my character as a trader is blasted; my property as a citizen embezzled; my intellects as a man suspected by a false and slanderous charge of insanity; every engine employed by a designing, needy, and desperate junto, for the absolute deprivation of my property; total destruction of *all* that those who respect themselves prize more even than life.   My lord, I claim the interposition of your authority as the first in law power—I supplicate your humanity as a man, a parent, a husband, that I may be permitted to confront my accusers at the House of Lords on to-morrow".

To justify the charge of lunacy against John Magee, it was alleged, among other pretexts, that he *had established* boat-races and foot-ball matches at *Dunleary,* and presided over them " in a round hat

and feathers".*   We cull a few passages from the
newspaper report:

"*The Chancellor*—' Mr. Magee, have you anything to
say?'

" ' As to what, my lord?'

" ' You have heard the matters with which you are
charged.   I am called upon to issue a commission to
try whether you are insane or not.   If you are found
insane, I am then to appoint a guardian of your person
and a guardian of your property, and you will become
a ward of the Court of Chancery.   Have you any
attorney?'

" ' No, my lord.   Some time ago I sent for Mr. Kenny
as my solicitor.   He came to me and found me sick in
bed.   I opened my case to him, and he promised to call
upon me next day ; but the first intimation I had of Mr.
Kenny afterwards was, that he was preparing briefs
against me for this prosecution.   Does your lordship
choose that I should call witnesses ?   My own physician
is here'.

" ' Has he made an affidavit ?'

" ' He has, my lord'.

" ' The chancellor declared that there was not the
shadow of ground for issuing a commission.   Supposing
all the charges true, they only amounted to acts of extravagance and indiscretion.   If he was to grant a
commission of lunacy against every man who did an
extravagant, an unwise, or even a bad thing, he was

* There is an anecdote of Magee traditionally preserved in the
office of the *Evening Post*, illustrative of his unawed demeanour
in the presence of Lord Clonmel, by whose domineering manner
even the bar were often overborne.   Magee stood up in court,
and addressed a few observations to the bench in justification
of his hostility to Francis Higgins.   But having styled him the
" Sham Squire", Lord Clonmel interrupted Magee, declaring that
he would allow no nicknames to be used in that court.   " Very
well, John Scott", replied the editor of the *Post*, resuming his
seat, " your *wish is* a law".

afraid he should have a great many wards. He had observed Mr. Magee during the whole time he had been in court, and he saw nothing insane about him. He must therefore refuse the application' ".

Magee's triumph began to date from this day. In the *Journals of the Irish House of Commons* (v. xiii. pp. 179–80) we find it " ordered that the proper officer do lay before the house an attested copy of the affidavit filed in the Queen's Bench, on which the chief justice ordered that a writ should issue, at the suit of Francis Higgins and others, against John Magee for £7,800. On March 3rd, 1790, the entire case was brought before parliament by George Ponsonby, afterwards Lord Chancellor of Ireland. He showed that the practice of issuing fiats under such circumstances was unconstitutional, and a direct violation of the Bill of Rights; and he reminded the House, that while Warren Hastings, who was accused of plundering India, murdering its inhabitants, and rendering the government corrupt and odious, was only held to £10,000 bail, an obscure Irish printer, on a mere individual affirmation, was held to bail for £7,800. Mr. Ponsonby ridiculed the idea of Higgins swearing that he " had been injured in his unspotted, unblemished reputation" by the lampoons of John Magee.

George Ponsonby was ably supported by Arthur Browne:* " Till of very late years the evil was moderate; but since a certain learned judge came upon the bench it has grown to an enormous height. Sir, under the auspices of that judge these doctrines

* For a notice of Arthur Browne, member for the University of Dublin, see *Review of the Irish House of Commons*, by Falkland, *i.e.* John Robert Scott, D.D., p. 30; *vide also Sketches of Irish Political Characters*, p. 211.

have been advanced, that any man may at his pleasure, with perfect impunity, deprive any other of his liberty by an affidavit swearing that he believes he has suffered damage, without showing when or how—that his fancy, or his perjury, is to be the guide of the judge's discretion, and the bail is to be accommodated to the ideal wrongs, to the fancied injuries, to the angry passions, or the wanton prevarication of a wicked or enraged prosecutor. What is the consequence? No man, however free from debt or unconscious of crime, shall walk in security in the public streets. He is liable to arrest for any amount; and if he seeks to punish the accuser he finds no spot on which to lay his hand. How can he indict the accuser for perjury? He only swore a general affirmative that he had been damaged. Who can prove a general negative that he had not? He only swore to the belief of damage. Who can arraign his capricious fancy, or convict it of perjury? If he had sworn to a particular instance—that his arm had been broken, that he had lost the setting of a house or the customers of his shop—I might prove the falsehood of the assertion by evidence. But upon a general charge nothing remains but submission and a prison.

" This power has been particularly directed against printers. Whoever presumed to print or publish without the leave or not under the direction of Francis Higgins, was in great danger of a fiat: numbers of printers have been run down by fiats whom the public never heard of. John Magee was more sturdy, and therefore his sufferings made more noise. Four fiats were issued against him in June, 1789, to the amount of £7,800; he was kept in prison from June to the end of November, before the question

whether this bail should be reduced was decided.
Mr. Higgins had now, by the practice of the courts
(which gives a plaintiff three terms before he need
try his action), power to keep Magee in prison till
November next, so that he may lie in prison nineteen months for want of bail before the action be
tried; perhaps afterwards have a verdict in his
favour, or only 8d. damages be given against him.
Each of the bail must swear himself worth twice
the sum for which he was security, *i.e.* £30,000,
and more in this case. What gentleman could find
such bail? It amounted to perpetual imprisonment.
We may talk of independence, but liberty is no
more—the security of our boasted emancipation is
a name, for we have nothing to secure.

" See what an instrument this doctrine might be
in the hands of private malice or public oppression.
Suppose a man willing to wreak his vengeance upon
his foe, and for that purpose recommending himself to the favour of the bench. Suppose a bad man
in possession of the ear of a judge, his old friend and
companion, perhaps instilling his poison into it, and
willing to make it the conduit through which to
wreak his vengeance on his foe; suppose him to recommend himself by every willing and base act to
a wicked judge—and such may be conceived. *Sup-*
pose him the minion of that judge, requiring a little
mutual favour for his multiplied services, and asking
the debasement of the bench as the price of former aid
in the elevation of that judge. * * * Suppose
the slanderous assassin, seeking for a fiat against a
far less criminal than himself, and fixing the sum
which he thinks sufficient to throw his neighbour
into eternal bondage; is it not possible that his
friendly judge may listen to his argument in me-

mory of old festivity, and grant him a fiat, even to
his heart's content, although by so doing, your
courts of law, instead of being the sacred fountains
of justice, should become the channels of malevo-
lence? If the wretched victims of this assumed
power do not find redress here, they know not
where to fly for refuge; on this House depends the
fate of all who are or may be subject to this tyranny.
If they do not find redress here, they must be lost;
but they will be lost in the wreck of the national
character. What an instrument might such a power
be in the hands of a bad government! what an instrument may it be against the liberty of the press!
How easily may any printer who presumes to open
his mouth against administration be run down by
it! We have called upon the administration to
correct this evil, and have met with a refusal. It
absurdly espouses a subject with which it has no
concern, and which it cannot defend".

. The practice of issuing fiats was soon after re-
stricted to a defined and definite sum. Intense was
the humiliation of Lord Clonmel at the victory obtained by Magee. Mr. Phillips informs us that his
heart withered from that day. Magee exposed his
errors, denied his merits, magnified his mistakes,
ridiculed his pretensions, and continually edging,
without overstepping the boundary of libel, poured
upon the Chief, from the battery of the press, a
perpetual broadside of sarcasm and invective.

"Save us from our friends; we know our enemies", is an old and trite adage. Groaning beneath
the weight of Magee's hostility, Lord Clonmel pursued the uneven tenor of his way; but when at
length the *startling* fact became evident that even
the fidelity of Higgins had begun to break down.

8

the Chief felt inclined to ejaculate, *Et tu Brute!*
Mr. Curran, in his *Bar Sketches*, relates, on the
authority of Bushe, a story which shows that in
1794 Lord Clonmel complained of having been lampooned by the *Freeman's Journal.* So much for
the instability of human friendship!

Lord Clonmel became at last singularly sensitive
to public criticism. Rowan's *Autobiography* records
a strange dialogue between the chief and a book-
seller named Byrne, into whose shop he swaggered
on seeing Rowan's trial advertised. One sentence
will convey an idea of the colloquy, as well as of
the times in which such language could be hazarded
by a judge. "Take care, sir, what you do; I give
you this caution; for if there are any reflections on
the judges of the land, by the eternal G—— I will
lay you by the heels".

Lord Clonmel's health and spirits gradually broke
down, and accounts of his death were daily circulated. On one of these occasions, when he was
really very ill, a friend said to Curran, "Well, they
say Clonmel is going to die at last. Do you believe it?" "I believe", said Curran, "he is scoundrel enough to live or die, *just as it suits his own
convenience!*" (See Addenda D.) Shortly before the
death of Lord Clonmel, Mr. Lawless, afterwards
Lord Cloncurry, had an interview with him, when
the chief exclaimed, "My dear Val, I have been
a fortunate man through life; I am a chief justice and an earl; but were I to begin the world
again, I would rather be a chimney-sweeper, than
connected with the Irish government".*

But we must not lose sight of the Sham Squire.
We now find him accused of " purloining a docu-

* *Personal Recollections of Lord Cloncurry*, p. 46.

ment from the office of the King's Bench, and committing erasures and alterations thereon, for the purpose of securing the conviction of a defendant, and depriving him of the benefit of a fair plea against judgment". "This", adds the *Post*, " is of a piece with the notorious theft committed on the grand jury bag in the town clerk's office, a few weeks since, of the bills against the markers and other vagabonds of the Crane Lane gambling-house. If such felonious audacities are suffered to escape with impunity, the dignity, the law, the equity of the bench, and the lives and properties of the honest part of the community, are no longer safe against the daring acts of cunning and villany".* Mr. Higgins denies the charge in the *Freeman's Journal* of the day; but the subject, notwithstanding, was brought before parliament, on March 5, 1790, when Arthur Browne stated that in "the suit, Higgins against Magee, it had appeared to the perfect conviction of every man in court, that two erasures and certain alterations had been made in the record; that a circumstance so momentous had astonished and alarmed all present, the court especially, who had promised to make a solemn investigation of it, and 'probe it to the bottom'. He had since heard from some friends, that it would not be proper to commence an inquiry until the suit, in which this record was involved, should be finally determined: no such objection had been offered by the court at the time of discovering the forgery; nay, the court, on the instant, had certainly commenced an inquiry, though he never heard they had carried it further.

"This dark and wicked transaction did, at the

* *Dublin Evening Post*, No. 1813.

time of its being discovered, greatly alarm the bar;
and in consequence a numerous and most respectable
meeting of barristers took place, at which meeting he
attended, and there did promise, that if the court of
king's bench did not follow up the inquiry with
effect, he would bring it before parliament: it cer
tainly was the business of the court of king's bench
to have taken it up; but they not having done so,
he was resolved to keep his promise, and never lose
sight of it till parliament should decide upon it.

"The inquiry was, whether the public records of
the highest court of criminal judicature, by which
the life and property of any man in the realm might
be affected, were kept with that sacred care that no
man could have access to alter or erase them? and
whether the officers of that court were so honest and
so pure, that they would not allow of any corrupt
access?"*

CHAPTER V.

Hair breadth escapes of Lord Edward Fitzgerald.—Testimony of
Lords Holland and Byron.—A dark picture of oppression.—
Moira House.—Presence of mind.—Revolting Treachery.—
Arrest of Lord Edward.—Majors Sirr and Swan.—Death of
Captain Ryan. — Attempted rescue. — Edward Rattigan.—
General Lawless.—Lady Louisa Connolly.—Obduracy of Lord
Camden.—Death of Lord Edward Fitzgerald.

SOME critics have been good enough to say that
an outline of the present narrative which appeared
a few years ago, possesses the interest of an effective
drama.   At this stage we propose to let the curtain

* *Irish Parl. Debs.*, v. 10, p. 382.

drop for an interval, during which eight years is
supposed to elapse.

*   *   *   *   *   *   *   *   *

Once more it rises, disclosing the dark and
stormy period of 1798. The scene is Leixlip Bridge
at the dawn of morning, with a view of the Salmon
Leap. Nicholas Dempsey, a yeoman sentinel, is
seen, with musket shouldered, pacing to and fro.
A young man dressed as a peasant with frieze coat
and corduroy knee-breeches, approaches the bridge
driving before him half a dozen sheep. Accosting
the sentinel, he asks if there is any available night
park at hand where he could put his tired sheep to
rest. The yeoman scans his face narrowly, and to
the surprise, and probably confusion of the drover
replies:—" No, *my lord,* there is no pasturage in
this neighbourhood". No other words pass; the
sentinel resumes his beat, and the drover proceeds
on his way.*

The person thus addressed by the yeoman was
Lord Edward Fitzgerald, of whom a cabinet minister, Lord Holland, deliberately writes:—

" More than twenty years have now passed away.
Many of my political opinions are softened—my
predilections for some men weakened, my prejudices
against others removed; but my approbation of Lord
Edward Fitzgerald's actions remains unaltered and
unshaken. His country was bleeding under one of
the hardest tyrannies that our times have witnessed".†

---

* We are indebted for this hitherto unpublished anecdote to
Mr. Ennis, of Kimmage, the grand-nephew of Nicholas Dempsey,
whose cartridge-box and sash are still preserved at Kimmage
House as an interesting memento of the man and of the incident. For a notice of the Yeomanry, see *Addenda* F.

† *Memoirs of the Whig Party.* Lord Holland adds:—
" *The premature and ill-concerted insurrections which followed*

" If Lord Edward had been actuated in political
life by personal ambition", writes Dr. MacNevin,
" he had only to cling to his great family connections

in the Catholic districts were quelled, rather in consequence
of want of concert and skill in the insurgents, than of any good
conduct or discipline of the King's troops, whom Sir Ralph
Abercrombie described very honestly, *as formidable to no one
but their friends.* That experienced and upright commander
had been removed from his command, even after those just and
spirited general orders in which the remarkable judgment just
quoted was conveyed. His recall was hailed as a triumph by the
Orange faction. Indeed, surrounded as they were with burning
cottages, tortured backs, and frequent executions, they were yet
full of their sneers at what they whimsically termed 'the cle-
mency' of the government, and the weak character of their
viceroy, Lord Camden. * * * * The fact is incontroverti-
ble, that the people of Ireland were driven to resistance, which,
possibly, they meditated before, by the free quarters and expenses of the soldiery, which were such as are not permitted in
civilized warfare, even in an enemy's country. Trials, if they
must so be called, were carried on without number, under martial
law. It often happened, that three officers composed the court,
and that of the three, two were under age, and the third an officer of the yeomanry or militia, who had sworn, in his Orange
lodge, eternal hatred to the people over whom he was thus con-
stituted a judge. Floggings, picketings, death, were the usual
sentences, and these were sometimes commuted into banishment,
serving in the fleet, or transference to a foreign service. Many
were sold at so much per head to the Prussians. Other less legal
but not more horrible outrages were daily committed by the
different corps under the command of government. Even in
the streets of Dublin, a man was *shot* and robbed of £30, on the
loose recollection of a soldier's having seen him in the battle of
Kilcullen, and no proceeding was instituted to ascertain the
murder or prosecute the murderer. Lord Wycombe, who was
in Dublin, and who was himself shot at by a sentinel, between
Black Rock and that city, wrote to me many details of similar
outrages which he had ascertained to be true. Dr. Dickson
(Bishop of Down) assured me that he had seen families returning
peaceably from mass, assailed without provocation, by drunken
troops and yeomanry, and the wives and daughters exposed to
every species of indignity, brutality, and outrage, from which
neither his remonstrances, nor those of other Protestant gentlemen, could rescue them. The subsequent indemnity acts de-
prived of redress the victims of this wide-spread cruelty".

and parliamentary influence.   They unquestionably would have advanced his fortunes and gratified his desires.   The voluntary sacrifices he made, and the magnanimous manner in which he directed himself to the independence of Ireland, are incontestable proofs of the purity of his soul".

"What a noble fellow", said Lord Byron, "was Lord Edward Fitzgerald, and what a romantic and singular history his was! If it were not too near our times, it would make the finest subject in the world for an historical novel".

The insurrection meanwhile, to which Earl Russell refers as one "wickedly provoked, rashly begun, and cruelly crushed",* was hastening to maturity. Dublin and Kildare were ripe for revolt: the mountains of Wicklow—the stronghold of Holt—were like slumbering volcanoes.   A great object was to procure, near Dublin, a place of concealment for the chivalrous nobleman who had espoused the cause of the down-trodden people; and a widow lady, named Dillon, who resided near Dolphin's Barn, undertook to give him shelter. Before he had been two days in the house, under an assumed name, an accident revealed his real one to the servant man.   In cleaning Lord Edward's boots he observed the noble stranger's name and title written in full; and he took occasion to tell his mistress that he knew who was the guest upstairs, but that she need not fear, as he would die in his defence.   The lady, with some anxiety, communicated the circumstance to Lord Edward, who expressed a wish to see the faithful adherent. "No", replied the servant; "I won't go up or look at him, for if they should arrest

* *Preface to Moore's Memoirs, vol. i., p. 18.*

me, I can then swear I never saw him or spoke to him".

Lord Edward Fitzgerald remained for five weeks in this retreat, when his friends suggested the expediency of removing to the house of a respectable feather merchant, named Murphy, who resided in Thomas Street, Dublin. Accompanied by William Lawless, who afterwards rose to the rank of general in the service of France, Lord Edward, wrapped in a countryman's great coat, arrived at Murphy's, where he remained for several days, during which time, dressed in female attire, he visited his wife and children in Denzille Street. He became by degrees more callous to risk, and we find him, early in May, riding, attended by Neilson only, to reconnoitre the line of advance from Kildare to Dublin. While executing this perilous task, he was actually stopped by the patrol at Palmerstown, but having, as Moore alleges, plausibly passed for a doctor hurrying to the relief of a sick patient, he was suffered, with his companion, to resume their journey.

In order to foil pursuit, Lord Edward was advised to remain not more than a night or two at any one house. Moore's and Murphy's, in Thomas Street, and Gannon's, in Corn Market, were the houses which afforded him shelter.

The proclamation offering a reward of one thousand pounds for such information as should lead to his apprehension had now appeared. On Ascension Thursday, May 17th, 1798, Major Sirr "received information", writes Moore, "that a party of persons, supposed to be Lord Edward Fitzgerald's body guard, would be on their way from Thomas Street to Usher's Island that night". The *precise object* or destination of this party, Moore

adds, has not been ascertained, but that it was supposed Lord Edward was going to Moira House,[*]
on Usher's Island, the residence of Lord and Lady
Moira, with a view to see his wife Pamela, who is
believed to have been then under their hospitable
roof.[†] Lord Edward's actual destination, however,—
and we have been at no ordinary pains to ascertain
it,—was the residence of Mr. Francis Magan, who
resided at 20 Usher's Island.

From the representative of the Moore family,
who gave Lord Edward ample shelter and protection when a thousand pounds lay on his head, we
have gathered the following valuable traditional
details; and, as will be found, they are interwoven
with the history of the Sham Squire. A carpenter,
named Tuite, was at work in one of the apartments
of Mr. Secretary Cooke's office on May 16th, 1798.
While repairing the floor within the recess of a
double door, he distinctly heard Mr. Cooke say,
that the house of James Moore, 119 Thomas Street,
should be forthwith searched for pikes and traitors.
Tuite, who was under some obligations to Moore,
with great presence of mind, noiselessly wrenched
off the hinge of the outer door, and asked permission to leave the Castle for ten minutes in order to
purchase a new hinge in Kennedy's Lane. Leave
was given; but, instead of going to the ironmonger's,
Tuite ran with immense speed to James Moore in

* Now the Mendicity Institution.
† It is not quite certain that Lady Edward Fitzgerald was, at
this time, at Moira House. The *Personal Recollections of
Lord Cloncurry* (2nd Edition, p. 130) rather favour an opposite
conclusion, by stating that " at the time of Lord Edward's arrest, his wife, Pamela, had taken refuge with my sisters, and
was at the time in my father's house in Merrion Street"—
namely, *Mornington House.*

Thomas Street, gave the hint, and returned to his
work. Moore, who was deeply implicated, and had
a commissariat for five hundred men on the premises,
fled to the banks of the Boyne, near Drogheda, after
previously telling his daughter to provide for the
safety of Lord Edward, who was at that moment
up stairs. Miss Moore had a high respect and friendship for Mr. Francis Magan and his sister, who resided at 20 Usher's Island. He was a Roman Catholic
barrister, and had been a member of the Society of
United Irishmen, though from prudential motives
he had shortly before relinquished his formal connection with them, but it was understood that his
sympathies were still with the society. Miss Moore
obtained an interview with Mr. Magan, and un-
bosomed her anxiety to him. Mr. Magan, at no
time an impassionable or impulsive person, seemed
moved: he offered his house as a refuge for
Lord Edward. The proposal was accepted with
gratitude, and it was thereupon arranged that Lord
Edward, accompanied by Mrs. and Miss Moore,
Gallaher, and Palmer, should proceed that evening from Moore's in Thomas Street, to Magan's on
Usher's Island. It was further astutely suggested by
Mr. Magan, that as so large a party knocking at his
hall door might attract suspicion, he would leave
ajar his stable door in Island Street, which lay immediately at the rere, and thus open access through
the garden to his house. Lord Edward, while under
Moore's roof, passed as the French tutor of Miss
Moore, who had been educated at Tours, and
they never spoke unless in French. On the pretext of being about to take a stroll through Galway's Walk adjacent, then a popular lounge, Miss
Moore, leaning on Lord Edward's arm, walked down

Thomas Street at about half-past eight o'clock on the evening of May 17th. They were preceded by Mrs. Moore, Palmer, and Gallaher, the latter a confidential clerk in Moore's employ, a man of Herculean frame, and one of Lord Edward's most devoted disciples. Of the intended expedition to Usher's Island the government early that day received information. Thomas Moore, in his diary of August 26, 1830, gives the following particulars communicated on that day by Major Sirr:—"Two ways by which he (Lord Edward) might have come, either Dirty Lane or Watling Street: Sirr divided his forces, and posted himself, accompanied by Regan and Emerson, in Watling Street, his two companions being on the other side of the street. Seized the first of the party, and found a sword, which he drew out, and this was the saving of his life. Assailed by them all, and in stepping back fell; they prodding at him. His two friends made off. On his getting again on his legs, two pistols were snapped at him, but missed fire, and his assailants at last made off".

As explanatory of the Major's statement we may observe that one of Lord Edward's bodyguard was despatched usually about forty yards in advance. Major Sirr speaks of men prodding at his prostrate body, but does not tell that he wore a coat of mail under his uniform. Gallaher used to say that he gave the Major seven stabs, not one of which penetrated. During the struggle Gallaher received from Sirr an ugly cut on the leg, which subsequently furnished a mark for identification. Meanwhile the rebel party hurried back with their noble charge to Thomas Street—not to Moore's, but to the nearer residence *of Murphy, who* had previously given his lordship *generous shelter.*

The original letter which conveyed to Major Sirr the information touching Lord Edward's intended visit to Usher's Island, still exists among the " Sirr MSS." deposited in the Library of Trinity College, Dublin. The following copy, has been made by Dr. Madden, who, however, seems to agree with Thomas Moore, in the opinion that Lord Edward's destination was Moira House.

"Lord Edward will be this evening in Watling Street. Place a watch in Watling Street, two houses up from Usher's Island;* another towards Queen's bridge;† a third in *Island Street, at the rere of the stables* near Watling Street, and which leads up to Thomas Street and Dirty Lane. At one of these places Lord Edward will be found, and will have one or two with him. They may be armed. Send to Swan and Atkinson as soon as you can

" EDWARD COOKE".

Mr. Cooke does not tell Sirr from whom he got this information; nor was the major, so far as we know, ever cognizant of it; but a letter written by Cooke for the eye of Lord Castlereagh, and printed in the Cornwallis correspondence, states unreservedly that all the information regarding the movements of Lord Edward Fitzgerald came through Francis Higgins, who employed a *gentleman*—for whose name Mr. Cooke considerately gives a dash—" to set" the unfortunate nobleman. The " setter" we believe to

* This precaution was obviously lest Lord Edward should enter by the hall door on Usher's Island.—W. J. F.
† Lest he should come by " Dirty Lane" instead of Watling Street. Magan's is the second stable from Watling Street, although his house on Usher's Island is the sixth from that Street.—W. J. F.

have been Mr. Francis Magan, barrister-at-law, of whom more anon.

Nicholas Murphy received his noble guest with a *cead mile failte;** but next morning both were thrown into a state of alarm by observing a detachment of military pass down the street, and halt before Moore's door.† The source from whence the espionage proceeded has hitherto remained a dark and painful mystery. Murphy hurried Lord Edward to the roof of the warehouse, and with some difficulty persuaded him to lie in the valley.

To return to Mr. Francis Magan. On the day following his interview with Miss Moore, he proceeded to her residence in Thomas Street, and with a somewhat careworn expression, which then seemed the result of anxiety for Lord Edward's safety, though it was probably occasioned by bitter chagrin at being baulked in a profitable job, said: "I have been most uneasy: did anything happen? I waited up till one o'clock, and Lord Edward did not come". Miss Moore, who, although a woman of great strength of mind, did not then suspect Magan, replied: "We were stopped by Major Sirr in Watling Street; we ran back to Thomas Street, where we most providentially succeeded in getting Lord Edward shelter at Murphy's".‡ Mr. Magan was consoled by the explanation, and withdrew.

* Anglice—A hundred thousand welcomes.
† For curious traditional details in connection with this incident see Mr. Macready's statement, Appendix F.
‡ Communicated by Edward Macready, Esq., son of Miss Moore, May 17, 1865. Miss Moore, afterwards Mrs. Macready, died in 1844. One of her last remarks was: "Charity forbade me to express a suspicion which I have long entertained, that Magan was the Betrayer; but when I see Moore, in his Life of *Lord Edward,* insinuating that Neilson was a Judas, I can no

The friends who best knew Magan, describe him as a queer combination of pride and bashfulness, dignity and decorum, nervousness and inflexibility. He obviously did not like to go straight to the Castle and sell Lord Edward's blood openly. There is good evidence to believe that he confided all the information to Francis Higgins, with whom it will be shown the Magan family were peculiarly intimate, and deputed him, under a pledge of strict secresy, to make a good bargain with Mr. Under-Secretary Cooke.

After Lord Edward had spent a few hours lying in the valley of the roof of Murphy's house he ventured to come down. The unfortunate nobleman had been suffering from a sore throat and cold, and general debility, and his appearance was sadly altered for the worse. He was reclining, half dressed, upon a bed, about to drink some whey which Murphy had prepared for him, when Major Swan, followed by Captain Ryan at some distance behind, peeped in at the door. " You know me, my lord, and I know you", exclaimed Swan, " it will be vain to resist".* This logic did not convince Lord Edward. He sprang from the bed like a tiger from his lair, and with a wave-bladed dagger, which he had concealed under the pillow, made some stabs at the intruder, but without as yet inflicting mortal injury.

longer remain silent. Major Sirr got timely information that we were going to Usher's Island. Now this intention was known only to Magan and me; even Lord Edward did not know our destination until just before starting. If Magan is innocent, then I am the informer". The Cornwallis Papers had not then appeared, furnishing a link which, although useless separately, powerfully tends to corroborate Miss Moore's suspicion.

* The *Express*, May 26th, 1798.

An authorized version of the arrest, evidently
supplied by Swan himself, appears in the *Express* of
May 26th, 1798, and goes on to say: " His lordship
then closed upon Mr. Swan, shortened the dagger,
and gave him a stab in the side, under the left arm
and breast, having first changed it from one hand
to the other over his shoulder (as Mr. Swan thinks).
Finding the blood running from him, and the im-
possibility to restrain him, he was compelled, in
defence of his life", adds Swan's justification, " to
discharge a double-barrelled pistol at his lordship,
which wounded him in the shoulder: he fell on the
bed, but, recovering himself, ran at him with the
dagger, which Mr. Swan caught by the blade with
one hand, and endeavoured to trip him up". Captain
Ryan, with considerable animation, then proceeded
to attack Lord Edward with a sword cane, which
bent on his ribs. Sirr, who had between two and
three hundred men with him, was engaged in
placing pickets round the house, when the report of
Swan's pistol made him hurry upstairs to his relief.
"On my arrival in view of Lord Edward, Ryan,
and Swan", writes Major Sirr, in a letter addressed
to Captain Ryan's son, on December 29th, 1838, " I
beheld his lordship standing, with a dagger in his
hand, as if ready to plunge it into my friends, while
dear Ryan, seated on the bottom step of the flight
of the upper stairs, had Lord Edward grasped with
both his arms by the legs or thighs, and Swan in a
somewhat similar situation, both labouring under
the torment of their wounds, when, without hesitation, I fired at Lord Edward's dagger arm, [lodging
several slugs in his shoulder,] and the instrument of
death fell to the ground. Having secured the
titled prisoner, my first concern was for your dear

father's safety. I viewed his intestines with grief and
sorrow".[*]

Not until a strong guard of soldiery pressed
Lord Edward violently to the ground by laying
their heavy muskets across his person, could he be
bound in such a way as prevented further effective
resistance.[†] When they had brought the noble
prisoner, however, as far as the hall,[‡] he made a
renewed effort at escape, when a dastardly drummer
from behind inflicted a wound in the back of his
neck, which contributed to embitter the remaining days of his existence. He was then removed
in a sedan to the Castle.

The entire struggle occupied so short an interval,
that Rattigan, who, the moment he received intimation of the arrest, rushed forth to muster the populace, in order to rescue Lord Edward, had not time
to complete his arrangements.[§] Rattigan was a respectable timber merchant, residing with his mother,
a widow, in Bridgefoot Street. In Higgins's
Journal of the day, we read :—

"A number of pikes were yesterday (Monday)
discovered at one Rattigan's timber-yard in Dirty
Lane ; as a punishment for which his furniture was

---

* *Castlereagh's Correspondence*, vol. i., pp. 463-'4.
† Moore's *Life of Lord Edward Fitzgerald.*
‡ Moore's *Diary*, vol. vi , p. 184.
§ "Recollections of the Arrest of Lord Edward Fitzgerald".
The *Comet* (Newspaper), Sept. 11, 1831 (p. 152).
The original Proclamation is now before us, offering a reward
of £300 for the " discovery" of Rattigan, Lawless, and others.
Rattigan escaped, entered the French service, and died at the
Battle of Marengo. Lawless, the attached friend and agent of
Lord Edward Fitzgerald, after undergoing a series of romantic
adventures, also succeeded in eluding the grasp of his pursuers,
and rose to the rank of General under Napoleon. For the
account of Lawless's escape from Dublin, furnished by the only
party competent to detail it, see Addenda G.

brought out into the street, and set fire to and consumed".

It does not seem to have been the wish of the higher members of the government, that Lord Edward should have fallen into the hands of their myrmidons. " Will no one urge Lord Edward to fly?" exclaimed Lord Clare. " I pledge myself that every port in the kingdom shall be left open to him".

It is not possible to overrate the fatal severity of the blow, which Lord Edward's arrest at that critical moment imparted to the popular movement. Had he lived to guide the insurrection which he had organised, his prestige and eminent military talents would probably have carried it to a successful issue. Four days after his arrest, three out of thirty-two counties rose; and to extinguish even that partial revolt, cost the government twenty-two millions of pounds, and twenty thousand men.

The late Lord Holland furnishes, in his *Memoirs*, many interesting illustrations of Lord Edward's sweet and gentle disposition:—

" With the most unaffected simplicity and good nature, he would palliate, from the force of circumstances or the accident of situation, the perpetrators of the very enormities which had raised his high spirit and compassionate nature to conspire and resist. It was this kindness of heart that led him, on his death-bed, to acquit the officer who inflicted his wounds of all malice, and even to commend him for an honest discharge of his duty. It was this sweetness of disposition that enabled him to dismiss with good humour one of his bitterest persecutors, who had visited him in his mangled condition, if not to insult his misfortunes, with the idle *hope of extorting* his secret. ' I would shake

9

hands willingly with you', said he, 'but mine are cut to pieces. However, I 'll shake a *toe*, and wish you good bye'".

"Gentle when stroked, but fierce when provoked", has been applied to Ireland. The phrase is also applicable, in some degree, to her chivalrous son, who had already bled for his king as he had afterwards bled for his country.[*] Murphy's narrative, supplied to Dr. Madden, says:—

" It was supposed, the evening of the day before he died, he was delirious, as we could hear him with a very strong voice crying out, ' Come on! come on! d—n you, come on!' He spoke so loud that the people in the street gathered to listen to it".

Two surgeons attended daily on Lord Edward Fitzgerald.[†]

This delirium is said to have been induced by the grossly indecent neglect to which his feelings were subjected by the Irish government. Lord Henry Fitzgerald, addressing the heartless viceroy, Lord Camden, "complains that his relations were excluded, and old attached servants withheld from attending on him".

[*] To his wounds received in active service, and his ability as a military officer, C. J. Fox bore testimony in the House of Commons on the 21st December, 1792. Cobbett said that Lord Edward was the only officer of untarnished personal honour whom he had ever known. Even that notoriously systematic traducer of the Irish popular party, Sir Richard Musgrave, was constrained to praise Lord Edward's " great valour, and considerable abilities", "honour and humanity", " frankness, courage, and good nature".

[†] One of the surgeons was Mr. Garnett, who, in a diary devoted to his noble patient, noted several interesting facts. Lord Edward manifested great religious feeling, and asked Mr. Garnett to read the Holy Scriptures to him. We are informed by *Mr. Colles*, Librarian of the Royal Dublin Society, that this *MS. is now in his possession.*

Epistolary entreaty was followed by personal supplication.

"Lady Louisa Conolly", writes Mr. Grattan, "in vain implored him, and stated that while they were talking, her nephew might expire; at last she threw herself on her kness, and in a flood of tears, supplicated at his feet, and prayed that he would relent; but Lord Camden remained inexorable".*

Lord Henry Fitzgerald's feelings found a vent in a letter, addressed to Lord Camden, of which the strongest passages have been suppressed by that peer's considerate friend, Thomas Moore:

"On Saturday my poor, forsaken brother, who had but that night and the next day to live, was disturbed; he heard the noise of the execution of Clinch at the prison door. He asked eagerly, 'What noise is that?' And certainly, in some manner or other, he knew it; for—O God! what am I to write?—from that time he lost his senses: most part of the night he was raving mad; a keeper from a madhouse was necessary".†

Lord Edward Fitzgerald died in great agony, mental and bodily, on the 4th of June, 1798, and was deposited in the vaults of St. Werburgh's Church. Hereby hangs a tale, which will be found in the Appendix.‡

* *Memoirs of Henry Grattan*, vol. iv. p. 387.
† Moore's *Life and Death of Lord Edward Fitzgerald*, vol. ii. p. 160.
‡ Appendix H.

CHAPTER VI.

A secret well kept.—The "setter" of Lord Edward at last traced —Striking in the dark.—Roman Catholic barristers pensioned.—A lesson of caution.—Letter to the author from Rev. John Fetherston-Haugh.—Just debts paid with wages of dishonour.—Secret service money.—An ally of "the Sham's" analysed.—What were the secret services of Francis Magan, barrister-at-law?—Shrouded secrets opened.

" One circumstance", says a writer, " is worthy of especial notice. Like Junius, an unfathomed mystery prevails as to who it was that betrayed Lord Edward Fitzgerald, and received the reward of one thousand pounds".*

When one remembers the undying interest and sympathy which has so long been interwoven with the name of Lord Edward Fitzgerald, it is indeed surprising that for sixty-one years the name of the person who received one thousand pounds for discovering him should have not transpired.† The secret must have been known to many persons in the Castle and the Executive; yet even when the circumstance had grown so old as to become the legitimate property of history, they could not be induced to relax their reserve. Whenever any inquisitive student of the stormy period of '98 would ask Major Sirr to tell the name of Lord Edward's betrayer, the Major invariably drew forth his ponderous snuff-box, inhaled a prodigious pinch, and solemnly turned the conversation. Thomas Moore, when engaged upon the *Life and Death of Lord Edward Fitzgerald*, made two special visits to Ireland for the purpose of

---

* Castlereagh Correspondence, vol. i., p. 468, First series.
† Francis Higgins received the £1,000 for having pointed out Lord Edward's retreat, but recent inquiries on the part of the *author have* ascertained that Counsellor Magan betrayed Lord *Edward to Higgins.*

procuring on the spot all the sadly interesting particulars of his lordship's short but striking career. The Castle was then occupied by an Irish Whig administration, but, notwithstanding Moore's influence with them, and their sympathy, more or less, with the hero whose memory he was about to embalm, he failed to elicit the peculiar information in which the Castle archives and library were rich. In 1841 Dr. Madden was somewhat more fortunate. He obtained access to a number of receipts for secret service money, as well as to a book, found under strange circumstances, in which the various sums and the names of the parties to whom paid are entered. But perhaps the most interesting entry was written in a way to defeat the ends of historic curiosity.

In the book of Secret Service Money Expenditure, now in the possession of Charles Haliday, Esq.,* the entry "*June 20th* [1798], *F. H. Discovery of L. E. F.* £1,000", appears on record. The researches of one of the most indefatigable of men proved, in this instance, vain. " The reader", says

* Doctor —— has given us the following account of the discovery of this document:—" When Lord Mulgrave, since Marquis of Normanby, was Lord Lieutenant of Ireland, some official in Dublin Castle cleared out and sold a quantity of books and papers, which were purchased in one lot by John Feagan, a dealer in second-hand books, who had, as his place of business, a cellar at the corner of Henry Street. I had the opportunity of examining the entire collection, but, not being much of a politician, I only selected two volumes, Wade's *Catalogue of the plants of the County Dublin,* and the *Catalogue of the Pinelli Library,* sold in London A.D. 1789, which I bought for 1s. 6d. They, and the others of the collection, had each a red leather label, on which in large gilt capitals was impressed, ' Library, Dublin Castle'. Among them was the MS. account of the expenditure of the Secret Service money, and of which I was the first to point out the possible value when it was about to be thrown, with various useless and imperfect books, into waste paper".

Dr. Madden, "has been furnished with sufficient
data to enable him to determine whether the initials were used to designate Hughes, or some other
individual; whether the similarity of the capital
letters J and F, in the handwriting, may admit or
not of one letter being mistaken for another, the F
for a J; or whether a correspondent of Sirr's, who
sometimes signed himself J. H., and whose name
was Joel Hulbert, an informer, residing in 1798 in
Monasterevan, may have been indicated by them".[*]
Watty Cox declared that Laurence Tighe, to
whose house the bleeding body of Ryan was borne
after Lord Edward's arrest, had played the spy;
while, on the other hand, Dr. Brennan, in his *Milesian Magazine*, broadly charged Cox with the perfidy. Murphy, an honest, simple-minded man, in
whose house Lord Edward was taken, has not been
exempted from suspicion. The late eminent anecdo-
tist, Mr. P. Brophy, of Dublin, used to tell that Lord
Edward's concealment became known "through an
artilleryman who was courting Murphy's servant
girl"; but Thomas Moore unintentionally disturbs
this story, which never reached his ears, by saying
"an *old* maid-servant was the only person in
Murphy's house besides themselves". The memory of
Samuel Neilson, one of the truest disciples who followed the patriot peer, suffered from a dark inuendo
advanced in Moore's *Life of Lord Edward Fitzgerald*, and echoed by Maxwell (p. 47), in his *History of the Irish Rebellion*. To one of the most
honourable of Lord Edward's followers, Charles
Phillips, under an erroneous impression, refers in a
startling note attached (p. 288) to the last edition
of *Curran and his Contemporaries*. He professes

* Madden's *Lives and Times of the U. I. Men*, v. ii. p. 443.

to know the secret, and adds: " He was to the last, apparently, the attached friend of his victim". In a memoir of O'Connell, from the pen of the late Mark O'Callaghan, it is stated in positive terms (p. 32) that John Hughes received the thousand pounds for the betrayal of Lord Edward. The son and biographer of the notorious Reynolds writes (v. ii. p. 194): " The United Irishmen, and their partizans, especially Mr. Moore, emboldened by the distance of time and place, have insinuated that my father was the person who caused the arrest of Lord Edward". Further on, at p. 234, Mr. Reynolds flings the onus of suspicion on Murphy, while Murphy in his own account of the transaction says: " I heard in prison that one of Lord Edward's bodyguard had given some information". Again, Felix Rourke was suspected of the infidelity, and narrowly escaped death at the hands of his comrades. Suspicion also followed William Ogilvie, Esq., who, as a near connection, visited Lord Edward at Moore's, in Thomas Street, a few days before the arrest, and transacted some business with him.* Interesting as it is, after half a century's speculation, to discover the name of the real informer, it is still more satisfactory that those unjustly suspected of the act should be finally acquitted from it. It is further useful as teaching a lesson of caution to those who, blindfold, strike right and left at friend and foe.†

* When Miss Moore heard this dark suspicion started, she said, " If so, I know not whom to trust. I saw Lord Edward take a ring from his finger and press it on Mr. Ogilvie as a keepsake. Tears fell from Ogilvie's eyes as he grasped Lord Edward's hand"— *Tradition of the Moore Family.*

† Never was stronger anxiety expressed to trace an informer, or fiercer maledictions hurled at his head. One stirring ballad descriptive of the arrest and death of Lord Edward, says:

One of the most valuable letters printed by Mr. Ross in his *Memoirs and Correspondence of Marquis Cornwallis* (v. iii. p. 320) is that addressed by Secretary Cooke to his Excellency, in which Mr. Francis Higgins and others are recommended as fit recipients for a share in the £1,500 per annum, which in 1799 had been placed for secret service in the hands of Lord Cornwallis. "My occupation", writes this nobleman on 8th June, 1799, "is now of the most unpleasant nature, negotiating and jobbing with the most corrupt people under Heaven. I despise myself every hour for engaging in such dirty work". And again: "How I long to kick those whom my public duty obliges me to court". It may be premised that "Mac" is Leonard McNally, the legal adviser and advocate of the United Irishmen. His opportunities for stagging were great, as, besides being a United Irishman himself, his name may be found for the defence in almost every state trial from Rowan's to that of the Catholic Delegates in 1811.* M'Gucken, the third name mentioned, was the solicitor to the United Irishmen.

" PENSIONS TO LOYALISTS.

" I submit to your lordship on this head the following: First, that Mac—— should have a pension of £300. He was not much trusted in the Rebellion, and I believe, has been faithful. Francis Higgins,

" May Heaven scorch and parch the tongue by which his life
    was sold,
And shrivel up the hand that clutched the proffer'd meed of
    gold:
May treachery for ever be the traitor's lot on earth,
From the kith and kin around him, in his bed and at his
    hearth".

* *See Addenda* K.

proprietor of the *Freeman's Journal*, was the person
who procured for me all the intelligence respecting
Lord Edward Fitzgerald, and got——to set him,
and has given me much information, £300".*

Mr. Under-Secretary Cooke and Francis Higgins
were old acquaintances.   The former came to Ireland in 1778 with Sir Richard Heron, chief secretary under Lord Buckinghamshire, and having effi-
ciently acted as his clerk, was appointed military
secretary in 1789, and obtained a seat in the Irish
Parliament.† During the Rutland administration Mr.
Cooke contributed papers to the *Freeman's Journal*
" under the auspices of the Sham Squire"; one, entitled *The Sentinel*, acquired some historic notoriety.‡
Mr. Cooke's services were further rewarded by the
office of Clerk of Commons with £800 a year, as well
as by the lucrative sinecure of Customer of Kinsale.

At a later period he became secretary to the treasury and under-secretary of state in the war and
colonial department. For some account of Mr.
Cooke's extraordinarily active and wily services in
promoting the legislative Union, see notice of Mr.
Trench, Addenda J.

*   *   *   *   *   *

Before we had thoroughly succeeded in unshroud-
ing Mr. Magan's share in the betrayal of Lord
Edward, the following and many more remarks,
tracing it on circumstantial evidence, were in type:

* It is strange that Mr. Ross, who has generally exhibited such
vigilance and research as editor of the Cornwallis Papers, should
print such a note as the following (v. ii. p. 339) : " The man
who gave the information which led to his arrest received £1,000,
but his name has never transpired".

† Castlereagh Correspondence, v. i. p. 113.

‡ *Irish Political Characters*, Lond. 1799, p. 130.

The considerate and cautious way in which Mr. Cooke leaves a blank for the name of the individual who performed the office of " setter", at the instance of Higgins, suggests that he must have been a person of some station in society, and one whose prospects and peace of mind might suffer, were he publicly known to have tracked Lord Edward Fitzgerald to destruction.* Mr. Cooke also leaves a blank for the name of Leonard MacNally, whose guilt did not transpire fully until after his death in 1820; but since then it has been but too notorious.

In the first volume of the second edition of Dr. Madden's *United Irishmen*, he furnishes, from page 364, an interesting account of " the Secret Service Money expended in detecting treasonable conspiracies, extracted from original official documents". At page 393 we learn that Mr. Francis Magan, a Roman Catholic barrister, not only received large sums down, but enjoyed to his death an annual pension of £200. On the back of all Mr. Magan's receipts, the Chief Secretary has appended a memorandum implying that Mr. Magan belonged to a class who did not wish to criminate openly, but stagged *sub rosa*. Dr. Madden remarks: " Counsellor Francis Magan's services to government, whatever they were, were well rewarded. Besides his secret pension of £200 a-year, he enjoyed a lucrative official situation in the Four Courts up to the time of his decease. He was one of the commissioners for enclosing commons".

In reply to an application addressed by us to an

---

* An old friend of Mr. Magan's informs us that he mixed in good society and held his head high. The same informant adds that he was stiff, reserved, and consequential; he often served with Magan on Catholic Boards, where, owing to these causes, *he was not a favourite.*

old friend of Mr. Magan's, it has been urged that the fact of his having received a pension from the crown is no presumptive evidence of secret service at the period of '98, inasmuch as nearly all " the Catholic barristers were similarly purchased, including Counsellors Donnellan, MacKenna, Lynch, and Bellew". Unluckily, however, for this argument, we find the following data in that valuable collection of state papers, the *Cornwallis Correspondence*, v. iii. p. 106: "In 1798", writes Mr. Ross, " a bill passed to enable the Lord Lieutenant (Lord Cornwallis) to grant pensions to the amount of £3,000, as a recompense to persons *who had rendered essential services to the state during the rebellion.* This sum was to be paid to the under secretary, through whose hands it was confidentially to pass.   By a warrant, dated June 23rd, 1799, it was divided as follows:—

Thomas Reynolds, his wife, and two sons*	£1,000
Mrs. Elizabeth Cope, and her three daughters†	1,000
John Warneford Armstrong‡ ...	500
Mrs. Ryan, widow of D. F. Ryan,§ and his daughters	200
MR. FRANCIS MAGAN, ...	200
	2,900
Balance to pay fees, etc. ...	100
	£3,000"

The counsellor's is the only name in this list which Secretary Cooke inscribes with a prefix of courtesy,

* The wholesale betrayer of his associates.
† Wife of Mr. Cope, " who managed Reynolds".
‡ Betrayer of John and Henry Sheares.
§ Mr. Ryan, who aided in the arrest of Lord Edward Fitzgerald.

and, no doubt, he was the mysterious gentleman whom Francis Higgins urged to "set" Lord
Edward Fitzgerald.   Between the Magan family
and Mr. Higgins a close intimacy subsisted for
many years.   The barrister's father was the late
Thomas Magan of High Street, woollen-draper, traditionally known by the sobriquet of " Whistling
Tom".*   In the *Dublin Directory* for 1770, his
name and occupation appear for the first time.   So
far back as June 30, 1789, we find it recorded in
the *Dublin Evening Post* that " yesterday Mr.
Magan of High Street, entertained Mr. Francis
Higgins" and others.   " The glass circulated freely,
and the evening was spent with the utmost festivity
and sociality".   The *Post* in conclusion ironically
calls him " Honest Tom Magan".   By degrees we
find Mr. Tom Magan dabbling in government politics.   The *Evening Post* of November 5th, 1789,
records:

   " Mr. Magan, the woollen-draper, in High Street, in
conjunction with his friend Mr. Higgins, are preparing
ropes and human brutes to drag the new viceroy to
the palace.   It was Mr. Magan and the Sham Squire
who provided the materials for the triumphal entry of
Lord Buckingham into the capital.   Quere—Should
not the inhabitants of Dublin who had their windows
broke on that *glorious illumination* order their glaziers
to entreat Mr. Magan and Mr. Higgins to cast an eye
on the *tots?*   Mr. Magan is really clever, and never
has flinched in his partiality and attention to the cause
of Mr. Francis Higgins—Mr. Magan has the honour,
and that frequently, to dine Messrs. Higgins, Daly,
Brennan, and Houlton.

   * The draper's father was "James Magan, apothecary, Skinner's Row", as we gather from a copy of the *Dublin Directory*
for 1769, in which an old man's hand-writing adds annota-
tively, " *Counsellor Magan's grandfather*".

The last two named, it will be remembered, were the Sham Squire's colleagues on the *Freeman's Journal.*

The *Post* further instances an act of great friendship which Mr. Magan performed with a view to serve Mr. Higgins. And there is good reason to believe that the Sham Squire was not unmindful of those services. In the *Directory* for 1794 we find Mr. Tom Magan styled " woollen-draper and mercer to his Majesty"—a very remarkable instance of state favour towards any Roman Catholic trader at that period of sectarian prejudice and ascendancy. George III., however, gave Mr. Magan no custom, and he died poor in 1797. With his son, who was called to the bar in Michaelmas Term 1796, Mr. Higgins continued to maintain a friendly intercourse. From the year 1796 Francis Magan resided with his sister until his death in 1843, at 20 Usher's Island. From the *Castlereagh Papers* (i. 459) we learn that Mr. Secretary Cooke received positive information of these movements of Lord Edward in the vicinity of Usher's Island, which preceded the final intelligence which led to his arrest some days afterwards in Thomas Street. Mr. Cooke's letter assures the viceroy that *all* the information respecting Lord Edward had come from Francis Higgins, who got some gentleman, for whose name the under-secretary considerately gives a dash, " to set" the unfortunate young nobleman.

Mr. Higgins at once claimed his blood-money, and on the 20th June, 1798, we find that one thousand pounds were paid to him. How much of this sum was given by the Sham Squire to his friend " the setter", or what previous agreement there may have been *between* them, will probably never be known.

We are rather disposed to suspect that Higgins tricked his tongue-tied colleague by pocketing the lion's share himself. Magan, by right, ought to have received the advertised reward of £1,000; but it appears from the Government records that this round sum went into Higgins's hand conjointly with a pension of £300 a year "*for the discovery of L. E. F.*" Magan obtained but £200 a year for the information of which Higgins was merely the channel; though later in life he received office, and sums for other discoveries. In 1799 an act was passed, placing a considerable sum at the viceroy's disposal, for the reward of secret services during the rebellion. Francis Magan is the only important member of the suborned staff of stags whose secret services until now have been historically unaccounted for. In the long array of items extracted by Dr. Madden from the Secret Service Book, per affidavit of Mr. Cooke, we find under date "September 11, 1800",

"Magan, per Mr. Higgins, . . £300".

The sums of £500 and £100 were afterwards privately presented to Mr. Magan, pursuant to the provisions of the Civil List Act, which placed money in the hands of the viceroy "for the detection of treasonable conspiracies". These douceurs were, of course, in addition to the payments made quarterly to Mr. Magan for the term of his natural life, and for which his receipts still exist.[*]

Mr. Magan possessed peculiar facilities, local and otherwise, for "setting" the movements of Lord

---

[*] One, by way of specimen, taken from the *Lives and Times of the United Irishmen*, v. i. 393, is subjoined :—
"Received from William Gregory, Esq., by William Taylor,

Edward Fitzgerald and the United Irishmen who habitually met in Con MacLaughlin's house, at 13 Usher's Island. Lady Edward, as we learn from Moore's Memoirs, was at Moira House, close to Mr. Magan's residence, while his lordship lay concealed in Thomas Street adjacent.

Francis Magan, who became a member of the Irish bar in 1796, found himself briefless, and without " connection" or patrimony. A drowning man, 't is said, will catch at a straw; and we have seen how he turned to mercenary account peculiar knowledge which he acquired. Yet he would seem to have made a false conscience, for with the wages of dishonour, he paid his just debts. The following letter, addressed to us by the Rev. John Fetherston-Haugh, is not without interest. It has been argued by one of the friends of Mr. Magan, in reply to a personal expression of our suspicion, that he who would do the one would scorn to do the other; but it must be remembered that Mr. Magan, subsequent to '98, was on the high-road to riches, and while the bond, to which he was a party, existed, he was, of course, legally liable.

" Griffinstown House, Kinnegad.

" MY DEAR SIR,—In reply to your letter, respecting Mr. Francis Magan, I beg to say that my grandfather, Thomas Fetherston, of Bracket Castle, was in the habit, for years, of lodging in High Street, Dublin, at the house of Thomas Magan, a draper, and departed this life in his house. My father, on inspecting my grandfather's papers, found a joint Esq., fifty pounds sterling, for the quarter, to 24th December last.

" Dublin, January 22, 1816. " F. MAGAN".

" Endorsed by Secretary of the Lord Lieutenant,
" January, 1816, £50, S. A. F. MAGAN".

bond from the draper and his son for £1,000, and on speaking to the draper respecting its payment, he told him he was insolvent,* so my father put it into his desk, counting it waste paper. Some years elapsed, and the son came to Bracket Castle, my father's residence, and asked for the bond, ' for what?' said my father. To his astonishment, he said it was to pay it. I was then but a boy, but I can now almost see the strange scene, it made so great an impression on me. Often my father told me Magan paid the £1,000, and he could not conceive where he got it, as he never held a brief in court. He was puzzled why the crown gave him place and pension. Believe me, etc.,

" I. FETHERSTON H.

As we have already said, in the official account of Civil Service Money expended in detecting treasonable conspiracies, the item,

" September 11, 1800, Magan per Mr. Higgins, £300",

arrests attention. In the hope that Higgins' journal of the day would announce some special discovery of treason, tending to explain the circumstances under which the above douceur of £300 was given, we consulted the files, but found nothing tending to throw a light on the matter, unless the following paragraphs published in the issues of August 12th and of September 9th, 1800:—

" Yesterday Major Swan took into custody a person named M'Cormick,† who is well known in the seditious

* The statement was doubtless correct. No will of Thomas Magan was proved in the Irish Probate Court.

† P. M'Cormick, a " noted" rebel, is mentioned in Madden's *United Irishmen*, i. 519, as residing in High Street. Did Mr. Magan's long residence in High Street furnish him with any *facilities* for tracing this man?

circle, and lodged him in the guard house of the Castle. He wore a green riband in his breast which had a device wrought upon it of two hands *fraternally united* by a grip, which, he said, was *the badge of a new* (it is supposed Erin-Go-Brach) Order".

The second paragraph refers to " recent discoveries" in general terms only, but the style is amusing.

" Some of these offenders who were concerned in the late conspiracies with United Irishmen, to whom the lenity of Government had extended amnesty on assurances of their becoming *useful* and proper subjects, having been *recently discovered* from their malignant tongues to be miscreants unworthy of the mercy and support extended to them, from their continual *applauses* of the common foe and his friends, and their maligning the first characters in the government and their measures, it is intended to dispose of these vipers, not as was at first intended, but in a manner that their perfidy and ingratitude merit".

Besides his pension of £200 a year and a place under the crown, given in recognition of secret services, Mr. Francis Magan further received, on December 15th, 1802, as appears from the account of secret service money expenditure, £500 in hand. This round sum, it is added, was given " by direction of Mr. Orpen". The secret service for which £500 was paid must have been one of no ordinary importance. Conjecture is narrowed as to the particular nature of the service by the heading of the document, *i.e.* " Account of secret service money *applied in detecting treasonable conspiracies* pursuant to the provisions of the Civil List Act of 1793". A study of the historical events of the time, with a comparison of the dates, find one or two dis-

10

coveries in which Magan may have been concerned.
In the year 1802 a formidable attempt was made to
rekindle the insurrection in the county of Cork.
Sergeant Beatty, its leader, after skirmishing with
the king's troops and killing several, escaped to
Dublin, where, while in the act of reorganizing his
plot, he was arrested and hung.* In 1802, Richard
F. Orpen, Esq., was high sheriff for the county of
Cork.† "He raised corps of volunteers for the sup-
pression of the Rebellion, was of an active mind,
and well acquainted with persons of rank and influence".‡ There is but one family of the name in
Ireland. It was, doubtless, this gentleman who
urged the reward of £500 to Magan in 1802; and,
probably, the secret service was the discovery of
the *Cork* conspirator.

The discovery of the plans of William Dowdall, a
confidential agent alike of Colonel Despard in England, and of Robert Emmet in Ireland, was also
made in 1802. Towards the end of that year, we
find him in Dublin, with the object of extending
their projects. Suddenly the news came that on November 13th, 1802, Despard and twenty-nine associates were arrested in London.§ Dowdall fled, and
after some hair-breadth escapes reached France. No
imputation on his fidelity has ever been made. That

---

* *Revelations of Ireland*, by D. O. Madden, p. 130 *et seq.*
See Addenda T. for fuller details.
† See files of the public journals for February, 1802.
‡ Letter from Richard F. John Orpen, Esq., August 16, 1865.
§ Plowden's *History of Ireland from the Union*, v. i. p. 176.
The Higgins journal of November 23, 1802, states, but without
sufficient accuracy, that "the major part are Irish". Lord
Ellenborough tried the prisoners, seven were hung and de-
capitated. — *Trial of Edward Marcus Despard*. London:
Gurney, 1803, p. 269.

Despard's plans extended to Ireland is not generally understood; but the Castlereagh Papers (ii. 3) show that he was one of the most determined of the Society of United Irishmen.

The Higgins journal of November 25th, 1802, records:—

"The lounging *Erin-go-Brachites* in this town seem somewhat frightened since they heard of the apprehension of Colonel Despard and his myrmidons. It marks a sympathy which, with the close whisperings and confabs that of late have been observable among them, incline some to think that they have not left off the old trade of dealing in baronial and *other constitutions*".

"Robert Emmet", says Mr. Fitzgerald, in a narrative supplied to Dr. Madden, "came over from France in October, 1802. He (Emmet) was soon in communication with several of the leaders who had taken an active part in the previous rebellion".[*] Emmet is probably included among the "Erin-go-brachites" thus indicated by the Higgins journal of November 2nd, 1802.

"Several Erin-go-Brachites have arrived in this city within a few days past, after viewing (as they would a monster) the First Consul. They do not, however, use the idolizing expressions of that character they were wont, which shows that he has not been courteous to the encouragers of *pike-mongering* in this country".

In the latter part of 1802, owing to private information, Emmet's residence near Milltown was searched by Major Swan.[†] The abortive insurrection of which he was the leader, did not take place

---

[*] *Lives and Times of the United Irishmen*, vol. iii. p. 330.
[†] Statement of Mr. Patten to Dr. Madden, Ibid., p. 339.

until July 23rd in the following year.   A memorandum of Major Sirr's, preserved with his papers in
Trinity College, Dublin, mentions, in contradiction
to a generally received opinion, that early intimation of Robert Emmet's scheme *did* reach the government.

The purchase of Mr. Magan by the government
was at this time unknown to his friends and the
public.   As a Roman Catholic and a member of the
former society of United Irishmen, no disposition
to suspect him seems to have taken possession of his
friends.*   The fact that he had been a member

* Dr. Brennan, in the second number of his *Milesian Magazine*, p. 49, enumerates the Roman Catholic barristers who had
received pensions.   Mr. Magan's name is not included.   Dr.
Brennan mentions the names of Donnellan, Bellew, Lynch, and
MacKenna.   The claims of Bellew and Lynch were for "Union
services".   Mr. Cooke, writing to Lord Castlereagh an account
of the Bar Meeting, September 10, 1798, says, "Bellew and
Lynch, two Catholics, were in the majority".   Mr. Sheil, in his
paper on the "Catholic Bar" contributed to the *New Monthly
Magazine* for February, 1827, thus specially refers to the above
four barristers:

"Every one of those gentlemen was provided for by Government.   Mr. Donnellan obtained a place in the revenue; Mr.
MacKenna wrote some very clever political tracts, and was
silenced with a pension; Mr. Lynch married a widow with a
pension, which was doubled after his marriage; and Mr. Bellew
is in the receipt of £600 a year, paid to him quarterly.

" Lord Castlereagh was well aware of the importance of securing the support of the leading Roman Catholic gentry at the
union, and the place of assistant barrister was promised to Mr.
Bellew.   It became vacant: Lord Castlereagh was reminded of
his engagement, when, behold! a petition signed by the magistrates of the county, to which Mr. Bellew was about to be nominated, is presented to the Lord Lieutenant, praying that a
Roman Catholic should not be appointed to any judicial office,
and intimating their determination not to act with him.   A
pension equivalent to the salary of a chairman was given to Mr.
Bellew, and he was put in the enjoyment of the fruits of the
office, without the labour of cultivation".

of the Lawyers' Corps awakened no misgiving. All
the Catholic barristers, as a matter of course, joined
it; and some of the most determined United Irishmen, including Macready and others, were known
to wear the yeoman uniform, merely with the object of cloaking themselves.*

A brother barrister and old friend of Mr. Magan's
informs us that he enjoyed some chamber practice;
but, though he sometimes appeared in the hall,
equipped for forensic action, he never spoke in court.
Mr. Magan, as one of the first and few Roman
Catholic barristers called on the relaxation of the
Penal Code, is very likely to have been consulted
during the troubled times of '98 and following
years, by his co-religionists who were implicated
in the conspiracy.

The influential leaders of the United Irishmen
were mostly Protestants, and Leonard MacNally,
who generally acted as counsel to the body, having
deserted the Catholic for the Protestant faith,
failed to command from Catholics that unlimited
confidence which a counsel of their own creed would
inspire. " Mac", writes Mr. Secretary Cooke, ad-

* All the Catholic barristers, with the object of averting suspicion or persecution, became members of the Lawyers' Corps.
Among others, Daniel O'Connell and Nicholas Purcell O'Gor-
man, both United Irishmen, belonged to the corps.
O'Connell served as a private in the corps. The uniform
was blue, with scarlet facings and rich gold lace.—See *Memoir
of O'Connell*, by his son, v. i. p. 13. In Mr. Daunt's *Recollections
of O'Connell*, v. ii. p. 99, O'Connell is found pointing out a house
in James's Street, which, when a member of the Lawyers'
Corps, he searched for "Croppies". This corps was disbanded
shortly subsequent to 1798; but in *Faulkner's Dublin Journal*
of April 9, 1803, an advertisement appears demanding its im-
mediate resuscitation, notwithstanding the absence of many influential members on circuit. For an account of O'Connell's
connection with the United Irishmen see Addenda B.

dressing Lord Castlereagh, "Mac—— was not much trusted in the rebellion".* Counsellor Magan, on the contrary, was not, for nearly half a century, suspected.† MacNally lived in Dominick Street, and later in Harcourt Street—a considerable distance from the more disturbed part of Dublin; but Mr. Magan's chamber for consultation lay invitingly open at No. 20 Usher's Island, in the very hotbed of the conspiracy.

The discoveries to which we have referred were made towards the latter end of the year 1802. On December 15th, 1802, one secret payment of £500 alone is slipped into the hand of "Counsellor Magan".

"In the month of March, [1803]", writes Lord Hardwicke, the then viceroy, "Government received information of O'Quigley's return, and others of the exiled rebels, and that they were endeavouring to sound the disposition of the people of the county of Dublin. A confidential agent was in consequence sent into that county, whose accounts were very satisfactory as to the state of the people, and of the unwillingness of any of the middle class, who had property to lose, to engage in any scheme of rebellion".‡

Whether Francis Magan was the confidential agent thus sent into the country we know not;

---

* Cornwallis Correspondence, v. iii. p. 320.

† The Irish Bar was sadly dishonoured in those days.—See Addenda K for the secret services of Leonard MacNally, and of that prince of duplicity, Samuel Turner, barrister-at-law, whose property was insincerely threatened with attainder by the crown.

‡ This original MS. statement of Lord Hardwicke's, of which *Dr. Madden* afterwards had the use, we fully transcribed in *1855.*

but it is at least certain that in the month of April, 1803, he is found within forty-seven miles of Dublin, and receiving money for political espionage.

" The account of secret service money applied in detecting treasonable conspiracies", contains the following entry:

" April 2, 1803, Magan, by post to Philipstown,   £100".*

The Philipstown assizes were held at this time. But so far from any important political trials being in progress there, from which Magan, in his legal capacity, might gather a secret, no business whatever was done, and, as the newspaper report of the day records, the chairman received, in consequence, a pair of white gloves trimmed with gold lace. We must look elsewhere for Mr. Magan's secret services at Philipstown in 1803.

Thomas Wilde and John Mahon were two of Emmet's most active emissaries, and in a statement of Duggan's supplied to Dr. Madden, it is stated that they proceeded to " Kildare, Naas, Maynooth, Kilcullen, and several other towns", in order to stimulate the people. The formidable character of Wilde and Mahon was known to Major Sirr, who in a memorandum preserved with his other papers, states that their retreat is sometimes " at the gaoler's in *Philipstown*, who is married to Wilde's sister".

Francis Magan, it is not unlikely, when one hundred pounds reached him by post at Philipstown in 1803, was quietly ascertaining the *locale* of Wilde and Mahon.

---

* An entry in the same form introduces the name of M'Gucken, the treacherous attorney for the United Irishmen, whose exploits will be found in our appendix:
"*January 1, 1801*, M'Gucken, per post to Belfast,   £100".

A letter from Captain Caulfield, written on December 17th, 1803, but to which the date "1798" has been by some oversight affixed in Dr. Madden's valuable work on the United Irishmen,* is also preserved among the Sirr papers, and details the progress of a search for Wilde and Mahon, first at Philipstown, and finally at Ballycommon, within two miles of it. Yeomanry and dragoons surrounded the house; a hot conflict ensued, "and", confesses Captain Caulfield, "we were immediately obliged to retire. . . . The villains made their escape. The gaoler of Philipstown and wife are in confinement".

John Brett, the maternal grandfather of the present writer, resided with his family in 1798, at 21 Usher's Island. No evidence of sedition existed against him, unless that furnished by the old aphorism, "show me your company, and I can tell who you are". John Brett was peculiarly intimate with Con MacLaughlin, and much intercourse existed between their families. James Tandy, son of the arch rebel Napper Tandy, was also a frequent visitor, and Mr. Brett possessed the friendship of Oliver Bond. One morning Mr. Brett's family were startled at the news that Major Sirr, with a chosen guard, were demanding admittance at the street door. Miss Maria Brett, the aunt of the writer, cognizant of only one act of political guilt, ran to her music-book, tore out a strongly national song, and flung the leaf, crushed up, on top of a chest of drawers. Major Sirr entered, precisely as this silly achievement had been completed, and found the young lady palpitating beneath the weight of her guilty

* *Lives and Times of the United Irishmen,* v. l. p. 522.

secret. A search for pikes was immediately commenced; drawers were rifled, wardrobes upset, beds diligently searched, and in the midst of the confusion what should turn up but the national song, which, had it been suffered to remain in the music-book, would never have excited attention. Major Sirr solemnly put on his spectacles, and read the democratic sentiments with a visage much longer than the lines in which they were enshrined. The search was resumed with renovated vigour, and from the beds in the sleeping rooms the soldiers now proceeded to uproot some recently dug beds in the garden. Major Sirr, baffled in his hopes and bitterly chagrined, withdrew; but he had a dexterous stroke of vengeance in store for John Brett. Next day an enormous detachment of soldiers' wives arrived, bag and baggage, at Usher's Island, loudly demanding hospitality, and producing an official order for that purpose. Mr. Brett was obliged to submit to the troublesome incubus, which remained for several weeks billeted upon his family. He could never guess the source which had suggested to the government the expediency of searching the house; but *we* are inclined to harbour the suspicion that the hint must have come from his vigilant neighbour next door, Mr. Francis Magan.

The files of the popular journals during the earlier part of the present century would, if diligently consulted, exhibit Francis Magan* as a zealous Catholic patriot. Thus, Mr. Magan's name may be found, in conjunction with those of Lords Fingal,

* It is not unlikely to Magan that the Duke of Wellington refers in his letter to Sir Charles Saxton, dated London, 17th November, 1808: "I think that as there are some interesting Catholic questions afloat now, you might feed —— with another £100"—*Irish Correspondence of the Duke of Wellington*, pp. 485–6.

Netterville, and Ffrench, Sir E. Bellew, Sir H. O'Reilly, Daniel O'Connell, Dr. Dromgoole, "Barney Coyle",* Con MacLaughlin,* Silvester Costigan,* Fitzgerald of Geraldine,* and others, convening an aggregate meeting of the Catholics of Ireland on the 26th of December, 1811, to address the Prince Regent " on the present situation of Catholic affairs". A few days previously, Lords Fingal and Netterville had been successively forced from the chair at a Catholic meeting by Mr. Hare, a police magistrate. Among the denouncers of the government at the aggregate meeting was Leonard MacNally!

The few surviving friends of Mr. Magan describe him as a prim and somewhat unsociable being, though moving in good society. He looked wise, but he never showed much proof of wisdom, and it was more than once whispered in reference to him, " Still waters run deep". For the last twenty years of his life he rarely went out, unless in his official capacity as commissioner. He never married, and lived a recluse at 20 Usher's Island. He became shrinking and timid, and with one or two exceptions, including Taxing Master C——, did not like to meet old friends. Since the year '98 it seemed as if his house had not been painted or the windows cleaned. The neighbours wondered, speculated, and pryed; but Magan's windows or doings could not be seen through.†

From this dingy retreat, festooned with cobwebs, Mr. Magan, almost choked in a stiff white cravat, would, as we have said, occasionally emerge, and

* Those persons had been United Irishmen.
† " The neighbours used to say that there was a mystery about the Magans which no one could fathom".—Letter from Sylvester E——d, Esq.

pick his steps stealthily to the courts in which he
held office.

This demeanour may have been owing to a secret
consciousness of dishonour, and was doubtless
aggravated by a shrewd suspicion expressed by the
late Mr. Joseph Hamilton.

To explain this, a slight digression is necessary.
In 1830, appeared Moore's life of Lord Edward
Fitzgerald, and it may be conceived with what tre-
pidation Mr. Magan turned over the leaves, fearful
of finding the long sealed secret told. " Treachery",
writes Moore, " and it is still unknown from·what
source, was at work".   Here the Counsellor, no
doubt, breathed freely, especially when he read:
" From my mention of these particulars respecting
Neilson, it cannot fail to have struck the reader
that some share of the suspicion of having betrayed
Lord Edward attaches to this man".   Hamilton
Rowan and the friends of Neilson indignantly
spurned the imputation, which Moore, further on,
sought to qualify. Mr. Joseph Hamilton made some
inquiries, and the result was a suspicion that Mr.
Magan was the informer.   He failed to find that
evidence which we have since adduced; but his
suspicion was deeply rooted, and he avowed it in
general society.

In 1843, Mr. Magan died. He was generally regarded as an honourable man; and an eminent
Queen's Counsel stood beside his death bed. It is
only right to add the accompanying letter from the
gentleman to whom we allude:

" I never, directly or indirectly, heard anything
of the alleged charge against Frank Magan during
his life.   I was on habits of intimacy with him to
the day of his death, and was with him on his

death-bed.   He always bore a high character, as far
as I could ever learn, either at the bar or in society.
Mr. Hamilton, to my surprise, wrote to me after his
death, cautioning me against taking any of the
money to which, he supposed, I was entitled as a
legatee.   I was not one, and never got a penny by
the poor fellow.   I can say no more".

Mr. Hamilton thought that it was beneath his
correspondent to accept a bequest derived from so
base a source.

Mr. Magan's will, drawn up hurriedly on his
death-bed, in January, 1843, and witnessed by his
parish priest and confessor, Rev. P. Monks, occupies
but a few lines, and bequeaths the entire of his property to Elizabeth, his sister.   Unlike his friend
the Sham Squire, who desired that his remains
should be interred with public pomp, Francis Magan
directs that his body may be buried with as much
economy and privacy as decency permits.*

Miss Magan, an eccentric spinster, continued to
reside alone at Usher's Island after her brother's
death.   She found herself, on his demise, possessed
of an enormous sum of money; and she became so
penurious, anxious, and nervous, that the poor lady
was in constant fear of being attacked or robbed.
From almost every person who approached her she
shrunk with terror.   Miss Magan felt persuaded
that designs on her purse, to be accomplished by
either force or fraud, were perpetually in process of
concoction by her narrow circle of friends.   Death
at last released Miss Magan from this mental misery.
She left considerable sums in charity, and, amongst
others, twelve thousand pounds, as the late Rev. Dr.

* Records of the Prerogative Court, Dublin.

Yore assured us, for founding a Lunatic Asylum at Clontarf. With the death of this lady the family of which she was a member became extinct, and we therefore feel the less hesitation in mentioning their names.

It may, perhaps, be said that any new suggestions or remarks regarding the informers of '98 should be left to Dr. Madden, who has devoted much time and space to the subject. But Dr. Madden himself does not seem to hold these narrow sentiments.

In the *United Irishmen* (vol. ii. 446), he throws out suggestions "to those who may be disposed to follow up his efforts to bring the betrayer's memory to justice".

It may also be objected that we have devoted undue space to tracing the betrayers of Lord Edward Fitzgerald; but the following remarks, expressed by the veteran historian of '98, show that the subject is one highly deserving of elucidation.

" And now", writes Dr. Madden, " at the conclusion of my researches on this subject of the betrayal of Lord Edward Fitzgerald, I have to confess they have not been successful. The betrayer still preserves his incognito; his infamy, up to the present time (January, 1858), remains to be connected with his name, and, once discovered, to make it odious for evermore. . . . . . Nine-and-fifty years the secret of the sly, skulking villain has been kept by his employers, with no common care for his character or his memory. But, dead or alive, his infamy will be reached in the long run, and the gibbeting of that name of his will be accomplished in due time".

It must be remembered that Dr. Madden was the *first to set inquiry* on a sound track, by citing from

the Secret Service Money Book the initials of the
Sham Squire—*i. e.* "F. H. for the discovery of
L. E. F., £1000". In 1858 the *Cornwallis Papers*
appeared, disclosing the name Francis Higgins. A
pamphlet from our pen appeared soon after, entitled
A Note to the Cornwallis Papers, in which were published many of the remarks contained in our sixth
chapter, and pointing, on purely circumstantial evidence, to Mr. Magan as the "setter" employed by
Higgins. The fourth volume of the *United Irishmen,* published in 1860, noticed the *Cornwallis
Papers,* and, indirectly, the pamphlet which followed its publication:

"These revelations", writes Dr. Madden (p. 579),
"leave us wholly uninformed as to the traitor who
actually betrayed Lord Edward — who sold his
blood to the agent of government, Mr. Francis
Higgins. All that we have learned, I repeat, from
the recent publication of the *Cornwallis Correspondence,* is, that Francis Higgins obtained the secret
for government of Lord Edward's place of concealment, but of the setter employed by Higgins we
know nothing, and all that we have reason to conclude is, that the setter was one in the confidence
of Lord Edward and his associates".

Now, we respectfully submit that the more recent
researches which will be found in our fifth and sixth
chapters prove to demonstration that the "setter"
was Counsellor Francis Magan.

CHAPTER VII.

Was Higgins guiltless of Oliver Bond's blood?—Walter Cox.—
Reynolds the informer.—William Cope.—Insatiable appetite
for blood-money.—A dark and painful mystery.—Lord Wycombe walks in the footsteps of Lord Edward Fitzgerald, and
spies follow in the footsteps of Lord Wycombe.

THERE is no man so bad but that he might be
worse; and the will of Francis Higgins, to which
we shall soon refer, shows that he was not incapable
of a generous impulse; but on the whole we cannot
divest ourselves of the suspicion that his general
policy was worse, and his dark deeds more numerous than have in black and white transpired. When
a man is once suspected and convicted of peculiar
turpitude, there is no limit to the suspicions which
ever after follow him.

A remarkable passage occurs in Walter Cox's
Irish Magazine for November, 1813, p. 52.*

"We hope," writes Cox, "no greater evil will be sustained by Mr. Scully than what this act of the *Free-*

---

* No one was better acquainted than Cox with the antecedents
of Higgins.   In his *Magazine* for October, 1810 (p. 436),
Cox writes, "If the illustrious shade of the Sham Squire can
witness the transitory scenes of this life, how exquisitely must
his exalted spirit feel, at the improved manner in which his
literary property is arranged, by a person so exactly after his
own mind, so fertile in stratagem, so guarded in his conduct,
and so various in management".
We further learn that the then editor was "exactly a minia-
ture copy of the Sham"; and then a secret or two transpires:
"After fixing his sentinels and dispatching his *Messenger*,
Con returns to the city to commence his literary labours on the
Sham's journal; there he figures in another character, since
that very immaculate paper was allowed to soar into the regions
of patriotism by having the little ballast of £1,200 a year thrown
over *board, that kept it floating over the Castle*".

man's Journal has inflicted; had we nothing more to record, to the prejudice of Irish interests, than such impotent, and we may say harmless nonsense, *Oliver Bond and Lord Edward Fitzgerald would be now alive,* and Tom Reynolds would have been only known as a harmless monster".

Cox, as an United Irishman, and one of Lord Edward Fitzgerald's body-guard, was cognizant of the various conflicting suspicions and surmises to which the unexpected arrest of their chief gave birth. Further, he was in the secrets of the government subsequent to 1798. Arthur O'Connor has said, that while a chance of success awaited the rebel movement, it possessed no more stanch partizan during thirty-five years that he personated the character of an indomitable patriot. But flesh is weak, and we find Cox in the receipt of a secret stipend from the government. Dr. Madden informs us that he played fast and loose—sometimes revealing the plans of the United Irishmen to the Castle, at other times disclosing to the popular party the secrets of the government and of its agents.

We are not aware that Dr. Madden ever noticed the passage just cited from Cox's *Irish Magazine.* Mr. Cox would seem to have formed a shrewd opinion in reference to Lord Edward's discovery; but he advances the charge so ambiguously that, unless with the light afforded by recent revelations, it is not easy to understand his meaning.

A dark and painful mystery enshrouds the death of Oliver Bond. Bond, an opulent merchant, residing in Bridge Street, Dublin, possessed, for many years, the fullest confidence of the United Irishmen, *who,* so early as 1793, formally addressed him on *the occasion* of his fine and imprisonment. From

1785 to 1797 we recognize him as an active member
of the two Northern directories of United Irishmen,
a body largely composed of Presbyterians.   At his
house in Dublin the Leinster directory regularly
met, until the night of March 12th, 1798, when,
Thomas Reynolds having betrayed his associates,
fifteen delegates were arrested, conveyed to Newgate, and sentenced to death.   Mr. Mark O'Callaghan, in his *Memoir of O'Connell*, p. 32, says: " It
is asserted on credible authority, that the secret
dungeons and state prisons of '98 were the scenes
of murder and assassination.   Among others, Oliver
Bond, a wealthy merchant, was generally allowed
to have been murdered by a government officer or
turnkey employed for the purpose, although it was
at the time given out that he died of apoplexy".
How far Mr. O'Callaghan may be correct in this
conclusion we know not; but a letter addressed by
the late James Davock to Dr. Madden, and printed
in the very interesting work of the latter, tends
much to corroborate it.

" The evening before his (Bond's) death I saw
him in the yard of the prison; he seemed then to be
in perfect health; the next morning he was found
dead in the passage outside his cell.   It was the
general opinion that he had been strangled.   Bond
had a free pardon signed at the castle at that time,
and was to have been sent out of the country with
the other state prisoners.   It was necessary for his
wife to obtain this pardon, to enable her to collect
in the debts, for he left about thirty thousand pounds
behind him; and his friends were afraid of impeding
her application, and thought it better to allow the
common report of his death arising from apoplexy
to pass unnoticed.

11

. . . . . . " The report in the prison was that he had been killed by the under-gaoler, Simpson. I was informed by Murphy, there was such an uproar in the prison all that night, that Murphy and others barricaded their doors on the inside, afraid of violence. The woman who first swore at the inquest that she had seen him die in ' the yard, afterwards, in a quarrel, accused Simpson of the murder; on which he kicked her in the back, of which injury she died".*

It may be added that Mr. Davock was for many years the intimate friend and close neighbour of Oliver Bond, who was a remarkably robust man, and not more than thirty-five years of age at his death.

Sentence of death on Bond and the fourteen delegates arrested at his house was commuted on condition of their signing a compact; but Bond was by far the most formidable man amongst them; and it may have struck some of the unscrupulous understrappers attached to the Irish Government that it would be desirable to get him out of the way. To make an exception in Bond's case by bringing him to the scaffold would be impossible. Of some of the darker doings which notoriously took place, the higher members of the government were, we have no doubt, ignorant.

From the Castlereagh Papers we find that two influential judges, Lords Carleton and Kilwarden, warmly urged the execution of Byrne and Bond. They were not of opinion that the offer made by Byrne and Bond to give information would counterbalance the discontent likely to be occasioned by

* *Lives and Times of the United Irishmen*, fourth series second edition, p. 164.

THE BLOODHOUNDS OF '98.   163

saving them from "the punishment due to their
crimes". Lord Carleton and his colleague also ex-
patiated on the injurious effects such an act of
mercy might have on the administration of criminal
justice, by discouraging jurors hereafter from coming
forward to discharge an odious duty. The viceroy
transmitted a paper to the Duke of Portland, dated
September 14, 1798, from which we gather that
" their reasoning did not altogether satisfy the lord
lieutenant. His Excellency, however, felt that he
could not do otherwise than abide by the opinion
of the first law authorities in Ireland". Byrne was
accordingly executed.* Oliver Bond was found
dead in his cell.

The Castlereagh papers do not seem to have been
consulted by those who professed to investigate the
circumstances attending the fate of Oliver Bond.

The Sham Squire, when a prisoner in Newgate,
we learn, made love to his keeper's daughter,
" whose friends, considering the utility of his talents
in their sphere in life, consented to her union with
the Sham, . . . and that the gaoler's interest procured Higgins admission to be a solicitor, in which
situation his practice is too notorious to require
particular statement".†

Did Francis Higgins, who seems to have enjoyed
a thorough immunity from legal pains and penalties,
and was unscrupulously officious in doing the dirty
work of the government, take upon himself to suggest to his intimate friend, the keeper, the expediency of getting rid of Oliver Bond? The Sham
Squire was too astute to do the deed himself; but

* *Memoirs and Correspondence of Lord Castlereagh*, vol. i.
pp. 347-8.
† *Sketches of Irish Political Characters*, Lond. 1799, p. 182.

he or his myrmidons may have got it done, and
then with complacency mused, "Shake not thy
gorey locks at me, thou can'st not say *I* did it".

To return to Cox. If we understand his aim
aright, he throws out the inuendo that Thomas
Reynolds would not have become an informer if it
had not been for Francis Higgins. At some future
day it may, perhaps, be ascertained that the Sham
Squire effected the corruption of Reynolds through
the mutual friend of both parties, the late Mr.
William Cope. The latter, after the plan had been
consummated, was openly recommended for a pension by Higgins in the *Freeman* of September 1st,
1798. The influential recommendation of the
Sham Squire proved, as usual, successful. Mr.
Cope received a pension of one thousand pounds a
year, which after his death was continued to his
daughter, an elderly spinster, who with her half-
sister, Miss G——, resided, until the last few years,
at Rhos Y Guir, opposite the Railway Station,
at Holyhead.*

It transpired that Mr. Cope, who received this
enormous pension for—as Lord Cornwallis remarks
—"certifying to the general credibility of Reynolds", held a bond of that person's for one thousand
pounds, which was not likely to be paid. Whether
Higgins was Cope's legal adviser we know not; but
the warm manner in which Cope was recommended
for a pension by Higgins favours the suspicion.
Cope was very intimate with Reynolds, and knew
all his secrets. By what judicious arrangement was
the bad debt settled? We can imagine some proposal
like this tendered: " Pay this bond, or I will get you

* Letter from Doctor ——, dated "Holyhead, January 4th,
1858". See Appendix.

arrested and imprisoned. Perform the double duty
of loyalty to your king and fidelity to a just cre-
ditor by revealing all you know. You will be
richly rewarded: refuse, on the other hand, and
the gallows may be your fate. It is your interest
as well as duty to take my hint". It is impossible
to know the exact words that passed, but we believe
we have given the substance. The tempter went
even further, and taking advantage of Reynolds's
notorious susceptibility to the dictates of vanity and
ambition, told him that the crown, regarding him as
a modern saviour, would probably prove their appreciation by giving him two thousand pounds a
year and a seat in parliament.* All this and more
was revealed at the trial. Reynolds, who held the
rank of colonel and delegate from the province of
Leinster in the rebel army, settled his terms, writes
Mr. Curran, "namely, 500 guineas in hand, and personal indemnity, through Mr. Cope, Dublin merchant".†

One by one he prosecuted his colleagues to con-

* Carrick's *Morning Post*, April 3, 1823, quotes the following
paragraph from the *Examiner*, then edited by Leigh Hunt:

MR. REYNOLDS.—A correspondent at Paris informs us, that
the Mr. Reynolds now in that capital, inquired about some time
back in our paper, is really the person who played such a conspicuous part in Ireland, and who for his meritorious services
on that occasion was rewarded by an appointment at Lisbon,
after which he was placed as Consul-General at Copenhagen—
from whence, about three years since, he proceeded to Paris,
where he keeps his carriage, and is reported to live expensively.
Our correspondent says, that Mr. Reynolds's family appear on
Sundays at the chapel of the English Embassy in seats reserved
for them close by the ambassador and Lady Elizabeth; and that
at his parties Lady Douglas (of Blackheath notoriety), Mrs. and
the Miss Reynolds, etc., form a portion of that company, for the
entertainment of whom the ambassador's salary is swelled out
to £14,000 a-year.

† *Life of Curran*, by his son. First ed., v. ii. p. 128.

viction. In contradiction to Mr. Cope's evidence, witnesses swore that they believed Reynolds unworthy of credence on oath. Curran lashed and lacerated him in passages which the government, out of tenderness for his fame, omitted from the published report.

" He measures his value by the coffins of his victims, and in the field of evidence appreciates his fame, as the Indian warrior does in fight, by the number of scalps with which he can swell his triumphs. He calls upon you by the solemn league of eternal justice, to accredit the purity of a conscience washed in its own atrocities. He has promised and betrayed—he has sworn and forsworn ; and whether his soul shall go to heaven or to hell, he seems altogether indifferent, for he tells you that he has established an interest in both. He has told you that he has pledged himself to treason and to allegiance, and that both oaths has he contemned and broken".*

Mr. Curran imagines that the reward of Reynolds did not exceed five hundred guineas. The *Life of Reynolds* by his son would fain persuade the reader that his emolument had been still smaller. The MS. book of secret service money expenditure, now in the possession of Mr. Halliday, and printed by Dr. Madden, reveals, however, that Reynolds received not only in 1798, £5000 in four payments, but in the following year a pension of £1000 a-year, besides which he long enjoyed several lucrative offices under the Crown. The total amount of money flung to satisfy his insatiable cupidity was about £45,740.†

* *Life of Curran*, by his son. First ed., v. ii., p. 134.
† *Lives and Times of the U. I. M.* By R. R. Madden, M.D., vol. i. p. 425, *et seq.*

The delivery of "a live lord" into the jaws of death proved so profitable a job to Francis Higgins, that we find him soon after in hot scent after another. John Earl of Wycombe, afterwards Marquis of Lansdowne, was committed more or less to the fashionable treasons of the time; he sympathised with the men and the movement of '98, and as the late John Patten, a near connection of Emmet's, assured us, his lordship was fully cognizant of the plot of 1803.   Had Higgins been alive during the latter year, Lord Wycombe might not have escaped the penalty of his patriotism.   His movements in Dublin and elsewhere were watched most narrowly by the Sham Squire.   In despair, however, of being able to gain access to Lord Wycombe's confidence or society, we find Higgins saying: " Lord Wycombe, son to the Marquis of Lansdowne, is still in Dublin.   He has gone to Wales and back again to Dublin several times.   His lordship has given many parties in the city, it is said, *but* they have been of a close, select kind".*

Higgins and his confederates, like " setters", pointed, and the scarlet sportsmen of the line immediately fired.   Lord Holland, in his memoirs of the Whig Party, mentions that his friend, Lord Wycombe, was fired at by common soldiers on the highways near Dublin, and narrowly escaped with his life.†

* *Freeman's Journal*, August 6th, 1798. His lordship's movements are further indicated by the same Journal on August 9th, 1800.

† See page 118, *ante.*

CHAPTER VIII.

Effort of conscience to vindicate its authority.—Last will and
testament of the Sham Squire.—Kilbarrack Church-yard.—
A touching epitaph.—Resurrectionists.—The dead watcher.—
The Sham Squire's tomb insulted and broken.—His bequests.

CHARITY, it is written, covereth a multitude of sins.
Let us hasten, therefore, to record a really meritorious act on the part of Mr. Higgins.   Anxious
to throw the utmost amount of light on a career
so extraordinary as that of Francis Higgins, we examined in the Prerogative Court, his "Last Will
and Testament".   From this document we learn
that the Sham Squire's conscience was not by any
means hopelessly callous.   On the contrary, while
yet comparatively young, it seems to have given
him a good deal of uneasiness; and it may not un-
reasonably be inferred, that, unscrupulous as we
have seen Mr. Higgins, his early life was chequered
by sundry peccadillos, now irrevocably veiled.
Whatever these may have been, they contributed
to disturb the serenity of his manhood, and conscience seems to have made an energetic effort to
assert its authority.   Unable any longer to bear the
reproachings of his ill-gotten wealth, Mr. Higgins,
on September 19th, 1791, then aged forty-five,
mustered up courage and bequeathed a considerable portion of it to charitable purposes.   It is
amusing to trace the feelings of awe which in the
last century filled our ancestors previous to attempting a voyage across St. George's Channel !   Mr.
Higgins's will begins by saying that as he meditates
a voyage to England, he thinks it prudent to prepare his will, and in humble supplication at the
feet of the Almighty, and by way of making atone-

ment for his manifold transgressions, he is desirous of leaving large sums of money to charitable purposes. But before he proceeds to specify them, the vanity of the Sham Squire shows itself in a command to his executors to commemorate his memory in a proper manner, on a slab " well secured with lime, brickwork, and stone", in Kilbarrack Churchyard. To defray the cost of this monument, Mr. Higgins left £30, and a further sum for his funeral. He adds, that in case he should die in England, his remains are to be removed to Ireland and " publicly interred". To a lady who had been of considerable use to Mr. Higgins, and had clung to him with great fidelity, but who suffered seriously from this circumstance, he bequeathed not only £1,000 as compensation, but all such property as might remain after paying the other bequests; and to his housekeeper, Mrs. Margaret Box, he left £100. But, perhaps, the most remarkable item in the will is £1,000 which he bequeathed to be laid out on landed security, in order that the annual interest might be applied to the relief and discharge of debtors confined in the city marshalsea on Christmas eve in each year.* This generous bequest has served, we trust, to blot out some of the Sham Squire's achievements, not alone at the hazard table, but by means of sundry pettifogging quibbles and doubles. Having been the means in early life of considerably increasing the number of inmates at the Lying-in-Hospital, Mr. Higgins now creditably bestowed £100 upon that institution. To an asylum

---

* See *Addenda* for some correspondence on the alleged nonexecution of this bequest. The Four Courts Marshalsea of Dublin, *previous to its* removal westward, stood in Werburgh *Street.*

for ruined merchants, known as Simpson's Hospital, he bequeathed £50, and ordered that a particular ward in it should be dedicated to his memory. To the Blue Coat Hospital, where his friend Jack Giffard* and other kindred spirits passed their youth, Mr. Higgins left the sum of £20. The Catholic and Protestant Poor Schools were remembered with impartiality by Higgins, who had been himself both a Catholic and a Protestant at different times. He bequeathed £10 to each of the Protestant schools, as well as a like donation to the Catholic Charity Schools of" Rosemary Lane, Adam and Eve, Bridge Street, and Lazor Hill". To Mr. (afterwards Colonel O'Kelly, of Piccadilly, London, the owner of the celebrated race-horse "Eclipse") £300 was left, "and if I did not know that he was very affluent", adds Higgins, "I would leave him the entire of my property". Father Arthur O'Leary, one of Curran's "Monks of the Screw", was also advantageously remembered by Mr. Higgins.† To that accomplished ecclesiastic he bequeathed the sum of £100: but O'Leary never lived to enjoy it, and passed into eternity almost simultaneously with the Sham Squire, in January, 1802. To George J. Browne, assistant editor, £50 was bequeathed, in order ·to purchase mourning for Mr. Higgins, as also certain securities held by Higgins for money lent to Browne. Several other bequests in the

* For a notice of Giffard see the 32nd note to General Cockburn's "Step Ladder", *Addenda, J.*

† Mr. Grattan in the *Life* of his father (ii. 198), mentions that O'Leary was very intimate with Colonel O'Kelly, and lived with him. O'Leary had a pension from the Crown for writing down the White Boys. Mr. Grattan adds, on the authority of *Colonel O'Kelly*, that Mr. Pitt offered O'Leary considerable *remuneration if he would write in support of the Union, but the Friar refused.*

same shape and under similar circumstances are made. Some young people who shall be nameless here, are advantageously mentioned,* probably on natural grounds. William, James, and Christopher Teeling,† are named executors; but it appears from the records of the Probate Court that they declined to act. In those days there was no stamp duty; and the sum for which Higgins' residuary legatee administered does not appear. The will was witnessed by George Faulkner.

In September, 1791, Mr. Higgins declares that he has £7,000 in Finlay's bank; "but my property", he adds, "will, I believe, much exceed this sum when all is estimated". Mr. Higgins having lived for eleven years subsequent to the date of his will, during which time he laboured with fiercer zeal, and reaped even richer remuneration than before, it may be inferred that his property in 1802 was not far short of £20,000.

Little further remains to be told regarding the Sham Squire. In 1799 we catch a parting glimpse of him in a work descriptive of the actors in the Union struggle. "From his law practice, his gaming-table contributions, and news-paper", says this work, "the Sham now enjoys an income that supports a fine house in a fashionable quarter of a

* In the third volume of the *Cornwallis Correspondence*, one of the name is found obtaining a pension of £300 a-year at the same time that Francis Higgins's services received similar recognition. A Christian name borne by the junior recipient is stated in the same work to have been "Grenville", he was probably born during the viceroyalty of George *Grenville*, Marquis of Buckingham, of whom Higgins was a parasite and a slave. See p. 79, *ante*, etc.

† Is this the party whose name appears in the Secret Service Money Act, viz.:—" Nov. 5, 1808, chaise for C. Teeling from the Naul, £1 6s. 0d".

great city, whence he looks down with contempt
on the poverty of many persons, whose shoes he
formerly cleaned".*

Mr. Higgins did not long live to enjoy the price
of poor Lord Edward's blood. On the night of
January 19th, 1802, he died suddenly at his house
in Stephen's Green, aged fifty-six. To the lonely
graveyard of Kilbarrack he bequeathed his body.
A more picturesque spot " where erring man might
hope to rest", it would be difficult to select. Situated
at the edge of the proverbially beautiful bay of
Dublin, the ruins of Kilbarrack, or as they are
sometimes styled, " the Abbey of Mone", have long
existed as a monument of that primitive piety
which prompted the Irish mariners of the fourteenth
century to erect a chapel in honour of St. Mary
Star of the Sea, wherein to offer up an orison for
their messmates, who had perished beneath the
waves.†

In accordance with Mr. Higgins's expressed
wishes, a large tabular tomb was erected over his
remains in 1804. Beside it repose the ashes of
Margaret Lawless, mother of the patriot peer Cloncurry, and near it lies the modest grave of John
Sweetman, a leading " United Irishman", from
whose house adjacent Hamilton Rowan escaped—
crossed in an open boat from Kilbarrack to the Bay
of Biscay, where it passed through the British fleet
—and although £1,000 lay on his head, was safely
landed in France by the faithful fishermen of Bal-

* Sketches of Irish Political Characters, p. 148.
† An interesting notice of Kilbarrack appears in Mr. D'Alton's
History of the County Dublin, pp. 113--118, but he does not sug-
gest the origin of its name, i.e. Kill Berach, or the Church of St.
Berach, a disciple of St. Kevin.

doyle, who were well aware of his identity. But the Sham Squire's ambitious looking tomb is the monarch of that lonely graveyard, and it is impossible to pass without one's attention being arrested by it. It records that "the legal representatives of the deceased deem it but just to his memory here to inscribe, that he has left bequests behind him, a memento of philanthropy, liberality, and benevolence to the poor and distressed, more durable than can sculptured marble perpetuate, as it will last for ever, and be exemplar to all those to whom Heaven has entrusted affluence". [Here the chief bequests are enumerated in detail]. "Reader", adds the epitaph, "you will judge of the head and heart which dictated such distinguished charity to his fellow-creatures, liberal as it is impartial, and acknowledge that he possessed the true benevolence which Heaven ordains, and never fails everlastingly to reward".

This epitaph suggests a curious comment on the question asked by a child after spelling the inscriptions in a church yard, "Mama, where are the bad men buried?"

The lonely and desolate aspect of the hallowed ruin which Higgins chose as his last resting place, contrasts curiously with the turbulence of his guilty life; and Old Mortality could not select a more fitting site for the moralising ruminations in which he loved to indulge.

Francis Higgins was wise in his generation, and astutely kept his own counsel. Some of his sins we have told, but the bulk are probably known only to the Searcher of Hearts. Of the guilty secrets which were buried in Higgins's heart, how many have found a *vent in the rank* hearts'-ease and henbane, which

spring from his grave. " Where", writes Nathaniel
Hawthorne, describing a dialogue between a doctor
and his patient, " where did you gather these herbs
with such a dark flabby leaf?" " Even in the
graveyard", answered the physician; " they grew
out of his heart, and typify some hideous secret
that was buried with him, and which he had done
better to confess during his lifetime".

" Perchance he earnestly desired it, but could not".

" And wherefore", rejoined the physician,
" wherefore not, since all the powers of nature call
so earnestly for the confession of sin, that these
black weeds have sprung up out of a buried heart,
to make manifest an unspoken crime?"

But why speculate upon it? It is not certain, after
all, that the storied urn of the Sham Squire really
enshrines his ashes. The deserted position of Kilbarrack graveyard rendered it, some years ago, a
favourite haunt with those who, under the nickname
of " sack-'em-ups", effected premature resurrections
for anatomical purposes;* and it is very possible that

* The *Irish Penny Magazine* for January 20th, 1833, contains
a picture of Kilbarrack churchyard undergoing spoliation at the
hands of medical students, who have succeeded, meanwhile, in
slipping a sack over the head of "the dead watcher". The
latter is made to tell a long story descriptive of his feelings
previous and subsequent to this *denouement*:

" One time I would picthur to myself the waves approaching
like an army a-horseback, and shaking their white tops for
feathers; and then I would fancy I saw the dead people starting
up out of their graves, and rushing down helthur skelthur to
purtect their resting-place, shouldering human bones for fire
arms—they grabbed thigh bones, and arm-bones, and all the
bones they could cotch up in their hurry, and when they would
make ready—present—back the waves id gallop nimble enough,
but it was to wheel about agin with more fury and nearer to
the inemy, who in their turn would scamper back agin with long
strides, their white sheets flying behind 'em, like the cullegion

the heart of Higgins may have been long since the subject of a lecture on aneurism of the aorta.*

Through life Higgins was the subject of popular execration, and in death this enmity pursued him. An alderman of the old Corporation, who resided at Howth, declared, in 1820, that in riding into Dublin, he could never pass Kilbarrack without dismounting from his horse for the purpose of ridiculing and insulting the Sham Squire's grave. The loathing in which Higgins had been held wreaked its vengeance in more formidable demonstrations. Many years ago some persons unknown visited his tomb, and smashed off the part on which the words, "sacred to the memory of Francis Higgins" were inscribed. The thickness of the slab is considerable; and nothing short of a ponderous sledge hammer could have effected this destruction. The same eccentric individual who, in the dead of night, well nigh succeeded in depriving an obnoxious statue of its head,† is likely to have been cognizant of the malign joke played on the Sham Squire's mausoleum. No one better knew the depth of his rascality than Watty Cox, who, in the *Irish Magazine*, makes reference to both his turpitude and tomb. Of the former, illustrations have been already given (p. 59 *ante*). Of the latter we read:

chaps of a windy Sunday, and grinning frightfully through the holes which wanst were eyes. Another time I would look across to Howth as it *riz* like a black *joint* betune me and the sky; and I would think if the devil that *is* chained down below there at full length in a cavern near the light-house was to break loose, what a purty pickle I'd be in".

* It has been remarked by Dr. Mapother and other physiologists that aneurism of the aorta is peculiarly liable to overtake the designing, selfish, and wrongly ambitious man. It kills suddenly.

† The *statue* of William III. in College Green.

"Con* was riding with his employer and lady by Kilbarrack Churchyard, where the remains of the Sham
are deposited under a magnificent tomb and splendid
inscription. The party naturally stopped to pay a
grateful tribute to departed worth; Con mounted the
flinty covering, and after reading with impassioned
energy the eulogium it bore, burst into tears, and declared upon his honour, the composition was unequalled
in the *history of sepulchral literature*".†

Nearly two generations passed away, and unless
by a few families, all memory of the Sham Squire became obliterated. Tourists visited Kilbarrack; and
disciples of Doctor Syntax, moved by the touching
epitaph and the romantic scenery around, perchance
dropped a tear upon the stone. Pedestrians made
it a halting point and resting place; the less matter-
of-fact mused on Erin's days of old,

Ere her faithless sons betrayed her,

cleared the moss out of the inscriptions, and prayed
for the nameless patriot and philanthropist who
mouldered below.‡ All remembrance of his life had

* Frederick William Conway, who conducted the *Freeman*
after the death of Higgins.
† *Irish Magazine* for November, 1813.
‡ On September 15, 1853, a gentleman published a letter in the
Freeman, requesting to know not only the name of the person
on whom so eulogistic an epitaph had been written, but the fate
of the trust-money named in it. "It is gross ingratitude", he
added, "and practical materialism, to allow the tomb and
memory of such a philanthropist to perish for want of a suitable
monument to mark his last resting-place, and I should only hope
that among so many benefited, one, at least, may be found to
turn to the grave of their common benefactor". A letter in
reply went on to say, "this will hardly satisfy your correspondent in regard to the trust bequest for poor debtors, or offer any
apology or explanation of why the tomb of such a charitable
testator should be left so totally neglected and defaced by the
highway". Twelve years later found another Jonathan Old-
buck poking among the stones of Kilbarrack, and addressing a

died out, although a tradition of his *sobriquet* still
floated about the locality, and by degrees the history
of Higgins degenerated into "the beautiful legend
of the Sham Squire":[*] which at last was cruelly
disturbed by the publication of the Cornwallis correspondence, the researches of the present writer, and
some patriotic scribe who since our first disclosures
on this subject has inscribed across the imposing
epitaph, surmounted by a picture of a pike and a
gallows,

> " Here lies the monster
> Higgins,
> Lord Edward Fitzgerald's
> Informer".

similar query to the *Irish Times*. The subject excited a considerable sensation, and became invested with almost romantic interest. Several leaders as well as letters appeared. "Kilbarrack", wrote the editor, "is as lonely and desolate a ruin as ever
an artist painted. A stray goat or sheep may be seen browsing
upon the old graves, half covered with drifted sand; or a flock
of sand larks sweeps through the wide and broken arches.
Round the forsaken tombs grow in abundance heartsease, ver-
onica, and the white harebell. There are pretty mosses on the
gray walls; but the aspect of the ruins oppresses the heart with
a sense of melancholy loneliness. Sometimes, when the storm
blows inshore, the waves dash in spray over the ruined walls,
and weep salt tears over the tombs"—*Irish Times*, Jan. 3, 1865.

" An Humble Debtor", dating from the Four Courts Marshalsea, and citing as his text, " I was in prison, and ye visited me
not"—*Matt.*, xxv. 43, 44, went on to say : " Your journal for the
last few days has given great consolation to the inmates of this
prison, by its insertion of letters bearing on the hitherto almost
unknown benefactions of Francis Higgins, of good memory".

The gentleman thus addressed was of opinion that the money,
if invested in land, ought to yield now, at least, £50 per annum;
but it has been stated by the chaplain to the Marshalsea that no
more than £15 a year. is received, and comes *not* from landed
security, but from some old houses in Cumberland Street.

[*] "The legend of the Sham Squire", full of romance, and
bearing *no resemblance to* the authentic details which we have
gathered, appeared in 1856 in a serial published by Mr. Chamney.

12

JOTTINGS

ABOUT

IRELAND AND THE IRISH

SEVENTY YEARS AGO:

BEING ADDENDA SUGGESTED BY ALLUSIONS IN THE FOREGOING TEXT

JOTTINGS

ABOUT

IRELAND AND THE IRISH

SEVENTY YEARS AGO:

BEING ADDENDA SUGGESTED BY ALLUSIONS IN THE FOREGOING TEXT

ADDENDA.

A.

BARATARIANA.

This book has always possessed peculiar interest for historic students of the period to which it refers ; and several communications have appeared from time to time in *Notes and Queries* touching it. In reply to an inquiry,[*] the late Right Hon. J. Wilson Croker promised to contribute particulars as to the writers of *Baratariana*,[†] but failed to do so, although he lived for several years subsequently.[‡] "That promise not having been fulfilled", observed a writer, "permit me to ask from some of your Irish correspondents materials for a history of this very curious volume";[§] and ABHBA expressed a hope that "Mr. Fitzpatrick would be induced to furnish us with a key to the characters which figure in the book".[||] In accordance with these suggestions, we gathered from a variety of sound sources, several well authenticated details.

Sir Hercules Langrishe, Mr. Grattan, then a young barrister not in parliament, and Mr. Flood, were, according to the *Memoirs of Flood* (p. 79), the principal writers of *Baratariana*. In *Grattan's Life* (vol. i., p. 185), there is an account of a visit to Sir Hercules in 1810 ; and the octogenarian is found repeating with enthusiasm some of his flash passages in *Baratariana*. The contributions of Sir Hercules to this bundle of

---

[*] First Series, vol. x., p. 185.   [†] *Ibid*, vol. x., p. 353.
[‡] *Ibid*.   [§] Second Series, vol. viii., p. 52.   [||] *Ibid*, p. 189.

political pasquinades are noticed in Grattan's elegy on the death of the patriot baronet (*vide* vol. i., p. 188). The late Hon. Major Stanhope informed us that Mr. St. George, a connection of his, held the very voluminous papers of Sir H. Langrishe, and not the present baronet. They threw, he said, great light on the political history of the time, and he promised to give us access to them if desired. The articles written by Grattan were, as his son informs us (vol. i., p. 185), "Posthumous", "Pericles", and the dedication of *Baratariana.* He read them to his friends, and they were struck by his description of Lord Chatham. Gilbert's *Dublin* (vol. i., p. 294) tells us, what the *Life of Flood* does not, that the articles signed "Syndercombe" were from Flood's pen. The volume of *Public Characters for* 1806, in noticing William Doyle, K.C., and Master in Chancery, remarks (p. 64) that he was "universally admired for his brilliant wit", and that "he contributed largely to *Baratariana*".

To the second edition of the book, published in 1773, there is appended the following so-called "key"; but the difficulty is to recognize, at this distance of time, the names which have been initialed, and to supply them.

1. Sancho	. . .	Lord T——d.
2. Goreannelli	. .	Lord A——y.
3. Don Francisco Andrea del Bumperoso	. .	Rt. Hon. F——s A——s.
4. Don Georgio Buticarny	.	Sir G——e M——y.
5. Don Antonio	. .	Rt. Hon. A——y M——e.
6. Don John Alnagero	.	Rt. Hon. J—n H——y H——n.
7. Don Philip	. .	Rt. Hon. P——p T——l.
8. Count Loftonso	.	L. L——s, now E. of E——y.
9. Don John	.	Rt. Hon. J—n P——y.
10. Don Helena	. .	R——t H——n, Esq.
11. Donna Dorothea del Monroso	. . .	Miss M——o.
12. Don Godfredo Lilly	.	G——y L——ll, Esq.
13. The Duke Fitzroyola	.	Duke of G——n.
14. Cardinal Lapidaro	.	The late Prim. S——e.

15. The Bishop of Toledo	. {	Dr. J——t B——e, late Bishop of C——k.
16. Don Edwardo Swanzero	.	E——d S——n, Esq.
17. Don Alexandro Cuning-ambo del Tweedalero	. {	Surgeon C——m.
18. Donna Lavinia	. .	Lady St. L.——r.
19. Don Ricardo	. . .	R——d P——r, Esq.

The first named is George Viscount Townshend, who became Lord Lieutenant of Ireland, October 14th, 1767, and continued in the government, until succeeded by Simon, Earl of Harcourt, November 30th, 1772.

2. Lord Annaly, Lord Chief Justice of the King's Bench in Ireland. As John Gore he represented Jamestown in parliament for several years; d. 1783.

3. The Right Hon. Francis Andrews. He succeeded Dr. Baldwin as Provost of Trinity College, Dublin, in 1758. Andrews had previously represented Dublin in parliament; d. 1774.[*]

4. Sir George Macartney, Knight,[†] born 1737; Envoy Extraordinary to the Empress of Russia, 1764, and Plenipotentiary, 1767; knighted October, 1764. In July, 1768, he was elected for the borough of Armagh. In 1769 he became Secretary to Lord Townshend, Viceroy of Ireland. In 1776 Sir George Macartney was raised to the peerage. He married the daughter of Lord Bute: hence the nickname *Buticarny*.

5. The Right Hon. Anthony Malone. For upwards of half a century an ornament to the Irish Bar; d. May 8, 1776. For a long account of him see Hardy's *Life of Charlemont* (vol. i. pp. 133–139; Taylor's *Hist. of the Univer. of Dublin* (pp. 395-6.); and Grattan's *Memoirs*, passim.[‡]

6. Right Hon. John Hely Hutchinson. In the *Direc-*

* Taylor's *Hist. of the Univer. of Dublin*, pp. 251-2; Wilson's *Dublin Direc.* (1770), p. 41.
† *Vide* "List of Privy Councillors", *Dublin Direc.* (1770), p. 41.
‡ In Wilson's *Directory* for 1770, Malone is styled "King's First Counsel at Law, Sackville Street".

tory of the day he is styled " Prime Serjeant and Alnager of Ireland, Kildare St.". He subsequently became Secretary of State and Keeper of the Privy Seal. For a long account of Hutchinson, see Hardy's *Charlemont* (i. 141.; ii. 185). Having obtained a peerage for his wife, he became ancestor of the Lords Donoughmore.* The *Sketches of Irish Polit. Char.* observes (p. 60): " Lord Townshend said of Hely Hutchinson, that if his Majesty gave him the whole kingdoms of England and Ireland, he would beg the Isle of Man for a cabbage garden".

7. Right Hon. Philip Tisdall, P.C., Attorney General. He represented the University of Dublin in parliament, from 1739 until his death in 1777. For a full account and character of Tisdall, see Hardy's *Charlemont* (i. 152–156). In the *Directory* of 1770 he is styled "Prin. Secre. of State, and Judge of the Prerogative Court, Leinster Street".

8. The Hon. Henry Loftus succeeded his nephew Nicholas as fourth Viscount Loftus ;† b. 11th Nov. 1709 ; advanced to the earldom of Ely, 5th Dec., 1771.‡

9. Right Hon. John Ponsonby, son of Lord Bessborough, Speaker of the Irish House of Commons, b. 1713; d. 12th December, 1789.§

10. " Robert Hellen, K. C., and Counsel to the Commissioners, Great Cuffe Street ; called to the Bar Hilary Term, 1755".‖

11. A Miss Munro was said to have been mixed up

* Burke's *Peerage* (1848), p. 315. For an account of his regime as Provost of Trin. Coll., see Taylor's *Hist. of Univer. of Dublin*, p. 253.

† His ancestor, A. Loft-House, accompanied Lord Sussex to Ireland. Various family links subsequently united the Loftuses to the house of *Townshend*. General Loftus married, 1790, Lady E. Townshend, only daughter of Marquis Townshend. Her daughter Charlotte married Lord Vere Townshend.

‡ Burke's *Peerage*, p. 371 (1848).

§ *Ibid.*, p. 93 ; Hardy's *Charlemont*, i. 184, 201, 293.

‖ *Wilson's Dublin Directories.*

with some of the political intrigues which characterized the Townshend and other administrations. "Dolly Munro" is traditionally described as a woman of surpassing beauty and powers of fascination. She was quite a Duchess of Gordon in the political circles of her time.

12. "Godfrey Lill, Esq., Solicitor General, Merrion Square, M——, 1743".*

13. Augustus Henry, third Duke of Grafton, b. 1735, filled the offices of Secretary of State and First Lord of the Treasury in 1765 and 1766, and that of Lord Privy Seal in 1771.

14. Primate Stone. He was the great political rival of Lord Shannon. Death closed the eyes of both within nine days of each other, in Dec. 1764.†

15. Dr. Jemmet Browne, consecrated Bishop of Cork, 1743; promoted to Elphin, 1772.‡

16. Edward B. Swan, Esq., Surveyor-General of the Revenue.§ He was the father of the famous Major Swan, who arrested the thirteen delegates of the United Irishmen at Oliver Bond's in 1798 (Plowden's *Hist. Ireland,* ii. 424), and who afterwards assisted in the capture of Lord Edward Fitzgerald? [*Castlereagh Correspondence,* vol. i. 463.]

17. "Surgeon Alexander Cunningham, Eustace Street", figures in the list of surgeons at p. 98. of Wilson's *Dublin Directory* for 1770.

18. Lady St. Leger. R. St. Leger (nephew of Hughes Viscount Doneraile, whose title became extinct in 1767) represented Doneraile from 1749 to 1776,

* Wilson's *Dublin Directories.*
† *Dublin Direc.* 1769, p. 42; Hardy's *Charlemont,* vol i. *passim*
‡ Wilson's *Dublin Direc.* 1774, p. 52.
§ *Dublin Direc.,* 1774 [*Com. Rev.*], p. 73. The Viceroy, at p. 228 of *Baratariana,* is made to speak of "his trusty friends, Swan and Waller". In the *Directory* for 1774, "George Waller, Clerk of the Minutes in Excise", is mentioned.

when his majesty pleased to create him Baron Doneraile as a reward for parliamentary services. He married Miss Mary Barry. She died March 3, 1778.*
This is probably the party referred to.

19. Richard Power, K. C.   In the *Directory* of 1774,
we find him styled "Third Baron of the Exchequer,
and Usher and Accountant-General of the Court of
Chancery, Kildare Street, Hilary, 1757".   Mr. Daunt,
in his *Recollections of O'Connell* (ii. 145), narrates an
extraordinary anecdote of O'Connell's in reference to
Baron Power, who, having failed to take Lord Chancellor Clare's life with a loaded pistol, proceeded to
Irishtown to commit suicide by drowning.   It was remarked as curious that in going off to drown himself, he
used an umbrella as the day was wet.   Baron Power
was a convicted peculator.

The *Anthologia Hibernica* for February, 1794, p. 154,
details the particulars of Baron Power's death.   Besides
his judicial office, he was Usher to the Court of Chancery,
and large sums were frequently deposited in his hands
for the security of suitors.   The Baron having pocketed
£3,000 in the Chandos suit, Lord Chancellor Clare was
appealed to, who ordered the Baron to appear in court
and answer for his conduct.   The Judge hesitated, declaring that he held a seat on the same bench with the
Chancellor in the Court of Exchequer Chamber.   Lord
Clare issued his command in a still more peremptory
tone ; and the tragedy detailed by Mr. O'Connell was
the result.   Sir Jonah Barrington's elaborately embel-
lished account of this transaction is most inaccurate.
He suppresses all allusion to the embezzlements—of
which, by the way, Barrington was himself convicted
as a judge*—and merely says that Lord Clare teased
Power to madness, because the Baron was arrogant

* Archdall's *Lodge's Peerage*, vol. v. p. 123.
† *Personal Sketches*, vol. i. p. 457-9.   See Notice of Barrington, Addenda P.

himself, and never would succumb to the arrogance of
Fitzgibbon, to whom in law he was superior.   Both
accounts, however, agree in saying that Power was im-
mensely rich.

The letters from Philadelphus, also published in
Baratariana, repeatedly mention the name *Pedro Pezzio.*
Dr. Charles Lucas (b. 1713 ; d. 1771) is the party
alluded to.

B.

TOPING SEVENTY YEARS AGO.

(See page 88, *ante*).

It did not need the example of the Duke of Rutland
to make hard · drinking the fashion in Ireland.   The
anecdote, " Had you any assistance in drinking this
dozen of wine ?"   " Yes, I had the assistance of a bottle of
brandy", gives an idea of the extent to which the practice reached.   Few songs were sung save those in praise
of wine and women.   Judge Day's brother, Archdeacon
Day, wrote a popular song called " One Bottle More".
Curran sung :

> " My boys, be chaste till you 're tempted ;
> While sober be wise and discreet ;
> And humble your bodies with fasting,
> Whene'er you 've got nothing to eat".

" It was an almost invariable habit at convivial meetings", observes an informant, " to lock the door lest any
friend should depart.   The window was then opened,
and the key flung into the lawn, where it could not be
again found without much difficulty.   An Irish piper
was stationed behind the door, where he jerked forth
planxty after planxty as the toasts progressed.   A certain baronet used to knock the shanks off each guest's
glass, to necessitate draining it to the bottom before he

could lay it down again. Gallons of buttered claret
were drunk, and morning found the convivialists lying
under the table in heaps of bodily and mental imbecility".

The late Dr. Henry Fulton informed us that he
heard from Mr. Dawson, one of the Volunteer Conven-
tion in 1782, and afterwards Chairman of Armagh, the
two following anecdotes, illustrative of Irish conviviality in the last century:

Sir William Johnson and his friend Dawson were
invited out to dine. Some time after dinner Sir William
came to him and said: "Dawson, am I very drunk?"
"No", said the other; "Why so?" "Because", said
the baronet, "I can't find the door". It would have
been hard for him, for the host had a mock bookcase
which moved on a spring, and when required closed up
the entrance. After making another trial, Sir William
gave it up, and quietly resumed his seat. Dawson
escaped out of a window, got up stairs to a sleeping
apartment, and knowing that all the party would remain
for the night, bolted the door and barricaded it with all
the furniture he could remove. Next morning he found
two of the gentlemen in bed with him, who had effected
an entrance through a panel of the door.

No gentleman thought of paying his debts, and the
extensive house of Aldridge, Adair, and Butler, wine
merchants in Dublin, sent a clerk to Connaught to collect money due to the firm. The clerk returned, pro-
testing that he was half dead with *feasting*, but could
get no money. Robin Adair then personally went down,
and arrived at the house of his principal debtor just in
time for dinner, and found a large party assembled.
In the course of the evening the following was composed and sung:

> " Welcome to Foxhall, sweet Robin Adair.
> How does Tom Butler do,
> And John Aldridge, too?
> Why did they not come with you,
>   Sweet Robin Adair?"

It is almost needless to add that he, too, returned without the debt.

To compensate for bad debts, a large margin for profit was fixed by the Dublin wine merchants of that day.

"Claret", writes Barrington, " was at that time about £18 the hogshead, if sold for ready rhino; if on credit, the law, before payment, generally mounted it to £200, besides bribing the sub-sheriff to make his return, and swear that Squire * * * * had 'neither body nor goods'. It is a remarkable fact, that formerly scarce a hogshead of claret crossed the bridge of Banagher for a country gentleman, without being followed within two years by an attorney, a sheriff's officer, and a receiver of all his rents, who generally carried back securities for £500". In the Irish Quarterly Review, vol. ii. p. 331, is quoted a French author's description of Holybrook, county Wicklow, the seat of Robin Adair, " Si famaux dans nombre des chansons". He was probably the head of the wine firm referred to by Dr. Fulton. Another Adair, equally noted for bacchanalian powers lived at Kilternan.

" Were I possess'd of all the chink
    That was conquered by Cortez, Hernan,
I'd part with it all for one good drink
    With Johnny Adair of Kilternan.
The soldiers may drink to their Cumberland brave,
    The sailors may drink to their Vernon,
Whilst all merry mortals true happiness have
    With Johnny Adair of Kilternan".

Owen Bray, of Loughlinstown, also figures in more than one song.

" Were ye full of complaints from the crown to the toe,
    A visit to Owen's will cure ye of woe;
A buck of such spirits ye never did know,
    For let what will happen, they 're always in flow ;
When he touched up Ballen a Mona, oro,
    The joy of that fellow for me".

Drinking clubs fanned the flame of political agitation and sectarian bitterness then so rife. One of these pandemoniums stood in Werburgh Street, where many a man with, as a song of the day has it,

> "——— ——— a goodly estate,
> And would to the Lord it was ten times as great",

drank himself to delirium, death, and beggary. The spirit of the times is shown in one of the club, who, having pitched a basin of filthy fluid from the window, which was hailed by a shriek below, exclaimed, " If you are a Protestant, I beg your pardon respectfully ; but if you're a Papist (*hic*), take it and bad luck to you !"*

The County Kildare was not second to Wicklow or Dublin in convivial indulgence. Some years ago, as we stood among the ruins of Clonshambo House, a song commemorative of its former occupant was chanted :

> " 'T was past one o'clock when Andrew got up,
> His eyes were as red as a flambeau ;
> Derry down, my brave boys, let us sleep until eve,
> Cried Andrew Fitz-Gerald of Clonshambo".

The windows of old Clonshambo House looked into a churchyard, which ought, one would think, to have preached a more salutary homily to the convivialists than the event seems to have proved. Adjoining it is a crumbling wall glassed, and displaying many a sturdy old neck with the cork still lodged in it.

The judges of the land, vulgarly regarded as almost infallible, were no better than their neighbours, and the phrase, " as sober as a judge", must for a time have fallen into disuse. Baron Monckton, being often *vino deditus*, as we are assured by Barrington, usually described the segment of a circle in making his way to the seat of justice. Judge Boyd, whose face, we are told, resembled " a scarlet pincushion well studded", *possessed* a similar weakness ; and a newspaper, in

---

* Tradition communicated by F. T. P——, Esq.

praising his humanity, said that when passing sentence of death, it was observable that " he seldom failed to have *a drop* in his eye". Of the first judge named it might be said, as of the Geraldines, *Ipsis Hibernis Hibernores,* for Baron Monckton was imported from the English Bar.

Hard drinking continued fashionable in Ireland within the last forty years. A late eminent polemic habitually drank, without ill effects, a dozen glasses of whiskey toddy at a sitting. Bushe, on being introduced to the late Con. Leyne of the Irish Bar, asked " Are you any relation to Con of the Hundred Battles ?" " This is Con of the Hundred Bottles", interposed Lord Plunket.

A well-known person, named Led——ge, who lived at Bluebell, having met a favourite boon companion, was induced by him to partake of some refreshment at an inn, where he speedily consumed sixteen tumblers of punch. He was rising to leave, when the friend suggested that he should " make up the twenty". " The parish priest is to dine with me", replied Led——ge, " and I should not wish him to see the sign of liquor on me".

C.

HOW LORD BUCKINGHAM PUNISHED JEPHSON AND PURCHASED JEBB.

Magee's lampoons on the Sham Squire's patron, the Marquis of Buckingham, were met by retorts in the same vein. The chief writer of these retaliative epigrams was Robert Jephson, Master of the Horse at Dublin Castle. Lord Cloncurry, in his *Personal Recollections,* observes : " He lived at the Black Rock, in a house which still remains, nearly opposite Maretimo, and was, for a considerable period, the salaried poet *laureate* of the viceregal court. He lost place and pension by an untimely exercise of his wit, when dining one day at my father's house. The dinner was given to the Lord Lieutenant, the Marquis of Buckingham, who happened to observe, in an unlucky mirror, the reflection of Jephson in the act of mimicking himself. He immediately discharged him from the laureateship".

Public writers were corrupted without stint during the administration of Lord Buckingham. By far the ablest man in Ireland, at that day, was Dr. Frederick Jebb, the Irish Junius. Under the pseudonym of Guatimozin, he published powerful letters in sustainment of his country's cause. The viceroy, writing to Lord North, says: "As the press was exceedingly violent at that time, and had greater effect in inflaming the minds of the people, it was recommended to me as a measure of absolute necessity, by some means, if possible, to check its spirit. On this a negociation was opened with Dr. Jebb, who was then chief of the polical writers, and he agreed, upon the terms of my recommending him for a pension of £300 a year, to give his assistance to government, and since that time he has been very useful, as well by suppressing inflammatory publications as by writing and other services, which he promises to continue to the extent of his power".* After the death of Dr. Jebb the pension was continued to his children.

D.

LORD CLONMEL.

Among the many searchingly critical notices of Lord Chief Justice Clonmel, contributed by Grattan, Barrington, Rowan, Cloncurry, Cox, Magee, and others, no allusion has been made to the circumstances in *which his* wealth may be said to have originated. We

* *Memoirs of Grattan,* by his Son, v. ii., p. 175.

are informed by a very respectable solicitor, Mr. H——, that in looking over one of Lord Clonmel's rentals he was struck by the following note, written by his lordship's agent, in reference to the property "Boolnaduff": "Lord Clonmel, when Mr. Scott, held this in trust for a Roman Catholic, who, owing to the operation of the Popery laws, was incapacitated from keeping it in his own hands. When reminded of the trust, Mr. Scott refused to acknowledge it, and thus the property fell into the Clonmel family".

In Walker's *Hibernian Magazine* for July, 1797, we read, p. 97:—"Edward Byrne, of Mullinahack, Esq., to Miss Roe, step-daughter to the Earl of Clonmel, and niece to Lord Viscount Llandaff".[*]

Hereby hangs a tale. Miss Roe was understood to have a large fortune, and when Mr. Byrne applied to Lord Clonmel for it, his lordship shuffled, saying: "Miss Roe is a lapsed Papist, and I avail myself of the laws which I administer, to withhold what you desire". Mr. Byrne filed a bill in which he recited the evasive reply of Lord Clonmel. The Chief Justice never answered the bill, and otherwise treated Mr. Byrne's remonstrances with contempt. These facts, which have never been in print, transpire in the legal documents held by Mr. H——.

Too often the treachery manifested by the rich in positions of trust, at the calamitous period in question, contrasted curiously with the tried fidelity observed by some needy persons in a similar capacity. Moore, in his *Memoirs of Captain Rock*, mentions the case of a poor Protestant barber, who, though his own property

---

[*] Lord Clonmel married first, in 1768, Catherine, only daughter of Thomas Mathew, of Thomastown; secondly, Margaret, only daughter of Patrick Lawless, of Dublin (Archdall's *Lodge's Irish Peerage*, v. vii. p. 243). The late Apostle of Temperance, Father Theobald Mathew, was a native of Thomastown, and a member of the family into which Lord Clonmel intermarried.

13

did not exceed a few pounds in value, actually held in
fee the estates of most of the Catholic gentry of the
county.   He adds that this estimable man was never
known to betray his trust.

The proximity of the residences of Lord Clonmel
and Sir Jonah Barrington has been noticed at p. 89.
It may amuse those familiar with the locality to tell an
anecdote of the projecting bow-window, long since
built up, which overhangs the side of Sir Jonah's former
residence, No. 14 Harcourt Street, corner of Montague
Street.   Lord Clonmel occupied the house at the opposite corner, and Lady Clonmel affected to be very
much annoyed at this window overlooking their house
and movements.   Here Lady Barrington, arrayed in imposing silks and satins, would daily take up position, and
placidly survey a portion of the world as it wagged.
Sir Jonah was remonstrated with, but he declined to
close the obnoxious window.   Lady Clonmel then took
the difficulty in hand, and with the stinging sarcasm
peculiarly her own, said: "Lady Barrington is so
accustomed to looking out of a shop window for the
display of her silks and satins, that I suppose she cannot
afford to dispense with this".

The large bow window was immediately built up,
and has not since been re-opened.   Lady Barrington
was the daughter of Mr. Grogan, a silk mercer of
Dublin.   Lady Clonmel was a Miss Lawless, related to
the Cloncurry family, who rose to opulence as woollen
drapers in High Street.   The Lawlesses held their
heads high, and more than once got a Roland for an
Oliver.   The first Lord Cloncurry having gone to see
the pantomime of Don Quixote, laughed immoderately
at the scene where Sancho is tossed in a blanket.
On the following morning the Sham Squire's journal
contained the following epigram:

> " Cloncurry, Cloncurry,
>   Why in such a hurry,
>   To laugh at the comical Squire?

For though he's tossed high,
You cannot deny
   That blankets have tossed yourself higher".

The *Diary of John Scott, Lord Clonmel,* has been privately printed by his family. It shows, while recording many weaknesses, that he was a man of rare shrewdness, and gifted with a considerable amount of political foresight. A few excerpts from this generally inaccessible volume will interest the reader :

"Lord! what plagues have false friends proved to " me. The idea of *friendship* and the very word should " be expunged from the heart and mind of a politician. " Look at Lórd Pery" (p. 211).

"In last month I became a viscount; and from " want of circumspection in trying a cause against a " printer (Magee), I have been grossly abused for several " months. I have endeavoured to make that abuse " useful towards my earldom". . . . . (Sept. 20, 1789, 348.)

On Oct. 19, 1789, he says that unless he adopts the discipline of Pery and others, "I am actually dis- " graced, despised, and undone as a public man. Let " me begin to be diligent to-day. No other learning but " law and parliamentary reading can be useful to me; " let these be my study" (p. 349).

On Jan. 21, 1790, he writes: "Let me therefore " from this moment adopt a war discipline, and resolve " *seriously* to set about learning my profession, and " *acting* my part *superlatively* throughout" (p. 351).

Among his good resolutions recorded on 10th Feb. were: "To establish a complete reform from snuff, " sleep, swearing, sloth, gross eating, malt liquor, and " indolence".

The Diary finds him constantly engaged in a battle with his own weaknesses, which unhappily in the end generally win the victory. At p. 362, towards the *close of the book,* we read: "By neglect of yourself

" you are now a helpless, ignorant, unpopular, accused
" individual; forsaken by Government, persecuted by
" Parliament, hated by the Bar, unaided by the Bench,
" betrayed and deserted by your oldest friends. Reform,
" and all will be well. Guard against treachery in
" others and passions in yourself". At p. 441, we learn:
" My three puisne judges are actually combined against
" me, and that ungrateful monster, Lord Carleton, has
" made a foolish quarrel with me".

Few men possessed a more accurate perception of
what was right to be done; and his *beau ideal* of a perfect Chief Justice is a model of judicial excellence
which a Mansfield or a Bushe might read with profit:
but poor Lord Clonmel signally failed to realize it. Day
after day, as we have said, finds this most extraordinary
man toiling in vain to correct his besetting weaknesses.
Sir Jonah Barrington's description of Lord Clonmel
perpetually telling, and acting, extravagantly comic
stories, is corroborated by the Chief's own Diary.
" I have made", he writes, " many enemies by the trea-
" chery of men and women who have taken advantage
" of my levity* and unguardedness in mimicry, and
" saying sharp things of and to others; and have injured
" myself by idleness, eating, drinking, and sleeping too
" much. *From this day, then,* let me assume a *stately,*
" *grave, dignified* deportment and demeanour. No buf-
" foonery, no mimicry, no ridicule". This is one of the
closing entries in the very remarkable Diary of John
Scott, Lord Chief Justice Clonmel. As a constitutional
judge he holds no place. In opposition to the highest
legal authorities of England, he held that one witness
was quite sufficient to convict in case of treason.

* It cannot be said of Lord Clonmel, as of Jerry Keller, an
Irish barrister, that some men have risen by their gravity while
he sank by his levity.

E.

THE IRISH YEOMANRY IN 1798.

The fidelity of Dempsey, the yeoman, to Lord Edward's cause is the more remarkable, when we remember that he belonged to a body which was notorious for its implacability to suspected persons. The personal narratives of Hay, Cloney, Teeling, O'Kelly, and the historic researches of Madden, furnish abundant anecdotes of their brutality. The following reminiscence, communicated to us by the late Mrs. Plunket, of Frescati—the former residence, by the way, of Lord Edward Fitzgerald—as it does not happen to have been printed, may be given here:—

Previous to the outburst of the Rebellion there was a noted bridewell at Geneva, in the county Wexford, wherein persons suspected of treasonable tendencies were incarcerated, and from thence removed soon after to some distant place of transportation. The betrothed of one young woman and the husband of another, both personally known to Mrs. Plunket, were cast into this prison. The women were permitted to visit the captives; they exchanged clothes, and the young men passed out unrecognized. When the young women were discovered occupying the cells, nothing could exceed the rage of the local yeomanry. They assembled a mock court-martial, found the fair conspirators guilty of having aided and abetted the escape of traitors, and then sentenced them to be tossed naked in a blanket. The yeomanry carried their decision into effect. They roughly tore the garments from the young women, stripped them stark naked, and then prostrated them on the blanket which was prepared for their punishment. They were tossed unmercifully, amidst the brutal laughter of the assembled yeomanry. A *Scotch* regiment present had the manly feeling to turn their backs. The married woman was pregnant, and died from the effects of the treatment she received. The younger girl, a person of great beauty, was seriously injured both in body and mind. Mrs. Plunket witnessed the less revolting part of the scene. She was a person of considerable energy of character, one of the Barringtons of Wexford, and a Protestant. Having married Mr. Plunket, a Catholic, she embraced that religion, to the great annoyance of her family, who brought her home, and kept her in detention. Mr. Plunket was arrested in Dublin on suspicion of treasonable intent; she escaped, walked the entire way to Dublin, and by her beauty and her tact, exercised in influential quarters, succeeded in getting her husband liberated. We have heard this lady say that an agent of Lord Camden's Government offered her £1,000 to inform on persons who were implicated in the rebellion, but she rejected the bribe with indignation.

About the same time, and in the same county, the yeomanry, after having sacked the chapel and hunted the priest, deputed one of their corps to enter the confessional and personate the good pastor. In the course of the day some young men on their way to the Battle of Oulart dropped in for absolution. One, who disclosed his intention and craved the personated priest's blessing, was retorted upon with a curse, while the yeoman, losing patience, flung off the soutanne, revealing beneath his scarlet uniform. The youth was shot upon the spot, and his grave is still shown at Passage.

Lord Cornwallis, the more humane Viceroy who succeeded Lord Camden, notices, in a letter to General Ross, the " ferocity and atrocity" of the yeomen, and that they take the lead in rapine and murder. He adds :—

" The feeble outrages, burnings, and murders which *are still* committed by the rebels serve to keep up

the sanguinary disposition on our side; and so long
as they furnish a pretext for our parties going in
quest of them, I see no prospect of amendment.

"The conversation of the principal persons of the
country all tend to encourage this system of blood;
and the conversation even at my table, where you
will suppose I do all I·can to prevent it, always turns
on hanging, shooting, burning, etc., etc.; and if a
priest has been put to death, the greatest joy is expressed by the whole company.   So much for Ireland
and my wretched situation".*

F.

MR. MACREADY'S STATEMENT.

[After we had received from Mr. Macready, the es-
teemed President of the Young Men's Society, a verbal
statement of the facts recited (p. 121, etc., *ante*), he
was good enough to commit to writing the subjoined
further details, which graphically illustrate the calamitous period in question.]

"Prior to the outburst of the insurrection in 1798,
and while espionage was active in its pursuit of Lord
Edward Fitzgerald, stimulated by the reward of £1,000
for his apprehension, he was stopping in my grandfather's house, No. 124 Thomas Street, and passing as
my mother's French tutor.   She was not long home
from France, having left it in consequence of the Revolution.   She was a woman of much strength of character, and carried the different letters between Lord
Edward and the other United Irishmen.   While acting
in this capacity she usually went as a patient in Dr.
Adrien's carriage, with her arm bandaged up, and her

* *Memoirs and Correspondence of Marquis Cornwallis.*   Vol.
II. p. 368.

clothes marked with blood. While Lord Edward was
at James Moore's, the only person he saw, exclusive of
Lawless and a few other trusted political friends, was
his stepfather, Mr. Ogilvie, who had been a tutor in
the Leinster family, and the duchess married him.
* * * * Lady Fitzgerald never visited him at
Moore's, as it was supposed every move of hers was
closely watched, but my mother brought his little
daughter to see him. She was a seven months' child,
and was afterwards married to Sir Guy Campbell,
who was head of the Constabulary of Ireland. [Here
the anecdote of Tuite, given at p. 121, *ante*, appears.]
I had this from my grandfather and Tuite. The former
promised to bury Tuite, but he outlived him by many
years.` It was considered unsafe for Lord Edward to
remain concealed at our house, and my grandmother
went down to Magan, a barrister, and friend of hers,
who lived on Usher's Island, and arranged with him
that to-morrow evening Lord Edward would go down
at seven or eight o'clock to his place, and, to avoid being
seen entering the front door, the stable in Island
Street was to be open to admit him. At eight o'clock
Mrs. Moore and Pat Gallagher, a clerk of ours, walked
out arm-in-arm, and my mother and Lord Edward
behind. They went along Thomas Street to Watling
Street, and turned down at the end of Watling Street,
and just at Island Street, near Magan's stable, Major
Sirr stopped Lord Edward. My mother screamed out
to Gallagher, who was a very powerful man. He at
once upset Major Sirr; and only the Major had a coat
of mail on him, his career was ended on that occasion,
for Gallagher tried his dagger on him. Major Sirr was
also a powerful man, wielded his dagger, and although
under Gallagher, contrived to drive it through the
calf of his leg. Finding himself wounded, and fearing
he would not be able to make his escape, and perceiving
that he could not wound Major Sirr, made the best of

his way off, having first knocked the Major down with a box, using the butt of the dagger to assist his blow. My mother and Lord Edward fled at the first part of the fray, and as Murphy's (now Graham and Dunnill's wool crane) was the nearest friend's place, they went into it. Mrs. Moore got home as she best could; of Gallagher I will speak hereafter. The accuracy of the carpenter Tuite's information to Moore was soon confirmed. The next day my grandfather Moore's house was taken possession of. The famous Dr. Gahan, the Augustinian friar, was visiting my mother, and she was seeing him to the door when the double knock came. The old priest in his humility stood partly behind the door to allow whoever it was to enter. A captain, a serjeant, and a large number of soldiers, rushed in. They seized the poor old priest, and by the queue or pig-tail, the then mode of wearing the hair, tied him up to a beam in the wareroom off the shop. My mother *cut him down.* She then remembered that the committee or council of the United Irishmen were sitting at a house in James's Gate (the house now occupied by Mr. Nulty). While the soldiers were taking possession and rifling the house, she ran up to James's Gate, and informed the parties there that her father's house was full of soldiers. The father of the Rev. George Canavan, late P.P. of St. James's, had a tan-yard outside the house wherein the Directory met. Into this yard they descended through a window, and escaped down Watling Street. My mother, when returning, met some of the soldiers; one of them recognized her, and said, 'There's that Croppy b——h again', making a drive at her with his bayonet which was screwed to the top of his musket. She stooped and escaped, but the bayonet cut her across the shoulders. There were some good shots on the *qui vive.* The occurrence just took place on the site of Roe's distillery, and a shot was forthwith fired from a house at the corner of

Crane Lane, which closed the loyal career of the soldier who wounded my mother. He was shot dead. The official report in the newspapers next day stated that they were so near capturing the Committee or Directory of the United Irishmen that in their flight they left the taper lighting, and the wax was soft with which they had been sealing their letters and documents. I should have mentioned that Magan went up the next morning to know had anything happened, as he was quite uneasy at not seeing Lord Edward and Mrs. Moore, and that he had stopped up until midnight expecting them. While on this point I may as well finish it. When Dr. Madden was getting information from my mother, he asked who she thought had betrayed Lord Edward. Whether she said this to him or not I cannot say; but just as he left, she said to me, " Dr. Madden asked me who I thought betrayed Lord Edward, and only fearing I should sin against charity, I would have said it was Magan, for *no one* but my mother and he knew that Lord Edward was to go down to his (Magan's) house on Usher's Island the night his lordship was stopped by Major Sirr. Poor Lord Edward himself did not know we were going to Magan's house till we set out for it. We told Magan next day what a narrow escape we had that night, and how Lord Edward had to take refuge in Murphy's. Lord Edward was arrested on the following day in Murphy's house'.*

" Gallagher, of whom I have already spoken, was brought out for execution ; but he put on a freemason's apron, having received an intimation that the captain of the guard was a member of the craft. By some

* It is more than probable that Mrs. Macready did not avow during that interview her suspicion of Magan. It took place, as we learn from the *Lives of the United Irishmen* (v. ii. p. 406) in the year 1842. Magan was then alive. Reminiscences contributed by Mrs. Macready appear, but Magan's name does not *occur in them.*

rule of *their faith*, one brother cannot see another hung. Be this as it may, the captain ordered his men away, and Gallagher was taken back to the Provost prison until some non-masonic hangman could be got. After or about this time the executions at the corner of Bridgefoot Street, in Thomas Street, were going on, and the blood flowing from the block whereon the poor rebels were quartered clogged up the sewers, and some dogs *were licking it up*. The Lady Lieutenant was driving past, and got such a fright from this horrible scene that she fainted in the carriage. Having arrived home, she wrote to her brother, who was high in the then government, for God's sake to stop this wholesale massacre of the defenceless. Her humane appeal had the desired effect; an order came to stem all further executions; *enough blood had been shed*. The rest of the prisoners were ordered to be transported, and vessels for that purpose were sent over. In one of these poor Gallagher was placed, heavily ironed. The night before the transport sailed, his young wife was permitted to see him, when his manacles, for that occasion, were taken off. His wife brought a coil of sash cord under her dress; night came on before she left, and Gallagher held one end, while she took the other ashore. The captain, as soon as he thought the wife was out of sight of the ship, ordered the prisoner to be put in irons again. When they went to him for that purpose he said, "Can you not wait *one* minute?" They paused, and he leaped overboard, and was towed by the rope safely ashore, before the sailors (who told the captain the man had leaped in) had time to overtake him in a boat. He was put aboard a smuggling lugger that conveyed salt to France, and in years afterwards James Moore, his former master, met him in London. He told him he was a wealthy hotel keeper in Bourdeaux, and the handsome landlady of course was the person who *pulled the cord* with him aboard the transport ship.

" My mother took £500 to the doctor who attended the prisoners in Bermingham Tower, Dublin Castle, where my grandfather was detained, and he certified my grandfather was mad! Whether he arrived at this conclusion from his professional skill or my mother's persuasive powers, deponent further knoweth not; but I even heard, in the event of my grandfather's escape, he was to be further convinced that my grandsire was mad. Major Sirr had not implicit faith in the doctor's word, for he went to the Tower to judge for himself. The prisoner must have acted the maniac to life, for he made Major Sirr run for his life after severely biting him. He then passed out of the Tower, and escaped up Castle Street. The government never re-arrested him, believing him insane.

" Major Sirr and Jemmy O'Brien the Informer were looking for pikes at the rere of my grandfather's stores in a field that is now occupied by Messrs. Fitzsimons, timber merchants, Bridgefoot Street. A croppy, named Clayton, saw them, and had them covered with his carbine; but as he could only hit one, he feared the other might escape, and that he himself would be captured. He told this to Casey, who said each of them were fully worth a charge of powder. This, perhaps, was the narrowest escape Major Sirr had, for he it was that was covered, and covered moreover by a man of unerring aim—the same who hit the soldier at Costigan's Gate".

JEMMY O'BRIEN.

O'Brien, to whom Mr. Macready refers, had obtained an unenviable notoriety for murder, burglary, and general chicane, when Major Sirr enlisted him in his service as a " bloodhound", who, to quote the words of Curran, " *with more* than instinctive keenness pursued victim

after victim". " I have heard", he added, " of assas-
sinations by sword, by pistol, and by dagger, but here
is a wretch who would dip the Evangelists in blood.
If he thinks he has not sworn his victim to death, he
is ready to swear without mercy and without end.
But, oh! do not, I conjure you, suffer him to take an
oath; the hand of the murderer should not pollute the
purity of the gospel, or, if he will swear, let it be by
the knife, the proper symbol of his profession". To
trace O'Brien through the bloody track of his progress
during "the reign of terror", would prove a repulsive
task. The following account of the circumstances
which led to his end, were given to us in 1854 by a
gentleman connected with the Irish Executive. In the
year 1800 O'Brien was deputed to scrutinize some persons who had assembled for the purpose of playing
foot ball, near Steevens' Lane. In scrambling over a
fence which enclosed the field, assisted by an old man
named Hoey, who happened to be on the spot, the cry
of " O'Brien the informer" was immediately raised, the
people fled, and O'Brien in his chagrin turned round
and illogically wreaked his vengeance by stabbing Hoey
to death. He was tried for the crime and sentenced to
execution by Judge Day, who was a just judge in bad
times, and disregarded the eulogiums with which Major
Sirr belauded O'Brien during the trial. The delight of
the populace was unbounded. A vast ocean of people
surged round the prison and under the gallows. A delay occurred; the populace became impatient, and
finally uneasy, lest the government should have yielded
to the memorial which was known to have been presented in his favour. A multitudinous murmur gradually gave place to a loud boom of popular indignation. The delay was caused by the cowardice of O'Brien,
who shrank from his approaching doom. Prostrate on
his knees, he begged intervals of indulgence according
as *the turnkey* reminded him " that his hour had come" .

At length Tom Galvin, the hangman, a person of barbarous humour, accosted him, saying, "Ah, Misther O'Brien, long life to you, sir, come out on the balcony, an' don't keep the people in suspense; they are mighty onasy entirely under the swing-swong".

G.

GENERAL LAWLESS.

Having some reason to doubt the accuracy of the account given on hearsay by the late Lord Cloncurry, and quoted by Dr. Madden, which represented Lawless effecting his escape in the guise of a butcher, carrying a side of beef on his shoulder, we instituted inquiries as to the real facts, and the parties exclusively competent to state them; and with this object we had an interview, in 1854, with the late Mrs. Ryan, of Upper Gardiner Street, then in her eighty-second year.

After the break-up of the Executive Directory by the arrests at Oliver Bond's, a new one, composed of John and Henry Sheares, William Lawless, and others, started into existence, determined to carry out the plans of the original founders. Proclamations appeared, and several arrests were made; but Lawless, owing to his own tact and the presence of mind of his friends, escaped. Lawless was proceeding to his mother's house in French Street at a rapid pace, through Digges Street, when his sister, perceiving his approach, appeared at the drawing-room window, and motioned him to retire. The house was at that moment undergoing a search by Major Sirr and his myrmidons, and had Lawless come up, his life would, doubtless, have paid the forfeit. It is a significant fact that, on the following day, Henry Sheares was arrested in the act of knocking at Lawless's door. The family of Mr. Byrne, of Byrne's Hill, in

the Liberty, was then staying at their country residence near Kimmage, where Mr. Byrne and his
daughters, of whom our informant Mrs. Ryan was one,
provided Lawless with an asylum. He was concealed
in a garret-bedroom, communicating with a small
clothes closet, into which he retired at every approach,
even of the servants, who were quite unconscious of
his presence. Days rolled over, and the search, but
without avail, continued. Military and yeomanry
scoured the country round. Major Sirr was so active,
that some swore he possessed the alleged ornithological
property of being in two places at once.

The Lawyer's corps having been on duty near Kimmage, it was suggested that Mr. Byrne's house should
be searched; but a gallant nephew of Lord Avonmore,
who commanded, refused to sanction this proceeding,
in consequence of Mr. Byrne's absence and the presence of several ladies in the house. Lawless thanked
his stars; but the fears of the family were greatly excited by the proximity of his pursuers, and they resolved
at all hazards to remove him to Dublin previous to
making one desperate effort to reach France. Word
was sent to Philip Lawless, an eminent brewer, residing
at Warrenmount, the elder brother of William, to send
his carriage to Mr. Byrne's to convey him to town.
Mrs. Ryan, then Miss Byrne, dressed Lawless in a
loose white wrapper of her own, and a close beaver
bonnet. As Lawless possessed a pale sallow countenance, Miss Byrne applied some effective touches, not of
ordinary rouge, but of lake paint, to his cheeks. The
outlaw, accompanied by Mrs. Ryan and her two sisters,
entered the carriage and proceeded openly at noon-day
to Dublin. The rebellion had not yet burst forth.
No opposition was offered to the ordinary transit of
vehicles. When half way to Dublin, a party of yeomanry scowled into the carriage, but not detecting
anything suspicious, suffered it to proceed. Having

arrived at the residence of Mrs. Lawless, the outlaw sent for a suit of sailor's clothes and donned them; but his long pale face was far from disguised. To effect this desideratum, Lawless placed upon his head an immense coil of cable, which he arranged so as that a large portion descended upon his forehead, and went far to baffle recognition. As he proceeded with this burthen in the direction of Sir John Rogerson's Quay, the redoubtable Major Sirr passed him closely, but the disguise was so perfect, that no suspicion seems to have been excited. Lawless gained greater confidence from this moment, reached the wharf, embarked on board a merchant vessel, and a favourable wind soon wafted him to the shores of France. He entered the military service of that country, gained distinction, lost a leg, and died a general in 1824.

One of the Irish refugees, Colonel Byrne, addressing the present writer in a letter dated " Paris, Rue Montaigne, February 18, 1854", says :—

" Lord Cloncurry committed a mistake in the work referred to, respecting the late General Lawless having lost his leg at Flushing, in August, 1809. He lost it at the battle of Lowenberg, in August, 1813. It appeared ridiculous that a colonel with but one leg should be put at the head of a regiment of infantry in a campaign by Napoleon".*

In Ireland Lawless had been a physician of great

---

* Colonel Byrne adds : " I have made notes of the principal events and transactions that came within my knowledge during the insurrection of 1798, as well as that of 1803. If I thought their publication could in any way tend to benefit my native country, I would cheerfully get them printed; but I am well aware that the present time is not a propitious moment. I trust a time may come when the publication of such documents will be encouraged. They will show the efforts and sacrifices that were made to procure the independence of Ireland". Colonel Byrne has since paid the debt of nature, an *the work in* question has been published under the auspices o *his widow.*

promise, and filled the chair of Physiology and Anatomy at the College of Surgeons. Another eminent medical man, Dr. Dease, Professor of the Practice of Surgery, was also deeply implicated; but he lacked the moral energy of Lawless, and, on timely information reaching him that a warrant was in progress for his apprehension, he retired to his study, and died, like Cato, by his own hand. A fine white marble bust of this physician, inscribed "William Dease, obiit 1798", is preserved in the Hall of the College of Surgeons. The old man's brow, furrowed by years of earnest honest labour, and the intelligent expression of his eye, prematurely quenched, awaken painful emotions.

William Lawless possessed a cultivated literary taste; and in the *Irish Masonic Magazine* for 1794 a number of poems from his pen may be found. He had been a member of the Royal Irish Academy; but *Faulkner's Dublin Journal* for 1802 announces his expulsion on political grounds.

H.

LORD EDWARD FITZGERALD.

A late eminent writer, Mr. Daniel Owen Maddyn, author of *Ireland and its Rulers, Revelations of Ireland, The Age of Pitt and Fox, Chiefs of Parties,* etc., in a letter to the author, written a few days before his death, strongly recommended that the present work, of which we gave him an outline, should be entitled, *Lord Edward Fitzgerald and his Bloodhounds,* and enclosed a story which he rightly considered would form an interesting note.

The story, whether true or false, ran to this effect:

"Lady Guy Campbell was most anxious to discover where her father was interred, so as to give him decent

14

sepulture. It was said that he had been buried in various places; but on examining them, it was found that the information was erroneous. After much investigation, she was at last referred to one old man, who, it was stated, could tell her.

"She accordingly went to this pauper's house, and found a man in bed, and no sooner did he see her than he said: 'I know who you are—you must be the daughter of Lord Edward Fitzgerald, you are so like him'. She told him the object of her visit, and then he related to her that he had lingered about Newgate when her father died, and that after nightfall he saw six men bearing out a shell, and that he followed them until they came to Werburgh's Church, and that he saw them take the coffin into the vaults of the church, and that, unperceived by them, he stole into the vaults after them, and saw where they deposited the coffin. From intensity of feeling, in the wildness of grief for his lost master, he stayed all that night in the vaults, and in order to mark the coffin he scratched the letters 'E. F.' on the lid of the coffin. In doing this he used a rusty old nail which he had picked up. He had great difficulty afterwards in forcing his way out through a grated window.

"He then put his arm into his breast and took out a rag of cloth, gave Lady Guy Campbell the identical nail, and told her to go to Werburgh's Church. She went there with her friends, and in the vaults she discovered the coffin exactly as it had been described by her informant, and the letters 'E. F.' incised on it several inches long.

"Such", adds Mr. Maddyn, "is the story told me by a member of the bar—a Tory, and a man moving in capital society".

In the churchyard of St. Werburgh is also buried Major Sirr, by whose hand Lord Edward fell. See *notice of Major* Sirr, Addenda J, note 29.

I.

JOHN AND HENRY SHEARES.

The Brothers Sheares were natives of Cork, whither the younger had proceeded, early in May, for the purpose of organizing that county. An energetic coöperator in this movement was a silversmith named Conway, a native of Dublin. The treachery of this man was so artfully concealed that his most intimate friends never suspected him.

"If those who join secret societies", writes a Cork correspondent, "could get a peep at the records of patriotic perfidy kept in the Castle, they would get some insight into the dangerous consequences of meddling with them. There is a proverbial honour amongst thieves; there seems to be none amongst traitors. The publication of the official correspondence about the end of the last century made some strange revelations. In Cork, there lived a watchmaker, named Conway, one of the directory of the United Irishmen there. So public and open a professor of disloyal sentiments was he, that on the plates of his watches he had engraved as a device a harp without a crown. For a whole generation this man's name was preserved as "a sufferer for his country", like his ill-fated townsmen, John and Henry Sheares. The *Cornwallis Correspondence* (vol. iii. p. 85) reveals the fact that Conway was a double-dyed traitor; that he had offered to become a secret agent for detecting the leaders of the United Irishmen, and that the information he gave was very valuable, particularly as confirming that received from a solicitor in Belfast, who, whilst acting as agent and solicitor to the disaffected party, was betraying their secrets to the executive, and earning, in his vile *role* of informer, a pension, from 1799 to 1804, of £150, and the sum of £1,460, the wages he received for his services".

The fate of the Sheares has been invested with something of a romantic interest ; and not a few traditional accounts describe their end as not less saintly than that of Charles the First. Into their case, as in that of other political martyrs, some romance has been imported ; and as truth is stranger than fiction, we may tell an anecdote communicated to us on November 21st, 1857, by the late John Patten, brother-in-law of Thomas Addis Emmet. The Sheareses, though nominally Protestants, were tinged with deistical ideas. "I heard it stated", observed Mr. Patten, "that when the hangman was in the act of adjusting the noose round the neck of John Sheares before proceeding to the scaffold, he exclaimed, 'D——n you, do you want to kill me before my time?' I could not credit it, and asked the Rev. Dr. Gamble, who attended them in their last moments, if the statement were correct. 'I am sorry to say', replied Dr. Gamble, 'that it is perfectly true. I myself pressed my hand against his mouth to prevent a repetition of the imprecation'".

J.

THE REIGN OF TERROR IN IRELAND.

Exception has been taken to impressions of the reign of terror in Ireland, whether derived from traditional sources which possess no personal knowledge of it, and, on the principle that a story never loses in its carriage, may be prone to exaggeration; or from the testimony of partisan participators in the struggle, who still smart from the combined effects of wrong received and unsatisfied vengeance.

The Viceroy, Lord Cornwallis, is at least a witness above suspicion. In a letter dated April 15th, 1799, *he writes:*—

"On my arrival in this country I put a stop to the burning of houses and murder of the inhabitants by the yeomen, or any other persons who delighted in that amusement; to the flogging for the purpose of extorting confession; and to the free-quarters, which comprehend universal rape and robbery throughout the whole country". And on the 24th July, 1798, we are assured, "except in the instances of the six state trials that are going on here, there is no law either in town or county but martial law, and you know enough of that, to see all the horrors of it, even in the best administration of it. Judge, then, how it must be conducted by Irishmen, heated with passion and revenge. But all this is trifling compared with the numberless murders which are hourly committed by our people without any process or examination whatever".*

To either of the objections just noticed, advanced by persons who are sceptical as to the extent of the Irish Reign of Terror, General Sir George Cockburn, who fought against the rebels, is not open. From his representative, Phineas Cockburn, Esq., of Shangana Castle, we have received several interesting MSS. in the autograph of the General, which possess much interest for the students of the calamitous period of '98.

"Sampson's papers", observes General Cockburn, in a letter to Lord Anglesey, "contained details of most horrible outrages on the people, of cruelty and foul deeds. Of course violence begets violence, and though the people, in many cases, were driven to retaliation, it was not before murder, burning, destruction of property, often on suspicion or being suspected, and flogging, drove them to desperation".

The following curious paper has, with others, been placed at our disposal by Mr. Cockburn:

* *Correspondence of Marquis Cornwallis*, vol. ii. p. 368.

THE STEP-LADDER, OR A PICTURE OF THE IRISH GOVERN-
MENT AS IT WAS BEFORE LORD CORNWALLIS'S ARRIVAL,
AND DURING THE SYSTEM OF TERROR, ETC.

No. 1.—The Cabinet, viz.	The Chancellor,	1
	Speaker,	2
	C. Cashel (Archbishop)	3
	Castlereagh,	4
	J. Reresford, Commissr.	5
No. 2 —Under-strappers to do.,	E. Cooke,	6
	Drogheda,	7
	Glentworth,	8
	Carhampton,	9
	J. Claudius Beresford,	10
No. 3.— Strong supporters of do., of Orangeism, jobbing, and corruption,	Enniskillen,	11
	Lees,	12
	Carleton,	13
	Perry,	14
	Isaac Corry,	$14\frac{1}{2}$
No. 4.—Servants to the Faction, viz.	Waterford,	15
	Annesley,	16
	Blaquire,	17
	Londonderry,	18
	Toler,	19
	Kingsborough,	20
No. 5.—Very mischievous men, and enemies to liberty,	Downshire,	21
	Dillon,	22
	Trench,	23
	Dr. Duignan,	24
	O'Beirne, Bp. of Meath,	25
	Tuam (Archbishop),	26
	Alexander, Mem. Derry	27

No. 6.—Ruffian Magistrates, always ready to murder, burn, etc.	Burns,	Meath.	
	Finley,	do.	
	Cleghorn,	do.	
	S. H. Mannix,	Cork.	
	Fitzgerald,	Tipperary.	28
	Jacob,	do.	
	Tyrrel,	Kildare.	
	Knipe,	do.	
	Griffith,	do.	
	Blaney,	Monaghan.	

No. 7.—Miscreants,	Sirr,	29
	Swan,	30
	Sands,	31
	Giffard,	82
	Hempenstall, Lt. M.	33
	Spectacle Knox,	34
	Higgins,	35

No. 8.—Spies, viz.	Armstrong,	36
	Reynolds,	37
	Cope,	38

No. 9.—Turnkey and Gaoler to the Faction,	Godfry,	39

A few remarks in illustration of the persons enumerated in the "Step-Ladder" of General Cockburn serves to disclose a condensed history of the time.

1. Lord Chancellor Clare was the son of John Fitzgibbon, who had received his education for the Roman Catholic priesthood, but, preferring civil to canon law, conformed, with a view to becoming a member of the bar. The subsequent Lord Clare was appointed attorney-general in 1784, and five years later attained the topmost rung of " the step-ladder", from whence he looked down with supercilious arrogance on those by whose aid he *had risen.* He rapidly covered all Ireland with his

partisans.   Both houses of parliament became his au-
tomatons.   Of coercion he was an uncompromising
advocate.   In 1784, as alleged by Plowden, he introduced a bill for demolishing Roman Catholic chapels.
In parliament he defended the use of torture.   In
private, as his letters to Lord Castlereagh show, he
upset the bill of Catholic relief, which, according to
Mr. Pitt's promise, was to have accompanied the Act
of Union.   But it should be remembered by the assailants of Lord Clare's reputation, that, unlike many
of the influential men enumerated in General Cockburn's "step-ladder", he, at least, was politically consistent, and did not commence his career in the ranks
of the tribunes.   In action he was impulsive, fearless.
and despotic.   Rushing to a political meeting con-
vened by the High Sheriff of Dublin, and attended by
one friend only, this, the most unpopular man in all
Ireland, interrupted a democratic orator in his address,
commanded the mob to disperse, almost pushed the
high sheriff from the chair, and threatened an *ex-officio*
information.   The sheriff, panic-stricken, dissolved the
meeting.   If hissed in the street, Lord Clare pulled out
pistols.*   He powerfully contributed to carry the Union.
His ambition was indomitable, and he aspired to transfer his boundless influence to the wider field of England.   He had placed several viceroys in succession
beneath his thumb.   Might he not also attain an ascendancy over the personage whom they represented ?

" If I live", said Lord Clare, when the measure was
brought before the House of Peers, " if I live to see
the Union completed, to my latest hour I shall feel an
honourable pride in reflecting on the little share I may
have had in contributing to effect it".   •

His first speech in the British parliament met with
interruption and rebuffs.   He abused the Catholics,

* *Diary of Lord* Clonmel, printed privately for his family,
p. *449.*

ridiculed his country, was called to order by Lord Suf-
folk, rebuked by the Lord Chancellor, resumed, was
again called to order, lost temper, and stigmatized the
opposition as " Jacobins and levellers".   " We would
not bear this insult from an equal", exclaimed the
Duke of Bedford; "shall we endure it at the hands
of mushroom nobility ?"   Even Mr. Pitt was disgusted.
" Good G—d", said he, addressing Mr. Wilberforce,
" did ever you hear, in all your life, so great a rascal
as that ?"   Mr. Grattan mentions, in the memoirs of
his father, that this anecdote was stated by Mr. Wilberforce to Mr. North.

Crestfallen, Lord Clare returned to Ireland, where
he found a number of hungry place-seekers awaiting
his arrival.   " Ah", said he, as he began to calculate
his influence, and found it wanting, " *I*, that once had
all Ireland at my disposal, cannot now nominate the
appointment of a gauger".   His heart broke at the
thought, and on January 28th, 1802, Lord Clare, after
a painful illness, and while yet comparatively young,
died.*   His death-bed presented a strange picture.
Charles Phillips says he ordered his papers to be
burned,† as hundreds might be compromised.   In

* A few days after the Sham Squire's demise. Lord Clare, notwithstanding his avowed tendency to foster political profligacy,
possessed the redeeming virtue of having snubbed the Sham
Squire.

† It has been mentioned by the *Athenaeum* (No. 1634), as a
significant fact, that nearly all those who were concerned in
carrying the Union had destroyed their papers, and Lord Clare,
Sir Edward Littlehales, with Messrs. Wickham, Taylor, Marsden, and King, were instanced. It is also remarkable, that all the
MSS. reports of the eloquent anti-Union speeches, with the MSS.
of many pamphlets hostile to the measure, were purchased from
Moore the publisher, and burnt by order of Lord Castlereagh.
See *Grattan's Memoirs*, vol. v. p. 180. Lord Clonmel, in his
last moments, expressed much anxiety to destroy his papers.
His nephew, Dean Scott, who assisted in the conflagration,
assured Mr. Grattan that one letter in particular completely
revealed Lord Castlereagh's scheme to foster the Rebellion of

Grattan's memoirs it is stated, on the authority of Loid Clare's nephew, that he bitterly deplored having taken any part in effecting the Union. Plowden states that he vainly called for the assistance of a Catholic priest; but we have never seen the allegation confirmed. His funeral was insulted by much of the indecency which attended Lord Castlereagh's in Westminster Abbey. In one of Lord Clare's speeches he declared, that he would make the Catholics as tame as cats. Dead cats were flung upon his hearse and his grave. Lord Cloncurry, in his *Recollections*, says that he was obliged to address the infuriated populace from the balcony of Lord Clare's house in Ely Place, ere they could be induced to relinquish the unseemly hooting which swelled the death-knell of John, Earl of Clare.

2. "Mr. Foster, we learn, was for several years not only the supporter, and indeed the ablest supporter of administration, but the conductor and manager of their schemes and operations ".* He sternly opposed the admission of Catholics to the privileges of the constitution; but Ireland must always remember him with gratitude for the determined hostility with which he opposed the Legislative Union.

Feeling that the papers of Mr. Foster (afterwards Lord Oriel) would throw great light upon the history of the Union, we asked the late Lord Massareene, who represented the Speaker, for permission to see them, but it appeared that the Honourable Mr. Chichester Skeffington "seized" the archives after Lord Ferrard's death, and Lord Massareene never saw them after.

'98 in order to carry the Union. The purchase of Lord De Blaquire's papers by the government appears in our notice of that personage. Mr. Commissioner Phillips tells us that the debates on the Union called into operation all the oratorical talent of Ireland, but their record has been suppressed, and that the volume containing the session of 1800 is so inaccessible, that it has been sought for in vain to complete the series in the library of the House of Lords.

* *Review of the Irish House of* Commons (p. 129).

3. Charles Agar, was appointed Archbishop of Cashel in 1779, translated to Dublin in 1801, and created Earl of Normanton in 1806. When we learn that his grace acquired £40,000 by a single renewal fine, the statement that he amassed a fortune of £400,000 is not surprising.* Lord Normanton would seem to have been more active as a privy councillor than as a prelate, for Archbishop Magee declared that " the diocese of Dublin had been totally neglected " by his predecessors.† A savage biographical notice of Archbishop Agar appears in Cox's *Irish Magazine* for August, 1809, pp. 382-4, together with some lines beginning:

> " Adieu, thou mitred nothingness, adieu,
> Thy failings many, and thy virtues few."

Yet amid the sectarian strife of that day it is pleasant to find " C. Cashel " in amicable epistolary correspondence with his rival, Dr. James Butler, Roman Catholic Archbishop of the same diocese. ‡

4. Lord Castlereagh, who, falsifying the hyperbolical apothegm of Dr. Johnson that " patriotism was the last refuge of the base", began political life in the ranks of the patriots. Of his hostility to the lordly interest, and identification with the reform or popular party, the autobiographies of Teeling and Sampson furnish curious particulars. His electioneering agent on those principles was Neilson the Rebel. Castlereagh's subsequent career is too notorious to require special detail. Dr. Madden calls him the Robespierre of Ireland, and says that his memory has " the faint sickening smell of hot blood about it ". Ireland, when weak and postrate from loss of blood, was robbed by Lord Castlereagh of its richest gem—a domestic parliament.

* Dalton's *Archbishops of Dublin*, p. 351.
† Charge delivered October 24, 1822 p. 33.
‡ Renehan's *Irish Church History*, edited by Rev. D. M'Carthy, p. 345.

The corruption he practised to silence opposition has been sometimes denied; but little attempt to disguise it appears in his own correspondence, notwithstanding the ample weeding which it admittedly underwent by Lord Londonderry.

"It will be no secret", writes the unprincipled statesman, " what has been promised, *and by what means the Union has been secured.* His appointment will encourage, not prevent, disclosures; and the only effect of such a proceeding on their (the ministers') part will be, to add the weight of their testimony to that of the anti-unionists *in proclaiming the profligacy of the means by which the measure has been accomplished*".[*]

5. The Right Honourable John Beresford, member for Waterford, discharged, besides his more legitimately recognized duties as commissioner of revenue, a peculiar office, similar to that held, during a later period, by the Right Honourable William Saurin. His influence penetrated every department of the state; and to every contemporary viceregal administration, except that of Lord Fitzwilliam, who paid the penalty of his independence, Mr. Beresford was the arrogant and dogmatical dictator. His family held places to the amount of £20,000 per annum. In Mr. Beresford's correspondence, rather recently published, much curious matter appears. Referring to some remarks of Denis Bowes Daly, Mr. Beresford writes: "No Lord Lieutenant could exist with my powers; that I had been a Lord Chancellor, a Chief Justice of the King's Bench, an Attorney General, nearly a Primate, and certainly a Commander-in-Chief; that I was at the head of the Revenue, and had the law, the army, the revenue, and a great deal of the Church in my possession; and he said expressly, that I was considered the king of Ireland".[†]

* *Memoirs and Correspondence of Viscount Castlereagh*, v. iii. p 331.

† *Mr. Beresford to Lord Auckland, Dublin, January 9, 1795, v. ii. p. 51.*

6. Mr. Under Secretary Cooke has already been noticed (p. 137, *ante*).

7. The Marquis of Drogheda was not a prominent character. "As an orator", observes a writer in 1779, "he is of no consideration; in fact he seldom speaks". Lord Drogheda's political labours were behind the scenes. He quietly promoted the Legislative Union, with other calamitous measures, and then as quietly applied for his reward. The Duke of Portland, in a private and confidential letter to the Viceroy, dated June 27, 1800, declares that Lord Drogheda's claims to be a member of the representative peerage were "irresistible".*

8. Lord Glentworth's services were much of the same order as those of the Marquis of Drogheda. So little was he known outside the backstairs of the Castle that he obtains no place in either of the contemporary publications which we have more than once consulted. It will be remembered that his was one of the three peerages which Grattan and Ponsonby offered to prove had been sold for hard cash, and the money laid out in the purchase of members in the House of Commons. The other two peerages were those of Kilmaine and Cloncurry.†

9. Of Lord Carhampton we have already spoken fully.‡ It is right, however, to give his memory whatever benefit is derivable from an excuse addressed by him to Colonel Napier, who, as a humane and chivalrous officer, protested against the demoralising license and brutality practised by the troops. "We are determined to use coercion only. Consider I am only an insignificant part of an administration, and must follow their system".§ "Like master, like man", would have been

* *Castlereagh Correspondence*, v. iii. p. 345.
† *Memoirs of Grattan*, v. iii. p. 291.
‡ Pages 57, 60, *ante*.
§ Moore's *Life of Lord Edward Fitzgerald*, v. ii. p. 300.

a fitting motto for the army when under the command-
ership of Lord Carhampton. He died poor, and we
have heard, from the representatives of Mr. Michael
Lewis, his attorney, that some bonds which Lord Carhampton left behind proved mere waste paper.

10. John Claudius Beresford, son of Mr. Commissioner
Beresford, already noticed, succeeded him as a member
of " the Irish Backstairs Cabinet". He expressed a wish
for the rebellion, that Mr. Pitt might see with what
promptitude it could be crushed. In conjunction with
Major Sirr, Mr. Beresford maintained a battalion of
spies, which octogenarians sometimes refer to as " Beresford's Bloodhounds". He largely helped to stimulate the
rebellion of '98 by generally a coercive policy, which
was cruelly followed up by the administration of torture. This was practised under the personal direction
of John Claudius Beresford, both at the riding school
in Marlborough Street and on the site of the present
City Hall. When Lord Castlereagh endeavoured to
ignore the charge, Mr. Beresford in parliament not
only admitted but defended the vile practice. He was
Secretary to the Grand Lodge of Orangemen, and in-
fused their views into almost every department of the
Irish government. The capriciousness of popular feeling in his regard was quite as remarkable as the mer-
curial movement of his own chequered career. Having
creditably filled the office of Lord Mayor of Dublin,
his carriage was drawn through the streets by the same
mob which had often previously execrated him.

The terrible vicissitude which marked the later
career of John Claudius Beresford strikingly contrasts
with his power anterior to the union. In partnership
with Mr. Woodmason he opened a bank at No. 2,
Beresford Place. One day the bank broke, and Beresford was a bankrupt, cut by those who had formerly
cringed. A man's good fortune often turns his head ;
but bad fortune as often averts the heads of his friends.

Beresford was, perhaps, an illustration of both ends of the apothegm. Some persons who had known him in his glory pitied the old attenuated man, with bent back and threadbare clothes—a well-known spectacle in the streets of Dublin for many years after, preaching in silent exposition, "*Sic transit gloria mundi!*" John Claudius Beresford strongly opposed the union, not, we fear, on patriotic grounds, but because it was likely to stem the torrent of his own ambition. His character was not without some good points, and he is said to have been charitable in disbursement, and of private worth in his family. In the Imperial Parliament he represented the County of Waterford, the great stronghold of his race, further noticed in our sketch of the Marquis of Waterford.

11. Lord Enniskillen, a vigorous speaker in the Irish Parliament, presided at a drum-head trial of a yeoman, named Wollagan, for murder, and acquitted him. "It was an atrocious murder", writes Plowden; "every aggravating circumstance was proved. No attempt was made to contradict any part of the evidence: but a justification of the horrid murder was set up, as having been committed under an order of the commanding officer, that if the yeomen should meet with any whom they knew or suspected to be rebels, they needed not be at the trouble of bringing them in, but were to shoot them on the spot; that it was almost the daily practice of that corps to go out upon scouring parties". Lord Cornwallis, the new viceroy, condemned the verdict, and disqualified Lord Enniskillen from sitting on any new court martial.*

12. Mr. John Lees, a Scotchman, accompanied Lord Townshend to Ireland as Private Secretary. He was appointed Secretary at War and Secretary to the Post-Office in Dublin, and in 1804 received the honour of a baronetcy.

* Plowden's *History of Ireland*, v. ii. p. 514.

13. Lord Carleton, the son of a trader in Cork,* was appointed Solicitor General in 1779, Chief Justice of the Common Pleas in 1787, Baron in 1789, and Viscount eight years later. In his policy on the question of the Legislative Union, Lord Carleton was not consistent. We find him at first giving his sentiments decidedly against it, and a few weeks later avowing himself a supporter of the measure.

Sir Jonah Barrington, in his *Personal Sketches* (i. 475), writes:—"Lord Carleton, as Justice of the Common Pleas, had rendered himself beyond description obnoxious to the disaffected of Ireland, in consequence of having been the judge who tried and condemned the two Counsellors Sheares, who were executed for treason, and to whom that nobleman had been *testamentary guardian* by the will of their father". The latter statement thus emphatically italicised by Barrington, is one of the startling myths in which he habitually indulged. The will of Mr. Sheares contains no allusion whatever to the Chief Justice.

14. Sexton Perry was originally a patriot of ultra energy, and considerable influence with his party. During the corrupt administration of Lord Townshend, Perry seceded from his popular principles. In the year 1771 he was appointed speaker, and in 1785 created Viscount Perry. Mr. O'Regan of the Irish Bar, writing in 1818, bemoans that Perry, Malone, and Avonmore should have no biographer: "What records have we of those who flourished for the last fifty years, the most memorable period of our history? Where, then, in what archives are deposited monuments of our illustrious dead? Where, but in *Lodge's Peerage*, are to be found any traces of Lord Perry?" †

We are able to answer one of the questions asked by the biographer of Curran. The historic investiga-

* *Sleator's Dublin Chronicle* for 1791.
† *Memoirs of Curran*, preface, p. xv.

tors of the life of Perry and his times may be glad to
know that at Dungannon Park, the residence of the
youthful Lord Ranfurley, is preserved an immense
collection of letters addressed to the late Lord Perry
when he was Speaker of the Irish House of Com-.
mons.*

14½. The Honourable Isaac Corry, Chancellor of the
Irish Exchequer, and M.P. for Newry, where his father
was a respectable trader, joined the Whig Opposition,
and for several years distinguished himself by the violence of his patriotism; but during Lord Buckingham's
administration he was appointed Surveyor of Ordnance
at a salary of £1,000 a year, which was followed by
further promotion. Official peculation had attained a
fearful pitch at this time. In the ordnance and treasury, the grossest frauds pervaded almost every department. The public stores were plundered with impunity
in open day. The arms, ammunition, and military
accoutrements, condemned as useless, were stolen out
at one gate, and brought in at the other, and charged
anew to the public account. Journeymen armourers,
who worked in the arsenal, seldom went home to their
meals without conveying away a musket, a sword, or
brace of pistols, as lawful perquisites, and sanctioned by
the connivance of the superiors. Clerks in subordinate
departments, with salaries not exceeding £100 per
annum, kept handsome houses in town and country,
with splendid establishments; some of them became
purchasers of loans and lotteries: all exhibited signs
of redundant opulence.† During the debate on the
Union, Grattan, with, we think, less point than usual,
stung the vulnerable ministerialist by calling him "a
dancing master"; Corry challenged his satirist; they

* Letter of Henry Alexander, Esq., guardian of Lord Ranfurley, dated Carlton Club, July 7 1860.
† Plowden's *History of Ireland* v. ii. p. 279.

15

left the House, and before the debate terminated,
Corry was shot through the arm.*

15. The Marquis of Waterford was the leading member of the powerfully influential family of the Beresfords.
In conjunction with his brother he hurled by their might,
the liberal viceroy, Lord Fitzwilliam, from office, and
provoked from the latter a remark in the English
House of Peers, to the effect, that it was impossible to
effect any good in Ireland unless the power of the
Beresfords could be destroyed.† Not until 1826 was this
desirable consummation achieved. At the Waterford
election in that year, the Beresfords received, from the
forty shilling freeholders, their death blow. "I did
not think", said Sheil, "that there was so much virtue under rags". This telling stroke was planned and
inflicted by Dr. Kelly, R.C. Bishop of Waterford.

17. Sir John, afterwards Lord De Blaquire, represents one of the Huguenot families of whom we have
spoken, p. 84 *ante.* Patronised by Lord Harcourt, he accepted the office of bailiff of the Phœnix Park, to which
the small salary of £40 a year was attached, with the
use of a little lodge, a garden, grass for two cows, and
half-a-crown per head for all cattle found trespassing
in the Park. The first piece of his cleverness was
shown in contriving to make the salary £50 per annum

* Grattan cultivated unerring aim in conjunction with accurate eloquence. In the secluded woods of Tenahinch he
might be, sometimes seen declaiming with Demosthenic
energy, and the next hour lodging bullets in particular trees
which still bear marks of the havoc.

† Lord Clare writing to the Right Honourable J. C. Beresford, says: "The more I consider the flagrant and unwarrantable calumnies which he [Lord Fitzwilliam] deals out so
flippantly against you, the more I am decided in my opinion
that you ought in the first instance to bring an action against
him for defamation, and lay it in the city of London. He had
fifty copies of this memoir made out by the clerks in the different offices in the Castle, which were distributed by his order".
—*Beresford Correspondence* v. ii. p. 88.

for his own life and that of the king's two eldest sons ;
with liberty to graze cattle to an unlimited extent.
Sir John was a pluralist in sinecures, and amongst the
rest filled the office of Director of Public Works.* He
applied for a more comfortable residence which the
Board of Works built for him at the public expense of
£8,000. Sir John, however, was not yet satisfied.
The garden being small, he successfully petitioned for
a larger one, whereupon, he took in about ten acres
which he surrounded by a wall, also at the expense of
the nation.† But it is De Blaquire's connection with
the Legislative Union, and the rare astuteness with
which he promoted the success of that measure, on
which his fame as a diplomatist historically rests. "Sir
John Blaquire is disposed to exert himself very much",‡
observes Lord Castlereagh in communicating the good
news to the Duke of Rutland on January 7, 1799.
"The entrance to a woman's heart", said the first
Napoleon, "is through her eye or ear ; but the way to
a man's heart is down his throat". De Blaquire illus-
trated the wisdom of the apothegm. "He enjoyed,"
says Sir Jonah Barrington, "a revenue sufficiently
ample to enable him to entertain his friends as well,
and far more agreeably, than any other person I had
previously met. Nobody understood eating and drinking better than Sir John De Blaquire ; and no man
was better seconded in the former respect, than he
was by his cook, Mrs. Smith, whom he brought from
Paris".§

For some notice of the intrigues with which De
Blaquire secured influential support to the Union, see
The Rise and Fall of the Irish Nation. A few years ago,

* *Personal Sketches* v. i. p. 194.
† *Irish Political Characters*, 1799, p. 150.
‡ *Memoirs and Correspondence of Lord Castlereagh* v. ii.
p. 85.
§ *Personal Sketches* by Sir Jonah Barrington v. i. p. 198.

one of his descendants found a trunk of old dusty papers calculated to throw great light on the history of the Union. This gentleman offered the entire trunk-full to the Wellington government for £100; his proposal was eagerly accepted; and we have heard him ridiculed by his friends for being so silly as not to have stipulated for a couple of thousand pounds, which would have been acceded to, they allege, with equal alacrity.

18. Lord Londonderry, father of Lord Castlereagh, was an active agent in checking the popular plots of the time; but that his lordship was not without misgivings as to the result may be inferred from the fact, mentioned in the *Castlereagh Papers* (ii. 331), that he would not take bank notes in payment of rent.

19. Of John Toler, Lord Norbury, it may without much injustice be said, that for thirty years he performed the triple *role* of bully, butcher, and buffoon. His services in the first capacity proved useful to the then government, and helped him far more than his law to judicial elevation.[*] His old passions and prejudices clung to him as a judge; he browbeat timid counsel; and has been known to suggest mortal combat by the remark, "that he would not seek shelter behind the bench, or

---

[*] Mr. Toler's powers of invective were quite startling. When he uttered such language in parliament as this, the license of his tongue elsewhere may be conceived, "Had he heard a man uttering out of those doors such language as that of the honourable gentleman, he would have seized the ruffian by the throat, and dragged him to the dust". (*Parl. Deb.*)

An extraordinary license of language was permitted by the Speaker in these days. A tradition of the period thus describes the denunciation of a certain family: "Sir, they are all rotten, from the honourable member who has just sat down, to the tooth-less hag that is now grinning at us from the gallery". The allusion was to the member's mother. Lord Castlereagh was upbraided with impotency by Grattan, in the presence of Lady *Castlereagh*, who occupied a seat in the Speaker's gallery during one of the debates on the Union.

merge the gentleman in the Chief Justice". His relish for a capital conviction was undisguised; a document before us mentions the almost incredible fact, that at a single assize, he passed sentence of death on one hundred and ninety-eight individuals, of whom one hundred and ninety-seven passed through the hands of Galvin, the hangman. With the black cap on his head, he joked as freely as though it were a cap and bells. "Ah, my lord, give me a long day", craved a wretched culprit. "Your wish is granted", replied the judge, "I give you till the 21st of June, the longest day in the year"! Lord Norbury's charges transcend description. "Flinging his judicial robe aside", writes Mr. Sheil, "and sometimes casting off his wig. he started from his seat and threw off a wild harangue, in which neither law, method, or argument could be discovered. It generally consisted of narratives of his early life, which it was impossible to associate with the subject, of jests from John Miller, mixed with jokes of his own manufacture, and of sarcastic allusions to any of the counsel who had endeavoured to check him during the trial".

Sir Jonah Barrington mentions that he has seen his "racket court"* convulsed with laughter by the appearance of the chief in a green tabinet coat with pearl buttons, striped yellow and black vest, and buff breeches—the costume of Hawthorn in "Love in a village", a character personated by Lord Norbury at Lady Castlereagh's masquerade; and he found the dress so cool that he frequently, in after years, wore it under his robes. On this particular occasion it was revealed accidentally by Lord Norbury throwing back his robes, owing to the more than ordinarily heated atmosphere of the court.

* This was a designation of Lord Norbury's own. "What's your business?" a witness was asked. "I keep a racket court". "So do I", rejoined the Chief Justice, puffing.

"That Scotch *Broom* deserves an *Irish stick*", exclaimed Lord Norbury, in reference to Lord Brougham, who had brought before parliament some unconstitutional conduct of which he had been guilty; and at a later period, it appeared, from the same source, that the old chief had fallen asleep on the bench during a trial for murder. In 1827 he resigned, and in 1831 he died. The late Mr. Brophy, state dentist, who was present at Lord Norbury's funeral, informed us that when lowering the coffin by ropes into a deep grave, a voice in the crowd cried, "Give him rope *galore,** boys; he never was sparing of it to others". As a landlord, Lord Norbury was by no means bad; and in his own house he is said to have been gentle and forbearing.

20. Lord Kingsborough had always been prominently zealous in promoting that system of coercion† which, as Lord Castlereagh admitted, aimed to make the United Irish conspiracy explode.‡ When the rebellion broke out, Lord Kingsborough, as colonel of the North Cork Militia, proceeded to join his regiment in Wexford, but was captured by the rebels, who held possession of the town. Lord Kingsborough owed his life to the personal interposition of Dr. Caulfield, Roman Catholic Bishop of Ferns.

21. General Cockburne regards Lord Downshire as a rotten rung in the step-ladder, and styles him "a very mischievous enemy to liberty". We think, however, that his hostility to the Union goes far to redeem his shortcomings. His policy on this question so displeased the government that he was dismissed from the lieutenancy of his county, from the colonelcy of his regiment, and even expelled from the Privy Council. It was further proposed to institute a parliamentary inquiry into the conduct of Lord Downshire.

* *Anglice*, in plenty.
† *Plowden's Ireland*, v. ii. p. 475.
‡ *Moore's Life of Lord E.* Fitzgerald, p. 110, Paris Edn.

22. Lord Dillon also pursued a policy in 1800 which covers a multitude of previous political sins.* At a meeting of influential anti-unionists in Dublin, he proposed that a joint-stock purse should be formed for the purpose of out-bribing the government. Until June, 1799. Lord Dillon exercised his property and influence, both con-siderable, in favour of the Union.

23. Mr. Trench formed, under curious circumstances, a majority of *one* in favour of the Union. His vote and voice disclosed a very painful instance of tergiversation and seduction. Mr. Trench declared, in presence of a crowded House, that he would vote against the minister, and support Mr. Ponsonby's amendment. "This", observes Sir Jonah Barrington, who was an eye-witness of the transaction, " appeared a stunning blow to Mr. Cooke, who had been previously in conversation with Mr. Trench. He was immediately observed sidling from his seat, nearer to Lord Castlereagh. They whispered earnestly; and, as if restless and un-decided, both looked wistfully at Trench. At length the matter seemed to be determined on. Mr. Cooke retired to a back seat, and was obviously endeavouring to count the House—probably to guess if they could that night dispense with Mr. Trench's services. He re-turned to Lord Castlereagh; they whispered, and again looked at Mr. Trench. But there was no time to lose; the question was approaching. All shame was banished; they decided on the terms, and a significant glance, obvious to everybody, convinced Mr. Trench that his conditions were agreed to. Mr. Cooke then went and sat down by his side; an earnest but very short conversation took place; a parting smile completely told the House that Mr. Trench was satisfied. These sur-mises were soon verified. Mr. Cooke went back to Lord Castlereagh; a congratulatory nod announced his satisfaction. But could any man for one moment sup-

* Plowden's *History of Ireland*, v. ii. p. 551.

pose that an M.P. of large fortune, of respectable
family, and good character, could be publicly, and
without shame or compunction, actually seduced by
Lord Castlereagh under the eye of two hundred and
twenty gentlemen? In a few minutes Mr. Trench
rose to apologise for having indiscreetly declared he
would support the amendment. He added, that he had
thought better of the subject; that he had been convinced he was wrong, and would support the minister ".
Mr. Trench accordingly became Lord Ashtown.

24. Dr. Duigenan has been already noticed at p. 74
ante.

25. Of Bishop O'Beirne much has been written, but
we never saw in print some curious details embodied
in a letter, dated April 22nd, 1857, and addressed to us
by the late Mr. William Forde, Town Clerk of Dublin.
" I can furnish", writes Mr. Forde, " an interesting
anecdote of the early history of that gentleman, which
I learned when very young, living within two miles
of the see house of the diocese of Meath. Dr. O'Beirne
was never ordained a Roman Catholic priest, but
was educated at the Irish College of Paris with a
view to his becoming a priest. His brother, Rev.
Denis O'Beirne, was educated at the same time
and in the same college, and died parish priest of
the town of Longford, of which his brother was the
rector. The name of the parish in the Church is Templemichael. The history of the bishop in early life was,
that having suspended his studies, owing to ill-health, he
returned home for a couple of years, and was returning
to the college, when the following incident, which altered his destinies for life, occurred to him :—He was
travelling on foot through Wales, when the day became
very boisterous and rainy, and took shelter in a poor
inn on the wayside, and after ordering his dinner, which
was a small bit of Welch mutton, he went into a little
sitting-room. In some time two gentlemen came in also

for shelter (they were on a shooting party, and were driven in by the violence of the storm), and asked the woman of the house what she could give them for dinner. She replied she had nothing but what was at the fire roasting, and it was ordered by a gentleman in the next room, adding in a low tone, she believed he was an Irishman; whereupon one of the gentlemen exclaimed, 'Damn Paddy, *he* have roast mutton for dinner and while we must fast; we will take it', whereupon O'Beirne walked down from his room, and asked who damned Paddy, and insisted upon getting his dinner, and added they should not have it by force, but if they would take share of it on his invitation he would freely give it, and they were heartily welcome; on which they accepted the invitation, provided he would allow them to give the wine, which they assured him was very good, notwithstanding the appearance of the place. They all retired to the sitting-room, and the two gentlemen began conversing in French, whereupon O'Beirne interrupted them, and informed them that he understood every word they uttered, and they might not wish that a third person should know what they were speaking about, and then the conversation became general, and was carried on in French, of which O'Beirne was a perfect master. They inquired of him what were his objects in life, when he told them his history—that he was a farmer's son in Ireland, and his destiny was the Irish Catholic priesthood. When they were parting, one of the gentlemen asked would he take London on his way to Paris, to which he replied in the affirmative. He then gave him a card with merely the number and the street of his residence, and requested he would call there, where he would be very happy to see him. O'Beirne walked to London, which took him a considerable time, and on arriving there did not fail to call at the place indicated by the card. When he got to the house, he thought there must be some mistake ; but nothing daunted, he rapped, and met a hall porter, to whom he presented the card, and told him how he came by it, but supposed it was a mistake. The porter replied : 'Oh no ! his grace expected you a fortnight ago, and desired you should at once be shown in', and ushered him in accordingly to the study, where his Grace the Duke of Portland introduced himself to him. He had been appointed Governor of Canada, and O'Beirne's knowledge of the French language, and his education and general information, were matters that made him a desirable private secretary to deal with the French Canadians, and O'Beirne accepted the proposal of going out private secretary to the Duke of Portland. It was in Canada he apostatized and became a minister of the Established Church. I understood all this from a clergyman. To the Duke of Portland O'Beirne owed his promotion in the Irish Church, first, to the parish of Templemichael, then to the see of Ossory, and finally his translation to the see of Meath, then valued at more than £8,000 per annum. He was married to a Scotch lady, a daughter of General Stuart. He had one son and two daughters. Neither of them married. At the time of his death he was an uncompromising opponent to Catholic Emancipation. I believe his brother the priest died before him. I always heard that it was Bishop O'Beirne married the Prince of Wales and Mrs. Fitzherbert, and that the marriage took place in France, where the party went to have the ceremony performed".

It may be added that the Honourable Charles Langdale, in his memoirs of his kinswoman, Mrs. Fitzherbert, expresses ignorance of the clergyman's name, though we are told the Pope recognized it as a valid marriage. Dr. O'Beirne is very likely to have been *the officiating* party. When studying for the Roman *Catholic* priesthood in Paris, he is said to have attained *deacon's* orders.

26. Wm. Beresford, D.D., another prominent member of the inexhaustibly influential sept of the Beresfords, was consecrated Bishop of Dromore in 1780; Bishop of Ossory in 1784, and translated to the archbishopric of Tuam in 1795.   He married the sister of Lord Chancellor Clare, and was created Lord Decies in December, 1812.   This influential prelate died September 6, 1819; and his personalty was sworn to as £250,000.

27. Mr. Henry Alexander, both a barrister and a banker by profession, represented Londonderry in the Irish Parliament.   Here he was an active member of the secret committee.   Having successfully promoted the Union, he entered the British Senate as member for Old Sarum.   He signally distinguished himself as an advocate for coercion; and on the 8th February, 1815, we find him strenuously defending the suspension of the *Habeas Corpus* Act in Ireland.   From the *Castlereagh Papers* (i. 348) we learn that Mr. Alexander was a relation of the Irish rebel, Oliver Bond.

28. To describe the exploits of the members of that body, styled by General Cockburn, " Ruffian magistrates", would be to write the history of the whole, and we are spared the painful necessity of detailing, *ad nauseam,* scenes of revolting barbarity.   As a specimen of his magisterial colleagues and cotemporaries, take Mr. Thomas Judkin Fitzgerald, High Sheriff for the County of Tipperary.   From the trial of Doyle *v.* Fitzgerald, we learn that the defendant, in the street, and for the purpose of flagellation, seized Doyle, who was a respectable tradesman in Carrick.   In vain he declared his innocence; and some of the most respectable inhabitants tendered evidence in support of that declaration.   Doyle was a yeoman, and he begged that Captain Jephson, his commanding officer, might be sent for; the request was refused. He offered to go to instant execution if, on inquiry, the shadow of

sedition could be advanced against him; but inquiry was declined. Bail was then offered to any amount for his appearance, but Mr. Fitzgerald would not be baulked in the sport of which he had a foretaste, and declaring that he knew Doyle by his face to be a "Carmelite traitor", tied him to the whipping-post, where he received one hundred lashes until his ribs appeared; his knee breeches were then removed, and fifty more lashes administered. Doyle's entire innocence was afterwards proved. He appealed at the Clonmel assizes for redress; the facts appeared to demonstration; but an Orange jury, packed by the sub-sheriff, acquitted the high sheriff, Mr. Judkin Fitzgerald.

Mr. Wright, a teacher of the French language, employed both by public schools and private families, having called on Mr. Fitzgerald, the latter drew his sword, exclaiming: "Down on your knees, rebellious scoundrel, and receive your sentence"—which was to be flogged first and shot finally. Wright surrendered his keys, and expressed himself willing to suffer any punishment if his papers or conduct revealed proof of guilt. "What! you Carmelite rascal", exclaimed the high sheriff, "do you dare to speak after sentence?" He then struck him, and ordered him to prison. The next day, when brought forth to undergo his sentence, Wright knelt down in prayer, with his hat before his face. Mr. Fitzgerald snatched the hat from him and trampled on it, seized Wright by the hair, dragged him to the earth, kicked him and cut him across the forehead with his sword, then had him stripped naked, tied up to the ladder, and ordered him fifty lashes. Major Rial came up as the fifty lashes were completed, and asked the cause. Mr. Fitzgerald handed him a note written in French, saying, he did not himself understand French, though he understood Irish, but Major Rial would find *in that letter* what would justify him in flogging the *scoundrel* to death. Major Rial read the letter. He found it to be a note for the victim, which he thus translated :

" SIR,

        " I am extremely sorry I cannot wait on you at the hour appointed, being unavoidably obliged to attend Sir Laurence Parsons.

                        " Yours,

                                " BARON DE CLUES".

" Notwithstanding this translation", observes Mr. Plowden, " Mr. Fitzgerald ordered Wright fifty more lashes, which were inflicted with such peculiar severity, that the bowels of the bleeding victim could be perceived to be convulsed and working through his wounds! Mr. Fitzgerald, finding he could not continue the application of his cat-o'-nine-tails on that part without cutting his way into his body, ordered the waistband of his breeches to be cut open, and fifty more lashes to be inflicted. He then left the unfortunate man bleeding and suspended, while he went to the barrack to demand a file of men to come and shoot him ; but being refused by the commanding officer, he came back and sought for a rope to hang him, but could get none.   He then ordered him to be cut down and sent back to prison, where he was confined in a dark small room, with no other furniture than a wretched pallet of straw, without covering, and there he remained seven days without medical aid" !*

Wright brought an action and—*miràbile dictu*— obtained a verdict ; but the effect of it was neutralized by the open indemnification of Mr. Fitzgerald for certain acts done by him not justifiable in common law.†
He received from the crown a considerable pension for his ultra-loyal services in 1798, and on August 5th,

* *Trial of Wright* v. *Fitzgerald, Plowden's History of Ireland,* v. ii., p. 546, etc.
† Barrington's *Personal Sketches,* v. iii., p. 267.

1801, was created a baronet.* Tipperary is full of traditions of his excessive political zeal. One represents him equipped in cocked hat and sword, mounting the altar steps of old Latin chapel during the most solemn part of the Mass, and endeavouring to recognize among the congregation some unfortunate man whom he desired to scourge.† On another occasion he ascended the altar in Tipperary chapel during the delivery of an exhortation by the parish priest. Mr. Fitzgerald for convenience placed his three-cocked hat on the same bench which bore the Blessed Sacrament, and it was thought, at the time, an act of most singular daring on the part of the priest to remove the terrorist's hat and hand it to an acolyte.‡ It was said that Mr. Fitzgerald used to steep his cat-o'-nine-tails in brine before operating. "I have *preserved* the country", he boasted. "Rather say that you have *pickled* it", replied Jerry Keller.

Cox, in his *Magazine*, furnishes a criminatory obituary of Sir Thomas Judkin Fitzgerald, who, execrated by the people, whom he had stung to fury and madness, sank into his grave September 24, 1810. "The history of his life and loyalty", observes Cox, "is written in legible characters on the backs of his countrymen".§ The painful manner in which the lives of the late baronets of this family terminated, presents some remarkable coincidences. Sir John Judkin Fitzgerald, son of the terrorist, was drowned in the "Nimrod" in its passage from Bristol to Cork. His son, Sir Thomas Judkin Fitzgerald—reduced to pecuniary straits—opened a blacking manufactory, and committed suicide in the year 1864 ; and again, his son, a fine boy, hanged him-

* Burke's *Peerage and Baronetage*, p. 399.
† Letter of Rev. Dr. Fitzgerald, P.P., Ballingarry, County Tipperary, July 10, 1865.
‡ Statement of Rev. W. Wall, P.P., Clonoulty, Cashel, September, 1865.
§ *Irish Magazine*, October, 1810, p. 482.

self accidentally while playing with "a swing" in the garden at Golden Hills.[*]

29. Major Sirr, who, acting upon the information supplied by Francis Higgins, shot at and captured Lord Edward Fitzgerald, is no stranger to the reader of these pages. For a pithy *resumé* of his life he would do well to consult Curran's speech in the case of Hevey *versus* Sirr.

" For the purpose of this trial", said he, "I must carry back your attention to the melancholy period of 1798. It was at that sad crisis that the defendant, from an obscure individual, started into notice and consequence. It is in the hotbed of public calamity that such portentous and inauspicious products are accelerated without being matured. From being a town-major, a name scarcely legible in the list of public incumbrances, he became at once invested with all the powers of absolute authority. The life and the liberty of every man seemed to have been surrendered to his disposal. With this gentleman's extraordinary elevation begins the story of the sufferings and ruin of the plaintiff".

The cessation of the rebellion, and the introduction of a milder system of government, found Henry Charles Sirr's occupation gone. He became a " picture fancier", cultivated the fine arts, frequented auctions, accumulated fossils and minerals, sonorously sung psalms, and exhibited the whites of his eyes rather than the blackness of his heart. Fifty years ago he was appointed police magistrate of Dublin, and continued to discharge its duties until his death in 1841, when "the remains of the assassin of Lord Edward",[†] writes Mr. Gilbert,

[*] Letter from W. L. Hackett, Esq , M.A., Ex-Mayor, dated, " Clonmel, April 16th, 1865".

[†] This phrase is not, perhaps, strictly accurate. The professor of medical jurisprudence in the University of Dublin, addressing the writer of these pages, says: " An inquest was held in Newgate on the body of Lord E. Fitzgerald, and on the evi-

"were deposited in Werburgh's churchyard", the same mortuary which contains Lord Edward's bones. "The stone, shaded by a melancholy tree", adds Mr. Gilbert, "does not explicitly state that the town major of '98 was buried under it, and appears to have been originally placed over the corpse of his father, who preceded him in that office, and was also distinguished by his bad character, a fact unknown to the biographers of Lord Edward Fitzgerald. A more infamous tool than Henry Charles Sirr was probably never employed; the bare relation of his atrocities would far exceed the wildest fiction which ever emanated from the brain of the most morbid romancist".

30. Identified with Major Sirr in most of his plans, perfidies, and perils, all that has been said of Sirr is applicable to Swan, with this exception, that Sirr professed to be a saint, while his deputy Swan, frank, jolly, and outspoken, claimed to be no better than an "honest "sinner". Of Swan's efficiency as a rebel-hunter the Sham Squire was a constant eulogist; and in one of his laudations, it is stated that the government proved their appreciation of "Major Swan's" services by awarding him the commission of the peace for every county in Ireland.

31. Major Sandys, perhaps the worst member of that terrible triumvirate of soi-disant majors, who daily stung the people to madness and death, filled the office of Governor of the Provost, the Bastile of Ireland. Here, cruelties the most revolting were hourly practised under the direction of Major Sandys, who, as the brother-in-law of Mr. Cooke, the Under Secretary to the Lord Lieutenant, enjoyed thorough connivance and immunity. Dr. Madden asserts that indulgences of air, light, and

dence of Surgeon Leake, a verdict returned of death from water on the chest. This fact is not known to many. I have *sometimes* mentioned it to my class when lecturing on forensic *medicine*".

food were sold to the state prisoners by Major Sandys, and that he remitted tortures at the triangle, on receiving either money, or written orders for goods, plate, or pictures, addressed by the prisoners to friends outside. The rapacity of Major Sandys, especially for plate, proved at last insatiable.   Curran's memorable speech *in re* Hevey, states: " A learned and respected brother barrister had a silver cup; the Major heard that for many years it had borne an inscription of ' *Erin go bragh*', which meant ' Ireland for ever'.   The Major considered this perseverance in guilt for such a length of years a forfeiture of the delinquent vessel. My poor friend was accordingly robbed of his cup".

These and even graver charges were made by Curran, not only in the lifetime of Major Sandys, but under the very flash of his eye.   " And I state this", exclaimed Curran, " because I see Major Sandys in court, and because I feel I can prove the fact beyond the possibility of denial. If he does not dare to appear, so called upon as I have called upon him, I prove it by his not daring to appear.   If he does venture to come forward, I will prove it by his own oath ; or if he ventures to deny a syllable I have stated, I will prove by irrefragable evidence that his denial was false and perjnred".

A terrible vicissitude, followed by a still more terrible disease, overtook the once potential Major Sandys. His family begged bread from door to door; and he himself died in extreme destitution and bodily suffering.

32. John Giffard, an illiterate and illiberal alumnus of the Blue Coat Hospital, began political life, like many a better cotemporary, as an ardent patriot and member of the Volunteer Association. 'He also practised as an apothecary, as did Lucas before him ; but he soon forsook the pestle for the pen, and acquired the sole editoral control of an influential newspaper, the *Dublin Journal*, which had been started, and for fifty years

16

ably edited, by George Faulkner, the friend of Swift and Chesterfield. Like the Sham Squire, whom he resembled in more ways than one, Giffard at once prostituted the newspaper to the worst purposes of the venal party which ruled supreme in Ireland some eighty years ago; and it has been stated that the paper disclosed such violence, virulence, vulgarity, and mendacity, that at the present date its advocacy would be held detrimental to the cause of any party. Yet Giffard was preferred to places of honour and emolument. Besides holding a lucrative office under the Back-Stairs Viceroy, Mr. Beresford in the Revenue, Giffard succeeded his brother journalist Higgins as sub-sheriff of Dublin. We have seen it stated by Mr. Gilbert in his *History*, that Giffard is understood to have received the latter appointment for the express purpose of packing the jury which in 1794 convicted Hamilton Rowan. Giffard was called "The dog in office", and his paper " The Dog's Journal". The artists who caricatured Sheriff Higgins were placed under arrest.* The same despotic policy pursued Sheriff Giffard's tormentors. The following paragraph, dated October 3d, 1794, doubtless refers to Giffard.

"A printer in South King Street was taken into custody by Messrs. Shee, etc., charged with printing and publishing a caricature of a dog in his last moments, with his confession and dying words. The picture and types were taken possession of".†

Hamilton Rowan and Dr. William Drennan were then under trial by Mr. Giffard's juries. The following admission we find in the *Beresford Correspondence*.

"Government are determined to hang Rowan, if possible, but they have not yet shown any suspicion of any person here being concerned in the plot, in order to lull them into security. No person knows as much

* See p. 85, ante.
† *Masonic Magazine* for October, 1794, p. 383.

as I now tell you except Lord Westmoreland, the
Attorney-General, and Sackville Hamilton".—*Beresford
Correspondence,* v. ii., p. 2ο.

Giffard sought to stab with his pen, and pike with his
tongue every friend to national progress. In reply to
a charge of treason, Grattan thus retorted : " It proceeds
from a hired traducer of his country, the excommuni-
cated of his fellow-citizens, the regal rebel, the unpun-
ished ruffian, the bigoted agitator. In the city, a fire-
brand ; in the court, a liar ; in the streets, a bully ; in
the field, a coward. And so obnoxious is he to the very
party he wishes to espouse, that he is only supportable
by doing those dirty acts the less vulgar refuse to exe-
cute". The quondam apothecary swallowed this box of
bitter pills. In 1817 Giffard ceased to edit the *Dublin
Journal.* In not less than twenty numbers, the following appeared, among other paragraphs affecting not
merely Mr. Giffard's reputation, but that of the party of
which he had long been the champion and the protege :
" Since Mr. Giffard ceased on the 1st of July, 1816, to
have directly or indirectly any concern with this paper,
it has rapidly increased in circulation, and we are now
satisfied that the public can fairly appreciate the value
of an independent print, which wishes to soothe and
not to irritate the angry passions which have so long
agitated the country".*

Giffard amassed a large fortune, and built himself a
handsome residence, known as Dromartin Castle, Dun-
drum.

33. Lieutenant Hepenstall is the person whom Sir
Jonah Barrington, in his *Historic Anecdotes of the Union,*
and afterwards in his *Personal Sketches* (v. iii., p 267–
271) describes as Lieutenant H—— " the walking
gallows". This notorious officer, originally an apothecary like Giffard, was a Goliah in stature, and a Nero
in feeling. If Hepenstall met a peasant who could not

* *Dublin Journal,* July 2nd, 1817.

satisfactorily account for himself, he knocked him down
with a blow from his fist, which was quite as effectual
as a sledge hammer, and then adjusting a noose round
the prisoner's neck, drew the rope over his own
shoulders and trotted about, the victim's legs dangling
in the air and his tongue protruding, until death at
last put an end to the torture.   These details, almost
incredible at the present day, have been authenticated
by several witnesses, and even admitted by Hepenstall
himself at the trial of Hyland when Lord Norbury
complimented him as having done no act which was not
natural to zealous, loyal, and efficient officer.   Prefixed
to the *Irish Magazine* for 1810 a picture of Hepenstall in
his capacity of executioner appears.   His features,
handsome in their conformation and seraphic in their
expression, present a puzzle to the students of Lavater's
theory.   The print is accompanied by a startling memoir
of Hepenstall's atrocities, which we find corroborated
by an article in the *Press* newspaper of January 11,
1798, and copied by Dr. Madden.   That article speaks
of Hepenstall as a person well known by the name of
" the walking gallows".   In conjunction with higher
colleagues, he had continued, long anterior to the outbreak of '98, to goad the people into revolt by such
brutalities as we have described.   Hepenstall did not
long live to enjoy the interval of repose which succeeded
his unsleeping vigilance in '98.   In 1800, as we are
assured by Cox, he became afflicted with *morbus pedicula-
ris;* his body was literally devoured by vermin, and after
twenty-one days' suffering, he died in great agony.   Dr.
Madden says that this event occurred in 1813 ; Mr. Cox
gives 1804 as the year ; but the Sham Squire enables
us to fix the date positively.   In his *Journal* of September 18, 1800, Mr. Higgins touchingly records :

" Died on Thursday night, of a dropsical complaint,
"*Lieutenant* Edward Hepenstall, of the 68th Regiment,
"*sometime* back an officer in the Wicklow militia—a

" gentleman whose intrepidity and spirit during the
" Rebellion rendered much general good, and himself
"highly obnoxious to traitors". And then follows a
tribute to " the *qualities which endeared Mr. Hepenstall
to his family and friends*".

Luckily, or unluckily, for Hepenstall's memory, his
fast friend the Sham Squire did not write his epitaph,
and the lieutenant's grave remains in St. Andrew's
churchyard uninscribed. It was once suggested by Dr.
Barrett that the inscription should be confined to two
lines :

" Here lie the bones of Hepenstall,
Judge, jury, gallows, rope, and all".

Lieutenant Hepenstall's brother, who survived him
for a few years, received a large pension soon after from
the crown. His relict was married by Archbishop Agar
to Dr. Patrick Duigenan, as we gather from an entry
in Donnybrook Parish Register, dated October 19,
1807, and printed in the Rev. B. H. Blacker's work
descriptive of the locality.

34. " Spectacle Knox", as General Cockburn styles
him, is Alexander Knox, whom Lord Macaulay calls
" a remarkable man". He began his career as assist-
tant private secretary to Lord Castlereagh, in whose correspondence and that of Mr. Wilberforce a mass of his
letters may be found, to say nothing of several volumes
ostensibly devoted to the preservation of his epistles.
Mr. Knox drew up the report of the Secret Committee,
and made himself generally useful as a scribe during
the reign of terror in Ireland. When the late Sir
Robert Peel came to Ireland as Chief Secretary, accompanied by a young and beautiful wife, Mr. Knox fell
wildly in love with her. He was fully sensible of the
madness and illegality of his passion, from which he
strove to fly—but in vain. In a state of temporary
mania he nearly destroyed himself by an act of bodily
mutilation. Our authorities for this story are the late

Surgeon Peel and Dr. Labatt, who professionally attended Mr. Knox, and communicated the facts to an eminent physician still living. Knox survived for many years after, but the vigour of his intellect had sunk, and his eye had lost its former sparkle.

36. Captain Armstrong. The arrests at Bond's were followed by the betrayal and execution of John and Henry Sheares. To those hapless victims—brothers by blood and barristers by profession—Captain J. W. Armstrong, of the King's County militia, had, with vampire instinct, obtained an introduction through the agency of a mutual friend. Carried away by the ardour of youth and the strong revolutionary current of the time, they unreservedly expressed their projects. Armstrong fanned the flame, helped their plans with hints derived from military reading and experience, wormed himself into their confidence, partook of their hospitality, mingled with their families, and, as has been stated by Mr. Curran, fondled on his knee the child of the parent whom he had marked out for death, while, to quote the reminiscence of one of the family, Mrs. Sheares sang at the harp for his amusement. Armstrong received promotion, a commission of the peace, and a pension of £500 a year. Fifty-six years subsequent to this tragedy, we heard with surprise that Armstrong was still alive! The late Maurice R. Leyne, addressing the present writer in 1854, says: "I saw the old scoundrel, Captain Armstrong, travelling by boat from Limerick. He was a passenger, and was attended by a body-guard of two policemen with loaded arms. He was the object of much observation and whisperings while on board; and as he was leaving the packet at, I think, Banagher, one of the boatmen with vengeful malice addressed him as '*Mr. Sheares*', pretending he had mistaken his name. He was known as 'Sheares Armstrong' among the *people*".

Soon after, the present writer, then a very young

man, addressed a letter to Captain Armstrong conveying some queries, which merely elicited the following note, suggesting a personal interview; but we recoiled from such close contact, and the matter dropped:

"Ballycumber, May, 17th, 1854.

"SIR—I have received your letter, I have no objection to a personal interview with you, and to give you every information in my power on the subject of your inquiries, but I decline writing anything about it.

"Your most obedient servant,

"J. W. ARMSTRONG.

"To W. J. Fitzpatrick, Esq.".

Captain Armstrong's seal displays the device of three arms outstretched in an attitude of hostility. His incorrigible longevity had heartily wearied and disgusted the Treasury. At length, one fine morning in 1858, he died, after having drawn altogether about £30,000. Whether his family inherit any share of his pension we have not been able to ascertain.

37. Thomas Reynolds has been already noticed, p. 164, *et seq., ante.*

38. To William Cope the same remark applies.

39. Of Justice Godfrey there is little of interest to tell. An instance of his magisterial activity may be found in the *Dublin Magazine* for December, 1799, p. 378.

It will be observed that Sir George Cockburn, in his list of the government of Ireland during the reign of terror, makes no allusion to the Viceroy, whom John Magee, for having styled "the cold hearted and cruel Camden", was prosecuted by the Orange Attorney-General Saurin, and heavily punished. The truth is that Lord Camden was a cypher. Watson Taylor acted as private secretary to his Excellency at this period, and he mentioned to Moore, on the 19th October, 1838, that "Lord Camden was constantly outvoted in his wish for a more moderate system of government by

Clare and Castlereagh". Watson Taylor, when in Ireland, was more busy writing songs than despatches; and we find that, among other effusions, he threw off the well-known, piece "Croppies, lie down".

K.

MACNALLY AND TURNER.

The *Cornwallis Correspondence*, published in 1859, confirms the allegation that Leonard MacNally, the confidential law adviser to, and eloquent counsel for, the leaders of the Irish rebellion of 1798, was in the pay of the unscrupulous Tory government of that day, and basely betrayed the secrets of his confiding clients. MacNally had been himself a member of the Whig Club, and the Society of United Irishmen, and went so far as to challenge and fight Sir Jonah Barrington, who had indulged in stinging animadversion of it. He was apparently a staunch democrat, and enjoyed the most unlimited confidence of the popular party. He survived until 1820; and with such consummate hypocrisy was his turpitude veiled, that men who could read the inmost soul of others never for a moment suspected him. The late W. H. Curran, in the *Life* of his father (i. 884-5), pronounces a brilliant eulogium on "the *many endearing traits*" in MacNally's character, and adds that he (W. H. Curran) is filled with "emotions of the most lively and respectful gratitude". We farther learn that "for three-and-forty years Mr. MacNally was the friend" of Curran, and that "he performed the duties of the relation with the most uncompromising and romantic fidelity". Years after, when the late D. Owen Maddyn urged W. H. Curran to bring out a new edition of the *Life* of his father, he replied that it would *be difficult* to do so, as he should have to cancel the *passage to* which I have referred, and indulge in severe reflections upon the memory of MacNally, a near relation of whom was practising in the court where Mr. W. H. Curran sat as judge. Curran's regard for MacNally was steadily consistent. In 1807, on the accession of the Whigs to power, Mr. Curran exerted the large influence which he then possessed, to obtain a silk gown for his friend. The Duke of Bedford, however, who was then viceroy, having discovered the base compact which subsisted between his Tory predecessors and MacNally, rejected the claim. But the reasons for the refusal were not then known, and the popular party regarded as a grievance this treatment of their favourite counsel. Charles Phillips, who practised for many years at the same bar with MacNally, thus notices, in one of the last editions of *Curran and his Contemporaries*, the report that MacNally had a pension :—" The thing is incredible! If I was called upon to point out, next to Curran, the man most obnoxious to the government —who most hated them, and was most hated by them —it would have been Leonard MacNally—that Mac-Nally, who, amidst the military audience, stood by Curran's side while he denounced oppression, defied power, and dared every danger!"

After the death of MacNally,* his representative claimed a continuance of the secret pension of £300 a-year, which he had been enjoying since the calamitous period of the rebellion. Lord Wellesley, the viceroy, demanded a detailed statement of the circumstances under which the unholy agreement had been made, and after some hesitation it was furnished. The startling truth soon became known. O'Connell announced the fact publicly, and used it as an argument for dissuading the people from embarking in treasonable projects.

The MS. volume containing "An account of the

* MacNally must have died intestate, as we can find no trace of his will in the Irish probate court.

Secret Service Money Expenditure", discloses the frequent payment of large sums to MacNally, irrespective of his pension, during the troubled times which preceded and followed the Union. This engine of corruption—as recorded by the same document—invariably passed through the hands of a Mr. J. Pollock.

It is suggestive of intensely melancholy ideas, to glance over this blood-tinged record. The initials of MacNally perpetually rise like an infernal phantom through its pages. Passing over the myriad entries throughout the interval of 1797 to 1803, we come to the period of Robert Emmet's insurrection. In the *State Trials* we find MacNally, on September 19, 1803, acting as counsel for Emmet at the Special Commission. Under date September 14, 1803, "*L. M.* £100", appears on record in the Secret Service Money Book. This retainer, doubtless, overbalanced poor Emmet's fee. The gifted young Irishman was found guilty and executed. No one is permitted to see him in prison, but MacNally, who pays him a visit on the morning of his execution, addresses him as " Robert", and shows him every manifestation of affection. On the 25th August, 1803, "Mr. Pollock, for L. M., £100", is also recorded. Sometimes MacNally signed the receipts for Secret Service Money "J. W.": but besides that the writing in these documents is identical with his acknowledged autograph, the clerk's endorsement "L. M. N." leaves no room for doubt. The original receipts were kindly shown to us in 1854 by Dr. Madden.

The masterly manner in which MacNally fortified his duplicity is worthy of attention. As I already observed, persons usually the most clear-sighted regarded him as a paragon of purity and worth. Defending Finney, in conjunction with Philpot Curran, the latter giving way to the impulse of his generous feelings, *threw his* arm over the shoulder of MacNally, and with *emotion* said : " My old and excellent friend, I have long known and respected the honesty of your heart, but never until this occasion was I acquainted with the extent of your abilities. I am not in the habit of paying compliments where they are undeserved". Tears fell from Mr. Curran as he hung over his friend.* Nineteen years after, Curran died; and he died with the illusion undispelled. From the *Freeman's Journal* of October 18, 1817, we gather that Judge Burton wrote from London to MacNally, as the old and tried friend of Curran, to announce the approaching death of the great patriot.†

Sir Jonah Barrington insinuates that MacNally was an unpopular companion in society. The late Dr. Fulton, addressing us in 1858, observed: " L. MacNally was a most agreeable companion—quite a little Curran, and his political views were considered even more democratic than Curran's. He made a bet that he would dine at the mess of the Fermanagh militia, an ultra Orange body. He joined them unasked, and made himself so agreeable, and every man there so pleasant, that he received a general invitation to their mess from that day. He was a most pleasing poet, and wrote, among other effusions, the well known song, 'Sweet Lass of Richmond Hill'".

Sir Jonah Barrington, who often sacrificed strict accuracy to sensational effect, has given us, in his *Personal Sketches*, a monstrous caricature of MacNally's outward man. Nevertheless, although, like Curran, of low stature, he had, as we are informed by O'Keefe, who knew him intimately, " a handsome, expressive countenance, and fine sparkling dark eye". ‡

Mr. MacNally must at least have had a rare amount of what is familiarly termed " cheek". In his defence of Watty Cox, at a public trial in Dublin, Feb. 26,

* *Life of Curran* by his Son, v. i. p. 397.
† We contributed to *Notes and Queries* some portions of this paper.
‡ Recollections of John O'Keefe, v. i. p. 45.

1811, he says, "few men become . . . informers until they have forfeited public character".[*]

The Duke of Wellington, in the following letter, probably refers to MacNally, whose insatiable cupidity is very likely to have prompted him to seek further recognition of his unworthy services by applying for some office in the gift of the crown:

"London, 29th June, 1807.

"MY DEAR SIR,—I agree entirely with you respecting the employment of our informer. Such a measure would do much mischief. It would disgust the loyal of all descriptions, at the same time that it would render useless our private communications with him, as no further trust would be placed in him by the disloyal. I think that it might be hinted to him that he would lose much of his profit, if, by accepting the public employment of government, he were to lose the confidence of his party, and consequently the means of giving us information. . . . . .

"Believe me, ever yours most sincerely,

"ARTHUR WELLESLEY.[†]

"To James Trail, Esq.".

The editor of the *Cornwallis Papers*, Mr. Ross, in enumerating with others (iii. 319), one Samuel Turner, who received a pension of £800 a year at the same time as MacNally, declares that he has been unable to obtain any particulars of this man. There can be no doubt that Mr. Turner belonged to the same school as MacNally.

---

[*] *Irish Magazine*, April, 1811, p. 45.

[†] Who is the "Catholic orator" referred to in the following note from Sir A. Wellesley to Lord Hawkesbury ? (p. 291).

"Dublin Castle, 8th Jan., 1808.

"The extracts of letters sent to you by Lord Grenville, were sent to us by ————, the Catholic orator, two months ago. The ———— mentioned is *a man who was desirous of being employed by government as a spy;* and his trade is that of spy to all parties. He offered himself to ————, Lord Fingal, and others, *as well as to* us; and we now watch him closely".

The old Dublin directories, in the list of "judges and barristers", record the name of Samuel Turner, Esq., who was called to the bar at Easter Term, 1788; and the following paragraph, which we exhume from the London *Courier* of December 5th, 1803, suggests a painful glimpse of the grounds on which Mr. Turner obtained a pension at the same time as MacNally:

"On Friday last, Samuel Turner, Esq., barrister-at-law, was brought to the bar of the Court of King's Bench, in custody of the keeper of Kilmainham prison, under a charge of attainder, passed in the Irish Parliament, as one concerned in the rebellion of the year 1798; but, having shown that he was no way concerned therein, that he had not been in the country for a year and seven months prior to passing that act, *i.e.*, for thirteen months prior to the rebellion, and therefore could not be the person alluded to, his Majesty's Attorney-General confessed the same, and Mr. Turner was discharged accordingly".

To return to MacNally:

A gentleman who conducted the leading popular paper of Dublin some forty years ago, in a communication addressed to us, observes: "It was in 1811, during the prolonged trial of the Catholic delegates (Lord Fingal, Sheridan, Burke, and Kirwan) that doubts were first entertained of MacNally's fidelity. MacNally took a leading part in the counsels of the delegates and their friends. We observed that the Orange Attorney-General, Saurin, always appeared wondrously well prepared next day for the arguments which we had arranged. MacNally, no donbt, used to communicate to the law officers of the crown all the secrets of his confiding clients".

MacGuicken, the attorney of the United Irishmen, of whom we shall speak presently, was also subsidized.

The world now knows the guilt of MacNally and MacGuicken. Their memory has been execrated. But

surely the seducer of these once honourable men deserves a share of the obloquy.   Who was the man who
first debauched the counsel and solicitor of the United
Irishmen ?

L.

JOHN POLLOCK.

In the *Memoirs and Correspondence of Marquis Cornwallis* (vol. iii. p. 320), a letter appears addressed by
Mr. Secretary Cooke to the Lord Lieutenant, in which
various persons are recommended, including MacNally
and MacGuicken, as fit recipients for a share in the
£1,500 per annum which in 1799 had been placed for
secret service at his excellency's disposal.   Mr. Cooke
thus concludes : " Pollock's services ought to be
thought of.   He managed Mac—— and MacGuicken,
and did much.   He received the place of Clerk of the
Crown and Peace, and he has the fairest right to indemnification".   Mr. Charles Ross, the editor, reminds his
readers that " Mac" is " Leonard MacNally, Esq., a
barrister of some reputation, who was regularly employed by the rebels, and was entirely in their confidence.   He was author of various plays and other
works ; born 1752, died 1820".

It may interest the students of that eventful period
of Irish history to learn some account of the unscrupulous and wily person who succeeded in corrupting the
counsel and solicitor of the unhappy men who staked
their lives and fortunes in '98.   On this nogociation
some important events hinged. · For almost every name
mentioned in the *Cornwallis Correspondence* Mr. Ross
has furnished an explanatory foot-note.   In the page
following the mention of Mr. Pollock's name the editor
says : " It has been found impossible to ascertain anything in regard to most of these individuals" ; and as

we have no note relative to Mr. Pollock, it may be presumed that Mr. Ross knows little or nothing of him.

Half a century ago John Pollock was a well-known solicitor in Dublin. In the *Dublin Directory* for 1777 his name appears for the first time, and his residence is given as 31 Mary Street. In 1781 he removed to 12 Anne Street, and in 1784 to Jervis Street. In 1786, Mr. Pollock was appointed " solicitor to the trustees of the linen manufacture"; in 1795 we find him Clerk of the Crown and Peace for the province of Leinster, and Clerk of the Peace for the County of Dublin. In the year 1800, Mr. Pollock is gazetted to the enormous sinecure of Clerk of the Pleas of the Exchequer.

The MS. volume, already noticed, containing an " account of secret service money expenditure employed in detecting treasonable conspiracies", chronicles the frequent payment of pecuniary stimuli to Mr. Pollock. On December 11, 1797, £300 is recorded; "April 20, 1798, John Pollock, £110", appears. June 15, £109 7s. 6d.; August 18, £56 17s. 6d; August 28, ditto; September 14, do.; and on January 18, 1799, the large sum of £1,137 10s., arrests attention. There are, however, various other payments to Mr. Pollock, which it would be tedious to enumerate.

As soon as he received the bloated sinecure of Deputy Clerk of the Pleas, Mr. Pollock removed from Jervis Street to No. 11 Mountjoy Square East, where, as I am informed by M—— S——, Esq. he lived in a style of lavish magnificence, and spent not less than £9,000 a-year. This reign of luxury lasted until the year 1817, when Mr. Pollock was suddenly hurled from his throne.

The sinecure office of Clerk of the Pleas of the Exchequer had been " in some measure created for Lord Buckinghamshire" as a reward for his important services in India,* as well as in Ireland, when discharging the

* *Sketches of Irish Political Characters*, London, 1799, p. 49

services of Chief Secretary. Sir J. Newport declared in parliament, on April 29, 1816, that his lordship's fees had amounted to £35,000 per annum. Lord Buckinghamshire died on Feb. 5 in that year. From the *Dublin Evening Post* of February 20, 1817, we learn that " Mr. Pollock still continues to fulfil the duties of the office, and the writs which had been authenticated by the signature of ' Buckinghamshire', are now signed 'John Pollock'". The duties of the office were indolently, inefficiently, and often fraudulently discharged: "Purchasers can have no security", observes the same authority ; " we have been informed of a judgment of £10,000 *omitted* in a certain certificate. It is one of the most lucrative and unnecessary offices in the country", continues the *Post* : " all the duty is performed by the deputy, Mr. Pollock, who derives about £5,000 a-year. All this is made up of fees on the distribution of justice in a single court of law. If this unnecessary office were now extinguished, how much would it cheapen justice to the public ! What a number of poor suitors would then procure justice who are now excluded from its benefits by their poverty !"

But the estimate of the *Post* would seem to have been "under the mark". On Monday, April 29, Leslie Foster declared that Mr. Pollock "drew £10,000 out of the profits, and on which he ought to pay the salaries of the other clerks; but, instead of this, he pocketed the whole of the money, leaving them to raise the fees upon the suitors on no other authority than their own assumptions !"

The son of a late eminent solicitor, in a letter addressed to us, dated Sept. 25th, 1865, thus refers to Mr. Pollock and the lax practices then prevalent :

" In 1816 my father died. Long before his death " my mother used to hear him and other professional " men talk of the general extravagance and demorali- "*zation* that existed among the officials of the Four

" Courts; several of whom, from poor clerks, were
" floated up to wealth by the rise of the times. Most
" of the higher class among them habitually antici-
" pated their incomes, availing themselves of the faci-
" lities for doing so then afforded by the paper-credit
" or kite-flying* system. As to Pollock, he lived mag-
" nificently in Mountjoy Square and in the country ;
" and like those, for the most part, who spend freely,
" he was not, indeed, disliked; though if, in taxing an
" attorney's costs, he received a note, in order, after
" deducting what was due him, to return the balance,
" he would, as it were by way of a joke, laugh, and
" say, ' We 'll talk·of this another time', and keep the
" note—the attorney not daring to object, lest he should
" be proportionately a sufferer when he 'd *next* have to
" get his costs taxed ! But, in time, the attorneys be-
" came sufficiently *up* to the great cost-taxer's failing
" as regards note-keeping, to be on their guard against
" it, by not letting him finger more than he was actually
" entitled to receive. Like ' robbers all at Parga', it
" should be added, that others of those gentry of the
" courts, Papists as well as Protestants, were Pollocks
" in their way, ' feathering their nests well', and even-
" tually purchasing estates. At last a government
" commission came, and reformed this very corrupt
" system".

The peculation upon which Mr. Pollock had so long
fattened soon began to enkindle a wide sensation. A
commission of inquiry was held, and some startling
facts came to light. Mr. Leslie Foster, afterwards
Chief Baron Foster, observed : " To show the progress

* This phrase greatly puzzled a member of the English bar,
Lord Redesdale, who was sent to Ireland as Chancellor. Plunket endeavoured to explain. " In England, my lord, the wind
raises the kite, but in Ireland the kite raises the wind". " I
feel no better informed yet, Mr. Plunket", replied the matter-
of-fact Chancellor. Possibly our readers may say the same.
—W. J. F.

17

of abuse, he might pursue the history of the place held
by this deputy. In 1803, his profits amounted to
£3,000 a year. After that time the office was placed
under regulations which reduced its emoluments to
one-third; and in consideration of what was called the
vested right of the possessor, he received a compensation of £2,000, which, joined to his fees, made up
£3,000, his original income. Instead of being worth
£3,000 at present, the office yielded £7,000 a year,
having increased £5,000 since 1803; which, with a
compensation of £2.000 for anticipated loss, amounted
to the £7,000 mentioned. All these abuses spring
from the circumstance that the power of taxation is
lodged in the hands of officers who were interested in
the sums they imposed, or in the abuses they con-
nived at".

At this time, as appears from the *Directory*, Mr. Pollock not only held the lucrative office of crown solicitor,
but various sinecures besides. The *Cornwallis Papers*
had not then divulged that all this emolument and
peculation was nothing more or less than the wages
earned by the corruptor of MacNally and MacGuicken!

It further appeared that £13,000 extra had been
seized upon and squandered by understrappers. The
commissioners pursued their inquiries. "They unex-
pectedly discovered", says the *Post* of May 4, 1817,
" an apparently humble satellite who obtained an income of £1,300 per annum from fees, and who, without being ambitious of even the celebrity which an
almanac confers, quietly revolved about the brilliant
orb of his superior, as much unknown to the public as
any of the satellites of Jupiter". A more monstrous
labyrinth of inveterate abuses had never before been
explored. Impeachment became unavoidable; and we
find the Attorney-General, Saurin, bringing forward
nine distinct charges against Mr. Pollock. One para-
graph will suffice for a specimen: " With respect to

the taxation of costs, the officer has exercised an arbitrary and discretionary power in demanding fees; and that the fees received have, in some instances, exceeded the amount of the costs themselves". In the Court of Exchequer, July 1, 1817, the Chief Baron O'Grady, afterwards Lord Guillamore, passed judgment on Mr. Pollock. He thus concluded: "We are obliged to declare, from the acts lately for the first time come to our knowledge, that he has abused his duty—abused his discretion—he has done acts without authority—by accepting gratuities he has degraded the court—he has permitted fictitious charges, and has raised the fees of this court to bring them to the level of higher fees of other courts, instead of bringing down what was highest to the level of those that were lower—these acts have tended to a perverse and mal-administration of justice; and it is, therefore, due to the public—to the ends of justice—to the authority and purity of the court—to the maintaining of the court's authority over its own officer—and to the end of the officer presiding with effect over those under him, that Mr. Pollock be removed, and he is thereby removed from the office of Deputy Clerk of the Pleas of this Court". The *Correspondent* and *Saunders*, of the day, do not report the case. The foregoing has been extracted from the *Freeman's Journal.* At the period in question, it does not seem to have been always easy for reporters to obtain access to courts of law during the progress of peculiar cases. The *Freeman* of July 12, 1817, devotes a leading article to the discussion of a petulant remark made by Mr. Jackson (Lord Chief Justice Norbury's registrar) to the effect that " he *would prevent the court from being turned into a printing office*".

Mr. S—— tells me that he remembers having noticed, with some pain, the once swaggering and influential John Pollock reduced to comparative poverty and prostration. Mr. Pollock did not long survive his humiliation. In 1818, Leonard MacNally saw his seducer consigned to the grave.

It may be worth adding, that Chief Baron O'Grady claimed the right of patronage in the appointment of successors to Lord Buckinghamshire and Mr. Pollock; and having named his son and brother to the overgrown sinecures, much comment was excited, which resulted in an elaborate public trial of the judge's right. Saurin contended that the king, not the court, had the right of appointment.

WALTER COX.

The seduction of the once indomitable patriot Watty Cox, who was eventually bought up by the Richmond government, was also due to Mr. Pollock.

Mr. John Pollock, in a letter addressed to Sir Arthur Wellesley, dated January 12, 1809, directing his attention to MacNevin's *Pieces of Irish History*,* goes on to say (p. 534):

"Whether this book was originally printed in New York is for the present immaterial; it is now in print in Dublin, and, no doubt, will be circulated through the country with indefatigable zeal. My information says it is the precursor of a French invasion; *and certainly the whole object of the book is calculated, and with great ability executed, in order to show the necessity of a separation of this country from England, and to procure a French army to be received here as allies.* Your means of information are, no doubt, most ample; it may, however, not be improper in me to say to you that *if you have Cox*† (who keeps a small book-shop in

* *Civil Correspondence and Memoranda of F. M. Arthur Duke of Wellington*; edited by his son.

† Mr Pollock was no stranger to Cox. who in his *Magazine* r 1811, pp. 353, 434, makes reference to him.

Anglesea Street), he can let you into the whole object of sending this book to Ireland at this time; and further, if you have not Cox, believe me that no sum of money at all within reason would be misapplied in riveting him to the government. I have spoken of this man before to Sir Edward Littlehales and to Sir Charles Saxton. He is the most able, and, if not secured, by far the most formidable man that I know of in Ireland". He was " secured" accordingly; but Lord Mulgrave, afterwards Marquis of Normanby, on his accession to the viceroyalty, deprived Cox of his pension. Under the regime of the Duke of Richmond was also accomplished the seduction of an able Roman Catholic satirist, Dr. Brennan, who continued until his death to enjoy a pension of £200 a year for ridiculing in his *Milesian Magazine* the Catholic leaders of that day.

A correspondent, Mr. C. C. Hoey, sends us the following note touching Walter Cox:—

" Scattered through the pages of Cox's (Watty) *Irish Magazine* from 1807 to 1814, now extremely scarce, may be found a great amount of uncollected information that may be advantageously read with the light of the *Wellington Correspondence.* Though Cox was finally bought up to silence, he did good service for his creed and country. In those years, and that principally on the veto question, the career of this man was extraordinary, and notwithstanding his weak points, he is entitled to a distinct biography. The ' Shrewd Man' and the ' Gunsmith', alluded to under Secretary Trail's letter, was no other than Walter Cox. Cox's father was a bricklayer, who was dragged to prison by order of Lord Carhampton, and suffered some indignities and even torture, which never left the mind of his son, and finally made him resolve on turning author, to retaliate for the severities he witnessed in 1798. Cox himself was originally a gunsmith; he supplied military data to Lord Edward Fitzgerald, enjoyed

his confidence as well as others in the Directory, and
afterwards became his lordship's biographer in the
pages of his own magazine. Cox, though a youth in
1792, held the command of the second company of
the Goldsmiths' Corps of Volunteers, whose last meeting was announced to take place on the parade ground
of *St. Michael le Pole*, Great Ship Street, but was prevented by a proclamation of the government and. a
turn out of the whole garrison, similar to the Clontarf affair of '43. This, I believe, was the last attempted meeting of the volunteers in Dublin. Dr.
Madden inserts a query in the fourth volume of the
last edition of his *United Irishmen* (p. 599) as to
whether some Mr. Cox who received secret service
money in 1803 was identical with Watty Cox; but it
is not likely, as from Lord Hardwick's official vindication of his government it appears that it was meditated in 1803 to place the formidable gunsmith under
arrest as a dangerous democrat. Cox suffered imprisonment and the pillory several times for his writings in
the *Irish Magazine;* the most noted was "the Painter
Cut; a Vision", of which he was found guilty and sentenced to pay a fine of three hundred pounds, and enter
into security himself for one thousand, with two others
of five hundred pounds each, to keep in good behaviour
for seven years, as well as suffer one year's confinement
in Newgate. A great portion of the priesthood exerted
themselves in striving to put down his *Magazine* for the
part he took against the veto, and he attacked the government so severely that Crown Solicitor Pollock suggested he should be bought up as being the most formidable character of the time. Archbishop Troy and Bishop
Milner (who subsequently became an anti-vetoist) and
Lord Fingal received no quarter at his hands. In his
Magazine may be found a good deal of matter connected
with those men, not to be found elsewhere. Sir Jonah
Barrington comes in for a share of castigation for his

shortcomings and backslidings ; he accuses him of bringing forward a motion in the Irish House of Commons
" to confiscate the property of Doctor Esmond, who
headed the rebel force at Prosperons, and thereby deprived his infant children of bread". He says Sir Jonah
Barrington printed his *History of the Union* in Dublin
in 1802, but, as he did not give it to the public then,
we presume he gave it to another quarter. There
is also some matter connected with the career of
Reynolds, O'Brien, Hepenstal, and many others, which
I think has not met the notice of the historians
of 1798. The admirably executed caricatures published in his *Magazine* were done by Mr. Brocas, who
afterwards was appointed head master of the Government School of Design, Royal Dublin Society. After
lying for some years in Newgate, Cox was at last bought
over. He resided for awhile in the house No. 12
Clarence Street, off Summer Hill, which still goes by
the name of " Cox's Cot", and his name appears on some
old leases connected with that quarter. He finally retired to Finglas, where he spent many years, and
mixed much in the sports and May-pole amusements
of that old village. I am hunting up for some information concerning his latter day, and I find that there
is at present alive a nephew of his, a working bricklayer". Cox died in 1837, having been prepared for
death by the Rev. Matthias Kelly, P.P. of St. Margaret's, Finglas. From some letters of Cox not generally accessible, we select a few in illustration of his
epistolary style :

" New York, December 18, 1819.

" MY DEAR FRIEND,—I am as uneasy as possible by remaining here, and I am determined to leave this hideous
climate and most detestable race of rascals, who call it
their own, and boast of it as a gift of Heaven, though
the wretches are hardly out of school when they die of
old age, or are swept away by yellow fever, which has

not spared any one within the range of its devouring
limits on the sea coast, from Boston to New Orleans.
The last summer, I escaped by flying to Quebec — a
distance of 562 miles; and from its lofty walls I despatched a letter to you on the 12th of October, and
returned here on the 11th of November, to see the
sickly wretched Yankees removing the fences that enclosed a considerable portion of this city, when, in their
fright, they attempted to put limits to the common
enemy, as judiciously as the wise men of Gotham attempted to keep in the sparrows, by placing a strong
railing round their town. They have perished in
thousands, and, in my opinion, the yellow fever would
confer a blessing on the human race by continuing its
capers.

" A work of interesting curiosity, I have almost
ready, to consist of two volumes, which, if I live until
summer, will be in the Irish press. I have seen Mr.
O'Connell's letter to the Catholics, and have got it
printed here. There never was a better or more season-
able *State Paper*, a dignity it most eminently deserves.
Remember me to your child; to B. Tell Mr. James
Crosbie, Attorney General to Toll-houses, that I hope
he is alive and well; but if he is dead, say nothing
about it until I call in person.

" Yours truly,

" WALTER COX.

" A considerable number of Dublin men are here,
captains, colonels, etc., who ran away from Generals
D'Evereux and L'Estrange, and from the burning sands
of Margaritta, famine and yellow fever, which the
orators and prophets of the Board of Health instituted
in Dublin for taking care of sick friends at a distance,
forgot to predict".

Mr. Cox did not continue an O'Connellite. In 1835
we find him brought up before the magistrate at Arran

Quay Police Office, charged by the reverend gentlemen of Church Street Chapel with having personally denounced in very violent language the collection of the O'Connell Tribute during its progress in the Chapel Yard.

"New York, Nov. 20, 1819.

"I have determined to return home, nor am I prepared, by my very sad experience, to encounter any more of the frightful climate and other miseries incident to the infernal state of society in this country, with the wretched penury to be met with in all parts of this land.

"You may conceive some faint idea of the health of this place, when I assure you even New York, the most salubrious city here, was entirely reduced to a solitude during the last summer, which, to avoid, I made a most expensive excursion to Quebec, a distance of 570 miles. Not an Irishman in Savannah that did not fall a victim to the yellow fever, among them, Mr. John Walsh, late of Usher's Quay; and his son and daughter; not an acre of ground occupied by white men in this extensive region, that did not feel the scourge of every species of fever hitherto known, besides thousands of a new variety.

"Cobbett has gone home, and then surely I may venture, as I would prefer the dry gallows at home to an inglorious sweating death under American blankets.

"P.S.—I will have ready for publication, on my arrival, a novel in true Irish style, which, I will venture to say, will be much superior in originality, style, and composition, to any of Lady Morgan's. What will the world say, when it is known I am turned novelist? Laughable, certainly, but true, as the existence of Essex Bridge.

"Yours,

"WALTER COX".

We are not aware that the formidable rival to *O'Donnell* and *Florence MacCarthy* ever appeared.

From other letters of Cox in our hands, we find him in June, 1821, residing at " Ingouville, Havre de Grace". He expresses himself in very laudatory terms of La belle France; invites some old friends to visit him "for three months", and by way of inducement promises no end of sparkling champagne.

ABSTRACTION OF PAPERS FROM THE CASTLE ARCHIVES.

We have received from Mr. S. Redmond, a respectable gentleman connected for many years, first with the Irish and later with the English press, the following letters, correcting the account given at p. 133, *ante*, of the disappearance from the Castle Archives of the Secret Service Money Book. It is right to premise, however, that having submitted Mr. Redmond's letter to Charles Haliday, Esq., J.P., perhaps the most extensive collector of rare and curious books illustrative of Irish history, he informs me that the Secret Service Money Book is in his keeping, and that Mr. Redmond's impression is somewhat erroneous. Mr. Redmond was a very young man in 1838, and probably the story told him did not lose in the carriage by Mr. Byrne. " The " Secret Service Money Book", writes Mr. Haliday, " was sold with other very curious documents as waste paper".

" 46 Salisbury Street, Liverpool,
" 22nd October.

" Sir,—Although I have not the honour of your personal acquaintance, I am very well aware of your name and character. I trust you will excuse me for addressing you on a subject which you have ventilated, and which is of deep historical interest. It is in reference to the foot note, referring to what your friend

Dr. —— told about the Secret Service Money Book. Perhaps the following facts may be of use to you, and if so, you are at liberty to make any use you think proper of them. The document in question was not 'cleared out and sold' by any official in the Castle—it was *stolen* with some other valuable documents, but it came into the hands of poor John Fegan in an honest and legitimate manner. He kept a stall at the corner of Off Lane and Henry Street, and was a man of great natural intelligence, had a limited education, but improved it wonderfully by self-culture. The doctor, I think, has made a mistake by stating that it was publicly exhibited for sale. No man in the world knew the value of such a document better than poor Fegan. He showed it to Mr. Edward Byrne (since dead), who kept a tavern at No. 6 Capel Street. I was then a very young man, connected with the reporting staff of the *Morning Register* newspaper (and subsequently for nearly ten years on the *Freeman's Journal*), and Mr. Byrne sent for me and showed it to me. Although young, I was immediately alive to the value of the treasure that lay before me, and I at once resolved to possess it. I appointed to meet Mr. Byrne and Fegan in the evening, and did so; but imagine my surprise when I found the treasure had flown. Mr. Byrne had taken it back to the Castle! Between the time I had seen him in the forenoon and my visit in the evening, a person from the Castle called on Mr. Byrne, and threatened to have him transported if he did not give up the document! Mr. B. was a very timid man, and at once proceeded to the Castle and delivered it up. It seems that, in consequence of the gossip raised by poor Fegan about it, it was missed from the Castle, and hot search made after it. The above is the result. This was in the latter end of 1838, or beginning of '39. I have often regretted the loss, for had I got it, no pressure would have extracted *it from me.*

" It may be interesting to you, when I state that many of Lever's and Carleton's best stories are founded on tales told them by Fegan. He was obliged to quit Dublin in '48, and subsequently kept a book-stall at the Custom House here. He lost his life, with his wife and three children, in a fire in the house where he lived in Shaw's Alley, in this town, three or four years ago. I wrote a short memoir of him in the journal to which I am attached. The public raised a handsome monument to the family, in Saint Anne's Church, Edge Hill.

" I have frequently seen the slab (a black stone, either marble or heavy dark limestone) over the grave of Higgins, in Kilbarrack Churchyard, but little did I think who lay beneath it. The last time I saw it (some years ago), it was partly on its side, apparently turned over. What a gigantic scoundrel he was, and to have done such a multiplicity of novel villanies in a life, comparatively short, surpasses comprehension. One would think that, to conceive and mature such an amount of Hell-born crimes, would have taken a couple of centuries; but when we find a human being capable of acting them, and dying at fifty-five, our astonishment becomes altogether lost. Poor Magee! *ought* he not have a statue some place *about College Green?* Fearfully as I felt my gorge rise at the treble-dyed damnation of Iscariot Higgins, I must say, with the utmost sincerity, that in all my life I never enjoyed such hearty laughter as I did at the description of the fetes at Fiat Hill; and when I meet with anyone troubled with the *hips*, I shall turn doctor and order the patient to read that part of the work twice, and I will insure him a radical cure. Many a day have I gambolled about these spots, little thinking that the ground was sacred to *Olympic pig races*, or that I would, in this country (to use a well-known phrase), nearly burst my sides reading of the scenes that were enacted on that now memorable hill.

" I am, etc.

" SYLVESTER REDMOND".

Mr. Haliday, as we have said, is positive in his impression that the document in question, with many other curious manuscripts, long preserved in the archives of the Castle, were sold as waste paper. The Duke of Wellington, in his Irish correspondence, more than once complains of the abstraction of papers from their legitimate repository. Among the curious papers alluded to by Mr. Haliday, is a voluminous correspondence between influential persons and viceroys of the day, soliciting place, promotion, pay, and patronage. One letter from Compton Domvile, Esq., M.P., of Santry House, addressed to the Duke of Richmond, asks for the peerage of Santry. The Lord Lieutenant writes across the letter—"A modest request! Answer this letter evasively.—Richmond". But the application was not, after all, very unreasonable, for an ancestor of Mr. Domvile's possessed the peerage of Santry, which he lost, according to O'Reilly's *Reminiscences of an Emigrant Milesian,** from having at a meeting of the Hell-Fire Club, in Saul's Court, Fishamble Street, compelled an unfortunate man to swallow brandy until his throat filled to overflow, when a lighted match was applied, and the sufferer slowly blazed into eternity !† But what little reliance can be placed upon hearsay stories, and how likely men are, after the lapse of many years, to confound the details of utterly distinct incidents, is exhibited in this *Reminiscence.* Lord Santry was tried by his peers, not for the above diabolical escapade, which, we believe, he never committed, but for having, at the village of Palmerstown, stabbed a man named Loughlin Murphy, who died of his wound on September 25th, 1738. The report of his

* Vol. iii., page 290.

† The Hell-Fire Club of Dublin was succeeded by the Cherokee Club. The late Mr. John Patten told us that the late estimable Earl of Charlemont was a member of it, and dressed in red and black—the devil's livery ! Lords Ormond, Enniskillen, and Llandaff also belonged to it.

trial is now before us. Lord Santry was sentenced to death; but there is an authentic tradition to the effect, that his cousin, Mr. Compton Domvile, having threatened to deprive Dublin of water, the noble convict's life was pardoned by the viceroy. The title, however, was forfeited, and Lord Santry's estates passed to Sir Compton Domvile..

It may be asked, how Mr. Domvile could deprive Dublin of water. The supply came from the Dodder at Templeogue, and ran through the Domvile property. By damming up or turning off this stream, which then was the sole conduit of supply to the Earl of Meath's Liberty and Dublin City, formidable inconveniences could not fail to arise.

The corporate records are said to contain some curious details of a quarrel in which Mr. Compton Domvile and the executive were occasionally engaged. It was more than once brought to a crisis by Mr. Domvile cutting off the water supply, sometimes in pique, sometimes in salutary pressure on the powers that were. On one occasion, as we are assured by an officer of the Corporation, the Lord Lieutenant was constrained to send out horse and foot, and forcibly wrest the water from the custody of Domvile's *retainers*. In 1775 the insufficiency of the supply from the Dodder, which for several centuries was the sole resource of Dublin, led the Corporation to resort to the Grand Canal. But matters were not much mended by the change. Dr. W—— of Dublin, who is still living, saw the troops cut the canal, when, owing to a dispute, the directors refused to continue to give water. A pure and abundant supply of soft water was long desired by Dublin, and this boon has been recently obtained for it through the energy of Sir John Gray.

O

TREASON IN ULSTER—HOULTON.

The repeated mention of Houlton's name in the history of the Sham Squire, leads to the query whether the miscreant named Houlton, described by Plowden, as having personated a rebel general in 1798, was connected with the colleague of Francis Higgins. Mr. Houlton, after an interview with the Irish Privy Council, Lord Redesdale presiding, was equipped with a superb rebel uniform, including a cocked hat and feathers, which was paid for by government, and sent on a mission to Belfast, to tempt, to prosleytize, to dupe, and to betray. An orderly dragoon repaired with instructions to General Sir Charles Ross, who commanded in Belfast, that Houlton was a confidential servant of the government, and on no account to be molested. Houlton, however, having set off on his mission in a postchaise and four, arrived at Belfast long before the advice of his advent, and the result was that, when in the act of spouting treason with startling volubility at a tavern, Houlton was arrested by the local authorities, paraded in his uniform round the town, and sent back under a strong guard to Dublin.[*]

A fine field for the profitable pastime of betrayal was spoiled by this contrariety. The North of Ireland, at one time ripe for revolt, never rose. Some interesting papers, formerly in the possession of General Nugent, who had the chief command in the North, are now in our hands, and reveal the formidable length to which the organization reached in Ulster.

The conspiracy was not confined to the men who had nothing to lose. Among those who staked their lives and fortunes on its issue, was Mr. Stewart of Acton, a gentleman of large property, noticed at considerable

* *Post-Union History*, v. i. p. 223.

length in "the Private and Secret" letters of Under Secretary Cooke, addressed to Lord Castlereagh, and published in the correspondence of the latter.*

The letters in question boast of possessing information calculated to criminate Mr. Stewart, but the details or even substance of the information is not given. The following letters are now printed for the first time. Lord Castlereagh's, we may add, was enclosed in the larger communication addressed by Lord Wm. Bentinck to General Nugent, Commander in Chief in Ulster.

(Secret.)   "Dublin Castle, June 24.

"MY LORD,—The information upon which I granted a warrant against Mr. Stewart, stated him, a very short time previous to the rebellion, to have accepted the situation of Adjutant-General for the County of Armagh in the rebel army.

"Your lordship's knowledge of the public mind of the North confirms me in a hope I have for some time entertained, that there has a salutary change of sentiment taken place amongst the Dissenters. I am not sanguine enough to hope that Mr. Stewart can, in so short a space of time, have become a good subject; however, under all the circumstances, it appears to me desirable that Mr. S. should, at least for the present, remain at large, under his bail, as taken by your lordship. Should any circumstance arise to make it advisable to proceed otherwise, I shall have the honour of communicating on the subject with your lordship before any steps are taken.

"I have the honour to be,

"Your lordship's very obedient servant,

"CASTLEREAGH.

"To Lord William Bentinck".

* Memoirs and Correspondence of Lord Castlereagh, v i. 253-60. See also the Personal Recollections of Lord Cloncurry, 2d Edit., pp. 64 and 66.

"Armagh, July 27, 1798.

" DEAR GENERAL NUGENT,—I send under the charge of one of our quarter masters, Mr. Stewart, a prisoner who was a man of very good property at the time he was apprehended under a warrant from Lord Castlereagh.

" I was at the time so convinced that all the leading people of this town whom I had known to be violent United Irishmen about a year and a-half ago, with the exception of one or two, had now changed their opinion, that upon their offer of very large bail I took upon myself to liberate him, and informed Lord Castlereagh that I had done so. And it is my opinion that the having liberated this man when I did, contributed very much to keep the people here in good humour, and as far as I can learn, they never had any intention of rising. Mr. Stewart confessed to me *privately* that he was an United Irishman, which confession appears to me, as being unnecessary and infamous to himself, is a proof of his innocence as to an insurrection. I send you Lord Castlereagh's letter to me. When I liberated him, I of course knew nothing of the charge against him, and since his release I cannot discover that he has been concerned in any way whatever with the rebels.

" You have a man of the name of Jackson at Belfast whom I apprehended here, and against whom by a letter from a Mr. Hamilton at Belfast, there appear to be no charges. It is of very material importance to the tranquillity of this part of the country that he should not return. He has always been remarkably active among the people, he is in all particulars very like Munro, who was hanged at Lisburn. He is the great leader here.

" I am, dear General, yours truly,
" W. BENTINCK".

"Lisburn, June 27th, 1798.
" SIR,—I am directed by Major-General Goldie to

18

send to you to Belfast, William Kean, a man who acted as aide-de-camp to Munro, and who was formerly a clerk in the *Star** office at Belfast. James Petticrew, Robert Fullerton, Charles Keanan, and John Sinclare, all prisoners, are positive evidence against him; Hugh Orr and Christopher Williamson, likewise prisoners, are circumstantial evidence against Kean. When Kean's trial is over, the General wishes you to send back these evidences, as they give information against people who are confined here. Hugh Reid is likewise sent, but the General desires me to say that he does not wish that this man should be brought to trial, as he is a very principal evidence against many people; and you will be so good as to send him up here when you are done with him. A man of the name of Fleeting is likewise sent, who says that he was employed by Dulry, who is now on trial with you, to make pikes, for whom he made about fourteen. Please to send him back when Dulry's trial is over.

> "I have the honour to be, Sir, etc.,
>
> "ALEX. McAULEY, M.B".

> "Antrim, Dec. 20th, 1798.

"DEAR GENERAL,—I enclose the examination against the man who was sent to Belfast yesterday, of the name of Duggan. The person who gave it may be heard of from Mr. MacGuicken, at the Sign of the Cock, in this place.

"I have also enclosed a state of our ammunition, and an application to have the deficiency made up.

"Information has just been given me of an intended meeting near Donegal Moat, about four miles from hence, this evening. I shall send out a party, which I hope will be successful.

> "I remain, dear General, etc.,
>
> "D. LESLIE".

* The *Northern Star*, edited by Samuel Neilson.

DUGGAN THE INFORMER.

The allusion to Duggan and MacGuicken, in the foregoing letter, reminds us that of both we have something curious to tell.

MacGuicken, already alluded to, and to whom we promised to return, invariably acted as solicitor to the United Irishmen. He performed with much skill the part of an ardent patriot, possessed the entire confidence of the popular party, was a member of the Northern Directory of United Irishmen, and long subsequent to 1798 spoke with much spirit at Catholic meetings. The *Cornwallis Papers* confirm the almost incredible statement, that MacGuicken revealed to the government, for money, the secrets of his clients and friends. In the trials which followed the partial outbreak in 1798, MacGuicken constantly figured as legal adviser for the rebel leaders of Ulster. This man was, as we have said, tampered with, corrupted, and eventually pensioned. He survived until 1817. Exclusive of his pension, he received, as gentle stimulants, various sums amounting altogether to nearly £1,500.

Bernard Duggan, a native of Tyrone, took a leading part in the rebellions of 1798 and 1803. Sir Richard Musgrave describes him as mounted on a white horse at the battle of Prosperous, and boasting that he was as good a man as the military commander of that district, Captain Swayne. In Robert Emmet's conspiracy of 1803, Duggan was a zealous ally. He wrote a narrative of his connection with that movement, and presented it to Mr. John C. O'Callaghan, who has kindly handed it to us for publication. Duggan was arrested and imprisoned; but he seems to have made terms with the government: no trial took place, and he was set at large "like a roaring lion, seeking whom he might devour". For forty years subsequently, we find Duggan regarded by the national party as a venerable and uncompro-

mising patriot, It awakens painful emotions to attempt
to estimate the extent of the mischief of which this
hoary-headed wretch was the father. It must, indeed,
have been enormous ; but, thanks to the vigilance of
Dr., now Sir John Gray, Duggan was at last unmasked.
On August 25th, 1858, we noted some interesting facts
regarding this discovery, communicated to us in conversation by Sir John Gray, who, in reply to a question
from us as to whether we are at liberty to publish them,
is good enough to reply affirmatively. We append the
original jottings, which Sir John Gray pronounces to
be perfectly accurate :

Spoke of the receipts for secret service money. Dr.
Gray went to Connaught in 1843, to see his father,
who was ill, and called on the Rev. Joseph Darcy Sirr,
rector of Kilcoleman, biographer of Archbishop Trench,
and son of the notorious Major Sirr. Dr. Gray found
him examining a mass of old documents spread over
his study table. " Here, you rebel repealer",* said Mr.
Sirr playfully, " some of these will interest *you:* they are
chiefly the communications of informers to my late
father". Dr. Gray read some of them over, and having
observed one particular letter, he started, saying, " I
have seen that handwriting before—can you tell me
who is ' D' ?" The letter, communicating the result of

---

* Repealer and rebel were not unfrequently regarded as
synonymous words, and the organs of Earl de Grey and the
Orangemen urged in prose and verse, that the Repealers should
be dealt with as Lords Camden, Castlereagh, and Clare dealt
with the United Irishmen. In November, 1843, the *Packet*
sang :

> " These, these are the secrets
>   Of peace in our land—
> The scourge for the back,
>   For the forehead the brand;
> The chain for the neck,
>   And the gives for the heel ;
> Till the SCAFFOLD lets loose
>   The base blood of Repeal !"

some mercenary espionage to the Major, was merely signed " D." " There are many other letters from the same party", observed Mr. Sirr. " I cannot discover who he can be; his letters extend over upwards of thirty years, and I think the writer has not less than thirty *aliases*. He was a most remarkable man, and if you wish to unravel the mystery, you can have all facilities, so send home your conveyance, and remain for the day". Dr. Gray embraced the proposal, and devoted several hours to following up the scent. He was familiar with the writing, though he could not recal to mind the name or individuality of the writer. At last a receipt for a small amount was discovered, signed "B. Duggan', the date of which was about 1806. Dr. Gray, in ecstacy, exclaimed : " I have him! I know him well! he was with me yesterday!" " Impossible", cried Mr. Sirr, "he must be dead long since". A comparison of the handwriting left no doubt of the identity of the scoundrel. The spy, who had grown hoary, and to outward appearances venerable, in his infamous employment, had repeatedly addressed letters to Dr. Gray breathing a strong spirit of patriotism and nationality. Dr. Gray, as editor of a highly influential organ of O'Connell's policy, was specially marked out for game by the designing Duggan, who, for forty years, enjoyed the reputation of an earnest and zealous patriot, was even entertained at dinner by a member of the Catholic Association, and contrived to insinuate himself into the confidence of many of the national party.

He was introduced by letter to Dr. Gray, by a leading member of the Young Ireland section of the Repeal Association Committee, who described him as a rebel of '98, who could assist Dr. Gray by his personal memory of events, in perfecting some notes on the history of the United Irishmen, on which Dr. Gray was then engaged. Dr. Gray soon ascertained that Duggan possessed much traditionary knowledge of the events

and of the men of the period, and gave Duggan a small
weekly stipend for writing his "personal recollections".
He observed before long that Duggan's visits became
needlessly frequent, and that he almost invariably endeavoured to diverge from '98 and make suggestions as
to '43.   This tendency excited more amusement than
suspicion, and the first real doubt as to the true character of Duggan, was suggested to his mind thus:
Duggan said he was about to commence business, and
was collecting some subscriptions.   Dr. Gray handed
him two pounds, and Duggan at once handed across a
sheet of blank paper, saying: " I will have twenty pounds
in three days, if you write the names of ten or twelve
gentlemen on whom I may call: they won't refuse if
they see their names in your handwriting".*   Almost in
the same breath he named half-a-dozen members of
the Repeal Association, most of them members of the
Young Ireland section, adding: " I know these gentlemen will aid me for all I suffered since '98".   The
former efforts of Duggan to get into conversation as to
present politics at once flashed across the Doctor's
memory, and he politely declined to write the required
list, which, possibly, was designed by Duggan and his
abettors to flourish at some future state trial, as the
veritable list of the Provisional Government of Ireland, in the handwriting of the proposer of the project
for forming arbitration courts throughout Ireland, as
substitutes for the local tribunals, that were deprived of
popular confidence by the dismissal of all magistrates
who were repealers.   It was during the same week
that Dr. Gray discovered Duggan's real character in
the course of the visit to the parsonage already described.   All the facts as here given, were rapidly told
to his reverend friend, who ascribing the discovery to a
special providence, begged the "life" of Duggan, ex-

* Mr. O'Callaghan informs us that Duggan also solicited him
to affix his signature to a document.

plaining that the papers before him showed that the fate of detected informers in '98 was death. The sincerity with which the good parson pleaded for the life of Duggan, was a most amusing episode in the little drama. His fears were, however, soon allayed by the assurance that Dr. Gray belonged to the O'Connell section of politicians, and that the only punishment that awaited Duggan was exposure. The parson would not be convinced, and under the plea that Dr. Gray was allowed as a private friend to see the papers that convicted Duggan, he extorted a promise that there should be no public exposure of Duggan, but allowed Dr. Gray within this limit to use the information he acquired at his own discretion.

Duggan was, in truth, a master of duplicity. In the Sirr papers he is found writing under various signatures. " At one time", said Dr. Gray, " he personated a priest, and on other occasions a peddler and a smuggler. He wrote to major Sirr for a hogshead of tobacco, and for £15 to buy a case of pistols for personal protection. In one year alone he got £500".

" As soon", added Dr. Gray, " as I discovered the character of this base spy, I returned to Dublin, and lost no time in apprising Duffy, Davis, Pigot, O'Callaghan, and every member of the national party, of the precipice on which they stood, and undertook to O'Connell that I would cause Duggan to make himself scarce without violating my promise to Mr. Sirr that he should not be exposed to public indignation".

A letter addressed to us on August 20, 1865, by Mr. Martin Haverty, the able author of *The History of Ireland Ancient and Modern*, supplies an interesting paragraph on the point we are now handling:

" One day, during the memorable repeal year 1843, Sir John Gray invited me to breakfast, telling me that I should meet a very singular character—a relic of '98, but intimating that he had his doubts about this person, and that the object of my visit was chiefly that their interview should not be without a witness.

"I may tell you that I never belonged to any political party in Ireland. I always felt an innate repugnance for the manner, principles, etc., of the Young Irelanders, and was convinced that I loved my country at least as sincerely, tenderly, and ardently, as any of them. I never had much faith in mere politicians, though my sympathies were O'Connellite, and Sir John Gray had perfect confidence in me.

"We were after breakfast when Bernard Duggan was brought into the room. I was introduced to him as a friend of Ireland before whom he might speak freely. It was easy enough to bring him out. He spoke at random about the pike-training in '98—that the people were now ready enough to fight—they only wanted to be called out—and the pike was the best thing for them. He appeared to me ridiculously sanguine of success, and to regard the men of the present day as poltroons for not taking the field.

"I believe I am too 'green' to detect dishonesty very readily; and the first impression the scoundrel made on me was two-fold—that he was a singularly hale old fellow for his age, and that he was an infatuated old fool; but, if I could have felt sure that he was an informer, I would have shrunk from him as from a murderer. Sir John Gray evidently understood the fellow better, and seemed perfectly able for him".

The grand *finale* of this curious episode remains to be told. Shortly after he introduced Duggan to Mr. Haverty, and after the old spy had time to develop the views indicated in Mr. Haverty's letter, the Doctor suddenly, with his eye fixed on him, as though he could read his inmost soul, exclaimed: "Barney, you think I do not know you. I know you better than you *know* yourself. Do you remember when you were dressed as a priest at Dundalk?" He writhed, and

tried to turn the conversation. Dr. Gray probed and
stabbed him, one by one, with all the points which he
had gathered from the informer's own letters to Sirr.
It was pitiable to watch the struggles and agonies
of the old man; he was ghastly pale, and he shook
in every nerve. He finally lost all self-command,
and flung himself on his knees at the feet of Dr. Gray,
imploring mercy. He seemed to think that pike-men
were outside ready to rush in and kill him. " Give
me", he said, "but twelve hours: I will leave the
country, and you will never see me again!" He tot-
tered from the room, left Ireland, and did not return
for many years. Amongst his first visits was one to
Dr. Gray, to whom he confessed his guilt, adding that
he was near his end. He received some trifling relief,
and shortly after died.

Preserved with Duggan's letters to Sirr, a note in
the autograph of the latter exists, stating that Duggan,
no doubt, shot Mr. Darragh, Terrorist, at his own hall-
door, in 1791, when in the act of pretending to hand
him a letter; and further, that Duggan was the man
who attempted the life of Mr. Clarke, in Dublin, on
July 22nd, 1803. In the London *Courier*, of the 30th
July following, we find this paragraph in a letter from
Dublin, descriptive of the then state of Ireland:—

"Mr. Clarke, of Palmerstown, a magistrate of the
county of Dublin, as he was returning from his attendance at the Castle, was fired at, on the quay, and
dangerously wounded, several slugs having been lodged
in his shoulder and breast. The villain who discharged
the blunderbuss at Mr. Clarke immediately cried out,
'Where did you come from now?' It appears that two
of them, taken by Mr. Justice Bell and Mr. Wilson,
were residenters in the neighbourhood of Mr. Clarke,
and had come to this city from Palmerstown".

That the man who, in 1803, was overflowing with in-
dignant disgust at the idea of a magistrate discharging

his duty by communicating at the Castle news of seditious proceedings, should suddenly tergiversate, and, throughout a period of nearly half a century, become a mercenary spy to the Castle, opens a wide field for thought to those who like to study weak humanity.

· We rather think that the long letter published in the Duke of Wellington's Irish correspondence, dated Nenagh, 6th Feb., 1808, is from Duggan.   The letter is addressed to an understrapper of the Castle, not to the Duke, who, however, prefaces it by saying that it "comes from a man who was sent into the counties of Tipperary and Limerick to inquire respecting the organization of Liberty Rangers".   "They are damned cunning in letting any stranger know anything of their doings", writes the spy.   "I assure you I could not find anything of their secrets, though I have tried every artifice, by avowing myself an utter enemy to the present constitution, and even drinking seditious toasts, though they seemed to like me for so doing, and still I could not make any hand of them anywhere, more than to find they are actually inclined to rebellion in every quarter of the country through which I have passed.   Even in the mountains they are as bad as in the towns".

Duggan, during the political excitement of the Repeal year, contrived to get himself introduced to many of the popular leaders; and when the intervention of a mutual friend was not attainable, he waived ceremony and introduced himself.   Among others on whom he called in this way was John Cornelius O'Callaghan, author of the *Green Book*, and designer of the Repeal Cards, to whom the Attorney-General made special reference in the state trials of the time.   Mr. O'Callaghan did not give Duggan much encouragement; but, in order to strengthen his footing, Duggan presented him with the following MS., written entirely in *his* own hand, which is now published for the first time.

The reader must bear in mind that the writer was originally an humble artizan, who had received no education beyond that furnished by a hedge school.

It will be observed that he speaks of himself throughout, not in the first person, but as " Bernard O'Dougan".

PERSONAL NARRATIVE OF BERNARD DUGGAN.

" At the time that Mr. Robert Emmet commenced his preparations for a revolution in Ireland, in the year 1803, he was after returning from France, and there came a few gentlemen along with him, Mr. Russell, and Counsellor Hamilton,* and Michael Quigley,† who had been nominated one of the rebel captains of 1798, and had signed the treaty of peace along with the other officers of the rebel party of the camp that lay at Prosperous, in the county of Kildare; where the Wexford and Wicklow men came and met the Kildare men, who were all invited by a flag of truce from government, and hostages given by the generals of the King's troops—namely, Major Cope and Captain Courtney, of the Armagh militia, who were kept in custody and in charge with Bernard Dougan, for the space of two hours, until eighteen of the rebel officers of the Wexford, Wicklow, and Kildare, returned back after signing the articles of peace, which was then concluded between the government and the people, and which put an end to the rebellion. The conditions were, a free pardon to all men acting in furtherance of the rebellion, except officers, who were to give themselves up to government, and to remain state prisoners until government thought it safe to let them go into any

---

* Dacre Hamilton is noticed in Moore's *Memoirs* (i. 62), as the attached friend of Emmet, though "innocent of his plans". There can be little doubt, however, that, like Russell, who lost his head, he was fully implicated in them.—W. J. F.

† Quigley survived until the year 1849. Successive notices of him appear in the *Nation* of that year, p. 137 et seq.

country they pleased, that was not in war with his Majesty, which conditions they had to sign, and it was called the Banishment Bill. They got three days of a parole of honour, to take leave of their friends, before they gave themselves up as prisoners. The breach of any part of these conditions was, not only to forfeit their pardon, but to be treated in any kind of way that the government should think proper. Now, Mr. Quigly broke these articles when he returned to Ireland after signing the Banishment Bill at his liberation and departure according to agreement, which caused him to assume the name of Graham in all companies, and none knew to the reverse but his own companions who were in the depot, and his particular acquaintances in the country, who were all true to the cause of his return with Mr. Emmet ; and none ever discovered or informed in any kind of way previous to the failure of the efforts for freedom on the 23rd of July, 1803, which caused great consternation to the government. The Secretary of State, Mr. Wickham, cried out with astonishment, to think that such a preparation for revolution could be carried on in the very bosom of the seat of government, without discovery, for so long a time, when any of the party could have made their fortunes by a disclosure of the plot, and remarked at the same time, in presence of Mr. Stafford, and the two Mr. Parrots, John and William, that it was because they were mostly all mechanical operatives, or working people of the low order of society, that the thing was kept so profound ; and said, that if any or a number of the higher orders of society had been connected, they would divulge the plot for the sake of gain. These expressions occurred at the Castle, when Quigly, Stafford, and the two Parrots were brought prisoners to Dublin from Artfry, in the county of Galway, where they fled to after the *death* of Mr. Emmet. Bernard O'Dougan was also at *Artfry,* but had escaped from being arrested by his

going in a sailing boat across the bay of Galway, to
make out a place of retirement for the whole party,
five in number, until they would get an account from
Dublin, where they sent a messenger, who had been
arrested and detained a prisoner, although being a
native of the county Galway, and no way connected
with Mr. Emmet, only going on a message to Dublin
for these five men, who passed off as bathers at the
salt water. The messenger was only known to some
of the party where he was sent, and could not be arrested without information of some of that party, who
have been found out since, and will be treated of in
another place. Mr. Emmet wished to get acquainted
with the men that distinguished themselves most in the
year 1798, and he was aware that Quigly knew these
men, which was one cause for bringing him (Quigly)
along with him from France. Mr. Emmet had also the
knowledge of the other men that had been in confidence in the year 1798 as delegates, some of whom
he employed as agents to forward his plans. James
Hope, from Belfast, was one that he, perhaps, got an
account of from some of the United Irishmen that
were in France. Although Hope did not distinguish
himself in battle, he was trustworthy, and lived in
Dublin at that time; he was a true patriot, and he
was soon found out for Mr. Emmet, and sent to Bernard O'Dougan, who lived in Palmerstown. At this
time, after O'D. had been liberated out of Naas gaol,
where he had been a state prisoner, he was obliged
to quit the county Kildare, where he had been tried
for high treason and the rebellion of 1798, the murder of Captain Swain, and the battle of Prosperous.
These facts were sworn against him and another young
man of the name of Thomas Wylde, and proved to the
satisfaction of the court, as may be seen by Lord Long-
ville's speech in the first Parliament after the union of
Great Britain and Ireland, but were both honourably

acquitted by the Amnesty Act (though detained as state
prisoners), which had been framed according to agreement of the peace between the government and the
rebels, as hath been explained heretofore. O'Dougan·
was called on also much at the same time by Quigley
and Wylde, on the same business as Hope had with
him, giving him to know what was intended by Mr.
Emmet. On this invitation, B. O'Dougan came into
Dublin and met Mr. Emmet's party. At the same time
there was but few in number, about five or six; but
they were confident in the disposition of all such of
their countrymen, as far as their influence went, which
was not a little at that time, that they would have
numbers to join their cause, and was the chief part
that did come at the day appointed. Henry Howley
was brought by O'Dougan, and Edward Condon also;
H. Howley took the depôt in Thomas Street, with its
entrance in Marshal Lane; then John Bourk, of Naas,
and Richard Eustace, from the same place, and also a
young man of the name of Joseph White, from the
county Kildare, near Rathcoffey; there was another
person of the name of Christopher Nowlan. These
men continued to collect into the depôt pikes from the
different places where the smiths would leave them
concealed; and also to bring in the timber for the pike
handles; and also powder and balls, and to make them
into cartridges, and put handles into the pikes. These
men, for the most part, were always attendant on the
depôt, preparing the pikes and cartridges, and bringing
in guns, pistols, and blunderbusses, and all other
requisites for rockets, etc. Pat Finerty was also employed in the depôt; and occasionally these men could
bring several of their own particular friends into the
depôt, to help the manufacture of cartridges and other
preparations for rockets, making pikes, and putting
handles in them. O'Dougan, Bourk, and Condon,
brought in the powder and balls from the different

places, but for the most part from Hinchey's, at the corner of Cuffe Street, who was licensed for selling gunpowder, and got it from the government stores, so that there was a vast preparation ; and all things went on well until the explosion of the depôt in Patrick Street, on the evening of the 16th, which deranged the projects that were in contemplation.   O'Dougan, Bourk, and Condon, were ordered by Mr. Emmet to go down to Patrick Street depôt to get the rockets filled.   It should be remarked that the men of the other depôts had no recourse to the one in Thomas Street, but the particular men of Thomas Street had recourse to all places ; and O'Dougan often went as a guard to protect Mr. Emmet, lest he should be surprised by any of Major Sirr's or any other spy from government. O'Dougan was appointed aide-de-camp to Mr. Emmet, but the circumstance of derangement from the time of that explosion put everything in confusion and disorder.   When these three men came into the depôt in Patrick Street, the preparation was not in readiness for the rockets, and many other disorders existed, which caused O'Dougan, Bourk, and Condon, to return back to the depôt in Thomas Street, as nothing could be done at that time.   It was McIntosh, and the Keenans, Arthur Develin, and George McDonald, and a few others, that were blown up at the time of the explosion, some of whom expired in Madame Steevens's hospital afterwards ; these were all in the depôt, and it is a great wonder they were not all blown up.   O'Dougan, Bourk, and Condon, were only about a quarter of an hour gone when the explosion took place.   It was occasioned by the experiments trying on the fuses to know the length of time they would burn, and by neglect, let the fire get into the joint of the table where there had been some meal powder which communicated to some saltpetre that had been out all day before the sun drying, after it had been purified, and which exploded,

and almost burst the house, and killed and wounded
three, and was near destroying all that were in the
place. The other powders escaped the flame, and nearly
all was got safe out of the place unperceived, but was
attacked by the watchmen who were soon knocked
over.   There were some secret cells in the depôt that
were not found out until after the arrest of Quigley,
which will be treated of elsewhere.   Some of the men
that belonged to the depôt of Patrick Street were
brought prisoners to Thomas Street depôt, and kept
confined until the night of the 23rd, particularly George
McDonald; but this shall be treated of in another place.
There was great apprehension entertained for fear of
discovery from that time of the explosion, and there
was great inquiry and look out on the part of Major
Sirr and his satellites, which caused a precipitant movement in Mr. Emmet's affairs.   The men in the different
counties might have time to act, as their look out was
the city of Dublin to free itself; but the orders from
the generals contiguous to the city, either not having
sufficient time to collect their men, or from other
neglect, prevented them from coming in according to
order and promise.   Dwyer was to come with his mountain battalions, and the Wexfords were to come in
thousands; but none of them made their appearance
up to four or five o'clock, nor any account of them;
none showed their faces but the men of the county Kildare, and part of the county Dublin that lay adjacent.
They came from Naas, Prosperous, and Kilcullen, a few
from Maynooth and Leixlip, and Lucan a few; Palmerstown turned out almost to a man.*   This was the
place where O'Dougan lived from the time of his liberation from prison for complicity in the rebellion of 1798,
and he had great influence among the people of that part
of the neighbourhood of Dublin, and they were very

* Duggan's attempt on the life of Mr. Clarke, of Palmers-
stown, p. 281, will be remembered.—W. J. F.

much attached to him; and O'Dougan had his friends
on the close look out, knowing as he did the artfulness
and the intrigue of government, being a state prisoner,
where experience teaches the depth of the artful
schemes of government, which no one can fathom except an experienced state prisoner or some supernatural
intelligence to instruct them.* O'Dougan was given
to understand that Mr. Clark† and Captain Willcock,
two magistrates of the county, were in the knowledge
of what was going on in Dublin by Mr. Emmet.
O'Dougan immediately let Mr. Emmet know of this;
whereupon Emmet, seeing how all the other expecta-
tions were likely to fail, which they did, ordered O'Dougan to do it himself, which caused him to take a few of
the bravest men he had in confidence, and placed some
between the Castle and the barracks, to stop any
despatch from one to the other, and a guard to keep
any communication to or from the commander-in-chief.†
There was but little time to be lost on either side. The
government had summoned a privy council to deliberate on what was best to be done on their part. Things
came so sudden on them, it seems they did not know
well how to act until they would consult. Mr. Emmet
thought on taking the whole of the privy council as
they sat in the Council Chamber,‡ and accordingly

* These observations are eminently rich when read in conjunction with Duggan's real history.—W. J. F.
† See the attempt on the life of Mr. Clarke, by Duggan, p.
281.—W. J. F.
‡ This was not, after all, a very visionary scheme. Mr.
Fitzgerald, in a narrative supplied to Dr. Madden, mentions
that he walked through the Castle Yard, at half-past seven
o'clock on the evening of Emmet's *emeute.* "There were no
preparations; the place was perfectly quiet and silent; the gates
were wide open!" Charles Phillips, in *Curran and his Contemporaries,* says, that on the night of Emmet's outbreak, there was
not a single ball in the Royal Arsenal would fit the artillery.—
This apathetic neglect contrasts curiously with the activity displayed in fortifying the Castle in 1848, and more recently
during the Fenian conspiracy.—W. J. F.

despatched Henry Howley for six double coaches to
carry six men in each coach, making in all thirty-six,
with blunderbusses and short pikes that sprung out
at full length with brass ferrules on them, to keep
them straight at full extent; but when Howley was
coming with the first coach, and got as far as the
lower end of Bridgefoot Street, a circumstance occurred that deranged the whole project. A soldier
and a countryman had a dispute and began to fight.
Howley stopped to see how the fight would end;
meantime Cornet Brown came up and took part with
the soldier; at seeing this, Henry Howley opened the
coach and advanced to this interfering officer, and a
struggle ensued, and Howley pulled out his pistol
and shot Cornet Brown on the spot, and suddenly perceived a sergeant and a party of soldiers coming over
Queen's Bridge, which caused him to withdraw and
leave the coachman and coach there and then; it was
then getting late, and no time to procure the coaches.
As the business of the coaches was left to Howley,
none else was sent, and all things seemed disappoint-
ment. A trooper, with despatches, was killed in Thomas
Street, and also Lord Kilwarden. There appeared no
better way to Mr. Emmet and his staff than to retreat
to the country and make their escape. They had a
little skirmish with the military at the upper end of
Thomas Street and Francis Street, and a little on the
Coombe. There were a few lives lost at their departure;
and they went out of town as far as the mountain
foot. At Ballinascorney they separated. Mr. Robert
Emmet returned into town, and his staff repaired to
the county Kildare. When O'Dougan returned from
his post, where he and his party kept the pass, and
cut off all communication to or from the commander-
in-chief, it was past eleven o'clock, and all silence
over the city; he came as far as the depot, and went
past through Marshal Lane and into Thomas Street,

s far as Crane Lane, where there was a guard of the army stationed, which he could discern by stooping, which he did frequently, for it was darkness all over the town, and the pikes lay in the street up and down, where they were cast away, and the men fled, every one to the best place they knew. O'Dougan did not know where they went, nor did he hear for the space of three days their destination; but on the third day he got intelligence and went to Rathcoffey, where he found a number of them who in a few days were proclaimed, and three hundred pounds reward offered for them; and, after Mr. Emmet's execution, all separated and went to different parts to conceal themselves from arrest, as they well knew their fate, for there was death without mercy, and the innocent as well as the guilty suffered; and the innocent suffered far more than the guilty, for there were but few concerned with Mr. Emmet that suffered, while numbers were hung on the evidence of Ryan and Mahaffy, who swore for the sake of getting fifty pounds for every one they hung. Mr. Emmet and Howley died for the cause; Redmond and Felix Rourke died friends to the cause, but they were not intimately concerned in the insurrection; all the rest", adds Duggan, " were hung innocent on false evidence!"

P.
SIR JONAH BARRINGTON.

Sir Jonah Barrington, whose name we have frequently mentioned, published a work entitled *Personal Sketches,* containing many anecdotes illustrative of the Sham Squire's times ; but we have been sparing in our references to that book, for, however pleasant as light reading, it is not wholly reliable as historical authority. The truth is, that Sir Jonah was in needy circumstances when the *Personal Sketches* appeared,

and no doubt exaggerated his already hyperbolical
style, in order to raise the wind still higher, though he
says in his introduction: "It was by no means commenced for mercenary purposes" (p. v. i.). We have
heard the late Mr. P. V. Fitzpatrick say, who as a *bon
raconteur* might be styled "Sir Jonah Barrington
secundus", that he heard him tell the stories very dif-
ferently from the sensational style of their subsequent
appearance, and that he knew Thomas Colley Grattan,
the novelist, to claim the chief merit of the *Personal
Sketches*, as having suggested the work and manipulated
the MS. But even in personal conversation, as we
have been assured by the late John Patten, Sir Jonah's
statements were always distrusted; although a judge,
he was not a man of truth or principle, and many pleasant anecdotes might be told illustrative of this remark,
but the Blue Book ordered by the House of Commons
to be printed the 9th of February, 1829, pillories Sir
Jonah on the most legitimate authority. This volume
has not been consulted by the writers who have hitherto
noticed the eccentric knight. Before examining it, we
may observe that the result of the disclosures therein
contained, was Sir Jonah's dismissal from the bench.
This was inconvenient, as the salary dropped at the
same time; but the knight's inexhaustible astuteness
in a dilemma proved, as usual, wonderful.

Barrington bethought him of a letter which he had
received, many years before, from the Duke of Clarence, who was now reigning as William the Fourth.
Barrington had shown considerable kindness to Mrs.
Jordan, at a time when his bar contemporary, Gould,
and others, had treated her slightingly, and even introduced her to his own family. The Duke wrote a warm
letter of thanks to Barrington, and expressed a hope
that it might be in his power, at some future day, to
attest his appreciation of kindness so disinterested.
Barrington overhauled his papers—which, by the way

he sold as autographs a few years later—and having found the old letter in question, forwarded it to the King. A rather stiff reply came by return of post, to say that no one knew better than Sir Jonah Barrington the very material difference which existed between the Duke of Clarence and the King of England, and that it was impossible to recognize, in his then position, every acquaintance whom he might have known when acting in a comparatively subordinate capacity. His Majesty, however, who possessed a heart of unusual warmth, and a memory of past friendship singularly acute and retentive, wrote a private letter to Sir Jonah by the same post which conveyed the official answer, recognizing the claim, and bestowing upon him a pension from the Privy Purse, exactly equal in amount with the forfeited stipend.[*]

To come now to the Blue Book.

Referring to the ship *Nancy* and its cargo, which were sold by the marshal under a commission of appraisement in December, 1805, we read: "It appears that in this cause alone Sir Jonah Barrington appropriated to his own use out of the proceeds £482 8s. 8d. and £200, making together £682 8s. 8d., and never repaid any part of either; and that the registrar is a loser in that cause to the amount of £546 11s. 4d."[†]

In the case of the *Redstrand*, Sir Jonah also netted some booty. On the 12th January, 1810, the sum of £200 was paid into court on account of the proceeds in this cause, "and the same day", adds the report, "Sir Jonah Barrington, by an order in his own handwriting which has been produced to us, directed the registrar to lodge that sum to his (the Judge's) credit in the bank of Sir William Gleadowe Newcomen, which he accordingly did. Subsequently a petition having been presented to the court by Mr. Henry Pyne Masters, one

[*] Communicated by the late P. V. Fitzpatrick, Esq.
[†] *Eighteenth Report on Courts of Justice in Ireland*, p. 8.

of the salvagers, Sir Jonah wrote an order at foot of it,
bearing date the 29th day of May, 1810, directing the
registrar to pay to the petitioner a sum of £40 ; and
at the same time he wrote a note to Mr. Masters, requesting that he would not present the order for two
months ; at the close of which period Sir Jonah left
Ireland, and never since returned"—*Ibid.*, p. 10.

Sir Jonah's circumstances at this time were greatly
embarrassed, and his last act on leaving Ireland was
one of a most unscrupulous character, as shall appear
anon. In the Dublin *Patriot*, then edited by Richard
Barrett, we read the following paragraph, which is
quite in Sir Jonah's style, having evidently for its object
the diversion of suspicion from the real grounds of his
exile. " His chest", it is true, was not in a satisfactory
state, but it was the money chest rather than the bodily
trunk which seems to have been chiefly affected.

" Sir Jonah Barrington has resided at Boulogne for
the last three years. His health, we regret to state, is
by no means perfect, but, on the contrary, has for some
years been very precarious. Under his patent he has
the right of appointing surrogates to act for him—a
right of which he cannot be deprived. The duties of his
situation have been, and continue to be discharged, in
his absence, by the very competent gentlemen who
have been appointed, Mr. Jameson, Mr. Mahaffy, and
Mr. Holwell Walshe".*

The commissioners requested Sir Jonah's attendance
in Dublin in order to give him every opportunity of
vindication ; but he declined on the plea of infirmity
and the difficulty of transit, for which, in 1828, he may
have had some excuse. The commissioners, before
closing their report, strained a point and enclosed to
Sir Jonah copies of the evidence. On the 2nd August,

* See *Patriot* of December 29th, 1822, and Carrick's *Morning
Post*, January 1, 1823.

1828, after acknowledging the receipt of the minutes, he wrote:

" Be assured, not one hour shall be unnecessarily lost "in transmitting to you my entire refutal; and I am " too impatient to do away any impression that such " evidence must have excited, that I cannot avoid an- " ticipating that refutal generally, by declaring solemnly, " ' So help me God', before whom age and infirmity " must soon send me, that the whole and entire of that " evidence, so far as it tends to inculpate me, is totally, " utterly, and unequivocally false and unfounded".

" This, and passages of a similar tendency in subse- quent letters", observe the commissioners, " are however the only contradiction or explanation of the foregoing facts given by Sir Jonah ; and, undoubtedly, although unsworn, so distinct and unqualified a contradiction would have had much weight with us, had the alleged facts been supported by the parol testimony only of the officer. But when *we find the handwriting of Sir Jonah himself supporting the statement of the witness, we cannot avoid giving credit to his evidence, and must lament that the judge did not adopt measures for reviving his recollec- tion, previously to committing himself to a general assertion of the falsehood of the entire evidence of Mr. Pineau, so* far as related to him, which is all that on this subject his numerous and very long letters have afforded us".

Some of Sir Jonah's defalcations in the Court of Admiralty were made good at the time by the registrar, Mr. Pineau, hoping to screen the judge from exposure, and trusting to his honour for reimbursement at a moment of less embarrassment. Mr. Pineau wrote to remind him of the liability ; and in a letter dated Boulogne, 4th August, 1825, we find Sir Jonah coolly saying : " I have no doubt you will believe me, I have not the most *remote recollection* of the circumstance in question".* And again : " Age (closing seventy) and

* *Report*, p. 154. Italics in orig.

much thought has blunted my recollection of numerous events".

The registrar drew up an elaborate statement of the circumstances, with facts and figures, but Sir Jonah's memory was still unrefreshed. In a letter dated 5 Rue du Colysée, Paris, 3rd Oct., 1827, he writes : " It is not surprising that (after closing twenty years) the concern you mention is totally out of my memory".[*]

Any person who has read the works of Sir Jonah Barrington, cannot fail to have been struck with the marvellous retentiveness of his memory for minute details. *The Rise and Fall of the Irish Nation* was published in 1831—six years after his letters to Mr. Pineau —and in 1830 appeared the memorable *Personal Sketches of his own Times*, in which, after alluding to a misunderstanding between Messrs. Daly and Johnson, Sir Jonah adds : " One of the few things I ever forgot is the way in which that affair terminated : it made little impression on me at the time, and so my memory rejected it".[†] The embezzlement of considerable sums could only be rejected by an eminently treacherous memory, although Sir Jonah in his memoirs tells us : " I never loved money much in my life".[‡]

Barrington's habitual exaggeration in story-telling would appear to be an old weakness. Describing the events of the year 1796, he says that " Curran and he" coined stories to tell each other ; the lookers on laughed almost to convulsion.[§] An indulgence in exaggeration, Sir Jonah seemed to regard both as a predominant passion and a venial sin. Sir Richard Musgrave, we are told, " understood drawing the long bow as well as

[*] *Report*, p. 156. Sir Jonah goes on to say " the *Irish Government* have NO *sort of authority* to order any returns from the officers of my court, and I *decline such authority*".
[†] *Ibid. Personal Sketches*, vol. i., p. 405.
[‡] *Ibid.*, vol. i., p. 227.
[§] *Personal Sketches*, v. i. p. 381.

most people".* Sir Jonah possessed a large share of
"cheek", and both as a marvellous story-teller and
successful negociator in money transactions, this
quality stood his friend.   So early as 1799, the author
of *Sketches of Irish Political Charac'ers* says: "He is
supposed to have pretty much the same idea of blushing that a blind man has of colours".

One very amusing illustration of Sir Jonah's astuteness as a trickster is not included in the Blue Book. He
had pledged his family plate for a considerable sum, to
Mr. John Stevenson, pawnbroker.   "My dear fellow",
said the knight, condescendingly, as he dropped in one
day to that person's private closet, "I am in the d—l
of a hobble.   I asked, quite *impromptu*, the Lord Lieutenant, Chancellor, and Judges, to dine with me, forgetting how awkwardly I was situated; and, by Jove,
they have written to say they'll come!   Of course I
could not entertain them without the plate; lend it to
me for one day, and lest you should have any fear on
the subject, come yourself to dinner, for, as a member of
the Corporation, you are perfectly admissible.   Bring
the plate with you, and take it back again, at night".
The pawnbroker was dazzled; although not usually
given to nepotism, he obligingly yielded, and embraced
the proposal.   During dinner, and after it, Sir Jonah
plied "his uncle" well with wine.   The pawnbroker
had a bad head for potation, though a good one for
valuation; he fell asleep and under the table almost
simultaneously; and when he awoke to full consciousness, Sir Jonah, accompanied by the plate, had nearly
reached Boulogne, never again to visit his native land!

Sir Jonah made another "haul" before leaving Ireland.   Mr. Fennell Collins, a rich saddler, who resided
in Dame Street, lent "the Judge" £3,000, on what
seemed tolerable security; but one farthing of the
money was never recovered.   A hundred similar stories

* *Personal Sketches*, v. i. p. 211.

might be told.*   Everybody has heard of Barrington, the famous pickpocket; but the equally dexterous though more refined achievements of his titled namesake will be new to many.

"The unrighteous borroweth and payeth not again", saith Psalm xxxii. v. 21.   Sir Jonah could not even return a book.   To assist him in his work on the Union, the late Mr. Conway lent him, for a few weeks, the file of the *Dublin Evening Post* for 1798; but it never could be got back, and was afterwards sold with Sir Jonah's effects.

We wish we could be sure that Sir Jonah's dishonourable acts were no worse than pecuniary juggling.   Dr. Madden is of opinion that Barrington, although a pseudo patriot, deserves to be classed among the "bloodhounds of '98".   In April, 1798, he dined in Wexford at Lady Colclough's, and on the following day with B. Bagenal Harvey.   Popular politics were freely talked; and on Sir Jonah's return to Dublin, as he himself tells us, he informed Secretary Cooke that Wexford would immediately revolt.   Nearly all Sir Jonah's friends whom he met at the two dinner parties—one a relation of his own—were hanged within three months; and on his next visit to Wexford, he recognized their heads spiked in front of the jail !

Colclough and Harvey were Protestant gentlemen of very considerable landed property in Wexford.   Their discovery in a damp cave on the Saltee Islands, through the bloodhound instinct of an old friend, Dr. Waddy, a physician of Wexford, is invested with a painfully romantic interest.   George Cruikshank has executed an effective sketch of this tragic incident.

---

* See *Life of Thomas Reynolds*, by his Son, p. 353, v. ii., etc.

Q.

EMMET'S INSURRECTION.

Emmet's revolt exploded on the evening of July 23, 1803. Mr. Phillips, in *Curran and his Contemporaries*, writes :—

"Lord Kilwarden, the then Chief Justice, was returning from the country, and had to pass through the very street of the insurrection. He was recognized, seized, and inhumanly murdered, against all the entreaties and commands of Emmet. This is supposed to have disgusted and debilitated him".

A curious reason is assigned in a MS. before us for Lord Kilwarden " passing through the very street of the insurrection". The MS. autobiography of the late Serenus Kelly, a well-known monk, was placed in our hands by the writer, on his death-bed, at Tullow, in 1859. Serenus was in Lord Kilwarden's house on the evening of his death :—

" Colonel Finlay sent a message to Lord Kilwarden at seven o'clock on the evening of his lordship's lamented death, apprising him that Dublin was about to be disturbed by a second rebellion, and an attempt to take the Castle. Lord Kilwarden ordered his carriage, and went over to speak to Colonel Finlay on the subject, to satisfy himself of the truth of the report. He took with him into Dublin his daughter and nephew, and directed the coachman to drive to the Castle through Dolphin's Barn, to avoid paying turnpike from his seat called Newlands, situate between Tallaght and Clondalkin, on the Naas road". [Here the usual details of the *emeute* are given.] " One of the insurgents asked who came there. The coachman answered, ignorant of their design, ' Lord Kilwarden'. With that they pulled his lordship out, saying it was he condemned the Sheares,* and they gave him, upon the spot, fourteen pike stabs, of which he died about eleven o'clock next morning. Mr. Downing, the gardener, went to see his lordship, and he heard Major Sirr say he would hang a man for every hair on his head: to which his lordship replied: 'Let no man suffer in consequence of my death unless by the regular operation of the laws'.

"This was said about eight o'clock on Sunday morning, while he lay in a guard-bed in Vicar Street, weltering in his gore. As to Emmet, I did not wish to witness his execution; but I saw the gallows erected, and a thrill of horror pervaded my blood as I observed the noose, black and greasy from the numbers it had launched into eternity".

EMMET'S INFORMER.

The person who received £1,000, on 1st November, 1803, for the discovery of Robert Emmet, still preserves his incognito. Dr. Madden, quoting from the Secret service money Record, says that " the above sum was paid into Finlay's Bank to the account of Richard Jones": and he adds that the circumstance of lodging the money in the hands of a banker leads to the conclusion that the informer was not of humble rank.

" Who was this gentleman Richard Jones?" asks Dr. Madden. For whom was the money paid to account of Richard Jones?

" In the county Wicklow there was a family of the name of Jones, of Killencarrig, near Delgany. In 1815 there was a brewery kept there by a family of that name. They were Protestants—quiet people, who did not meddle with politics.

* The mob confounded Lord Kilwarden with Lord Carleton. See p. 224, ante.

"In the County Dublin, at Ballinascorney, near where Emmet was concealed for some time, there was also a family of the name of Jones, small farmers, Catholics.

"There was a gentleman of the name of Jones, the Right Hon. Theophilus Jones, a member of the Privy Council, a collector of revenue. In 1800, being in Parliament, he voted for the 'Union', and he was a person of some distinction in 1798. He lived at Cork Abbey, Bray. He was a humane, good man in 'the' troubles', and interested himself much for the people.

"There were two attorneys of the name of Richard Jones living in Dublin at the period of Emmet's capture" (v. i. p. 392).

As Dr. Madden desires to ventilate this question, we will drop a suggestion, tending, perhaps, to throw some light on it. In the *Dublin Evening Post* of March 2nd, 1784, particular reference is made to Richard Jones, Esq., a very efficient justice of the peace, constantly on the foot in support of law and order, and praised by the Castle journals for his activity.

A receipt for secret service money, signed Malachy Dwyer, appears in the new edition of the *Lives and Times of the U. I. M.*, v. i. p. 391. "There is", writes Dr. Madden, "a very curious account of a person named Malachy (no surname mentioned) in those very remarkable papers entitled *Robert Emmet and his Cotemporaries*, published in the *London and Dublin Magazine* for 1825, and probably written by the late Judge Johnston, the author of *Roche Fermoy's Commentary on Tone's Memoirs*. The Malachy therein mentioned is described as the betrayer of his friend, Robert Emmet".

On the strength of these papers, suspicion has been raised against a brave and honourable man, the late Malachy Delany—a suspicion which we ourselves con-

tagiously imbibed some years ago;* and we deem it
due to the living and the dead to say, that the papers
cited by Dr. Madden are neither from the pen of Judge
Johnson, nor historically true in any one particular.
In correcting this oversight, it is right to add that Dr.
Madden is an author of great research and truth, and
most conscientious in his conclusions, and that the
above exceptional correction ought not to impugn his
general accuracy. Following the example usually set
by Dr. Madden, of giving the best authorities for every
allegation advanced, we subjoin the following conclusive letter from the editor of the *Liverpool Daily Post,*
an influential organ :

> " *Daily Post* Office, 25 Lord Street,
> "Liverpool, Sept. 14, 1858.

" DEAR SIR,—In reply to your note of the 12th, I
beg to say that the author of *Robert Emmet and his
Cotemporaries,* etc., was your humble servant. It was
originally intended for two volumes, but was cut down
for the magazine. It was a dull affair, so dull that Dr.
Madden has taken it for veritable history : see *Life of
Emmet* (orig. edn.) pp. 8, 195, 197, etc).

"When writing it, I could get no intelligence of
Emmet, or what manner of man he was. The remnant
of the cursed Celt is still in Ireland, for, like the Orien-
tals, they have (that is, the Irish) no appreciation for

---

* In the *Telegraph* newspaper of November 10, 1855, a long
letter appears in vindication of the character of Malachy
Delany ; and Dr. Madden, in the second edition of his United
Irishmen, v. i. p. 393, makes honourable compensation for some
ambiguous references to Mr. Delany, published in the 1st ed.,
3rd s., v. iii. p. 197. The vindication was signed " A Milesian";
and the writer shortly after introduced himself to us personally
as Mr. Luke Cullen, a monk of the Monastery of Mount St.
Joseph's, Clondalkin. Mr. Cullen died suddenly, in January,
1857, leaving behind him an immense collection of MSS. illustrative of the histories of '98 and 1803.

departed greatness. They are impressed only by the present. A living ass in their estimation is better than a dead lion.

"Dear sir, your obedient,

"M. J. WHITTY.

"W. J. Fitzpatrick, Esq.".

THE MYSTERY ENSHROUDING EMMET'S GRAVE.

Robert Emmet, when asked if he had anything to say why sentence of death should not be pronounced upon him, delivered an eloquent oration, which thus concluded:—"Let no man write my epitaph; for, as no man who knows my motives dare now vindicate them, let not prejudice nor ignorance asperse them; let them rest in obscurity and peace! Let my memory be left in oblivion, and my tomb remain uninscribed, until other times and other men can do justice to my character. When my country takes her place among the nations of the Earth, then, and not till then, let my epitaph be written. I have done!"

Notwithstanding the interest attaching to the name of Emmet, the locality of his final resting-place and uninscribed stone still remains undetermined.

A correspondent of the *Irishman* newspaper has requested information as to whether the "uninscribed "tomb of Robert Emmet is the one pointed out in St. "Michan's churchyard? I am aware that the question "has been often asked, and, as appeared to me, not "satisfactorily answered. I arrived at this conclusion "owing to the absence of any information by members "of the Emmet family. My reason for asking the ques- "tion is, being in the vestry of St. Peter's, Dublin, some "short time ago, I was told by the men connected

" therewith that Emmet was *positively* interred close to
" the footpath (left gate), or near to where the old
" watch-house stood, and was pointed out to them, as
" they stated, by some member or acquaintance of the
" family from America some few years ago. If there
" be nothing for it but the uninscribed tomb of Michan's,
" I would be inclined to think that Peter's was the
" place, as tombs of the above description are not so
" very rare".

It is not the remains of Robert Emmet, the gifted
orator and insurgent leader, but of his father, Robert
Emmet, State Physician, which are interred in St.
Peter's churchyard. The latter died on the 9th of
December, 1802, and was buried in St. Peter's, three
days afterwards, according to an official certificate fur-
nished to Dr. Madden. The mother of young Robert
Emmet is likewise interred in the same grave.

Another correspondent of the journal first quoted
said :— " No allusion has been made to James's parish
cemetery. The sexton told me about two years ago
that there was a registration of his having been interred there. This is not at all improbable, it being so
near the place of his execution. It is a sad thing that
such discrepancy should exist as to the place where
lie the remains of that pure-minded martyr".

Owing to this suggestion, we carefully examined the
Burial Register of St. James's Church, held by the
parish clerk, Mr. Falls, but no trace of Emmet's interment can be found in it.

We had the pleasure, soon after, of a conversation
with John Patten when in his eighty-seventh year.
This gentleman was the brother-in-law of Thomas Addis
Emmet. He told me that having been a state prisoner
in 1803, he was not present at Emmet's funeral. He had
no authentic information on the subject, but, according
to his impression, Robert Emmet had been buried in
Bully's Acre—also known as the Hospital Fields; and

that the remains were from thence removed to Michan's churchyard, where the ashes of Bond and the Sheareses rest. He added that Doctor Gamble, the clergyman who attended Emmet in his last moments, was a very likely person to have got the remains removed from Bully's Acre to St. Michan's. The uninscribed tomb is said to have been set up in St. Michan's churchyard, soon after the period that Mr. Patten believes the remains of Emmet to have been exhumed from Bully's Acre.

A literary friend of ours, Mr. Hercules Ellis, was speaking of Emmet and the uninscribed tomb at a dinner party, when a gentleman present corrected the error under which he conceived Mr. Ellis laboured respecting the place of his burial.

"It was not in Michan's churchyard", he said, "but in Glasnevin, and I speak on the best authority, for my late father was the incumbent there at the time, and I repeatedly heard him say that he was brought out of his bed at the dead of night to perform the burial service over Emmet. There were only four persons present, two women and two men. One of the men he understood to be Dowdall, the natural son of Hussy Burgh, and one of the ladies Sarah Curran, who had been betrothed to Emmet. The corpse was conveyed through a little narrow door leading into the old churchyard of Glasnevin from the handsome demesne of Delville, formerly the residence of Dean Delany".

With interest awakened by this tradition we visited the classic grounds of Delville, and the old graveyard adjacent, accompanied by Mr. Ellis, the great-grandson of the wife of Dean Delany, to the memory of both of whom a tablet, almost smothered in ivy, is set in the churchyard wall—the boundary which divides their former residence from their final resting place. We learned from the gardener who acted as cicerone that there was a tradition precisely to the effect of the state-

20

ment made by the clergyman's son. Our conductor
having unlocked a narrow door which leads to the little
cemetery, pointed out a grass-grown grave and uninscribed head-stone immediately to the left on entering.

The entire aspect of the place forcibly recalled to
our mind the beautiful description given by Moore of
Emmet's grave : —

> "Oh, breathe not his name, let it sleep in the shade
> Where, cold and unhonoured, his relics are laid;
> Sad, silent, and dark, be the tears that we shed,
> As the night-dew that falls on *the grass o'er his head.*
>
> But the night-dew that falls, though in silence it weeps,
> Shall brighten with *verdure the grave where he sleeps*".

This description, by the early friend and college chum
of Emmet, is entirely applicable to the picturesque green
grave near classic Delville and the deserted village of
Glasnevin,* but is inappropriate to the huge flat tabular flag, excluding every blade of grass, in St. Michan's,
Church Street, Dublin. It is not easy to understand
how a tomb thus situated could "brighten with ver-
dure". Moore would appear to have had rather the
grass-grown grave at Delville in his mind than the flat
dusty stone in a back street of Dublin.

The following letter from Dr. Petrie, to whom Irish
history and archæology are much indebted, tends the
more to corroborate our views,, as it was written by

---

* Many a pleasant day Addison, as he tells us, passed among
these picturesque grounds. Tickell, his executor, resided in the
adjacent demesne, now known as the Botanical Gardens, and
Parnell, the poet, was vicar of a neighbouring hamlet. Swift has
celebrated the beauties of Delville in prose and verse, to the in-
spiration of which Stella not a little contributed. In a retired
grotto may be seen a fine medallion likeness of Stella, in excellent preservation, from the artistic hand of Mrs. Delany, with
the inscription " *Fastigia despicit urbis*", composed by Swift.
Several old basement rooms are shown as the site of the private
printing presses employed by Swift and Delany.

the Doctor, before he had seen the above, or even heard
the substance of it:

"7 Charlmont Place,
"10th Nov., 1866.

"MY DEAR SIR—According to my recollection and
belief, derived from the best local information, the grave
of poor Emmet is in the churchyard of Carmerick, and
is situated at one side, the left as I enter, of a private
doorway, which gave to the family occupying Ferrica
House a direct passage to the church, and thus enabled
them to avoid coming round through the town to the
service.

"Believe me, my dear sir,
"most truly yours,
"George Petrie.

"P.S.—The above was written before I read the
printed paper which you enclosed."

CORRESPONDENCE OF NAPOLEON I. WITH EMMET.

Some time since we received from Colonel Glendowyn
Scott the following letter of inquiry. We believe that
by publishing it we are best helping to promote the
interesting object to which the Colonel wishes well.
We may add that he is the son of Mr. Scott, an eminent
barrister who defended one of the state prisoners
arrested with Arthur O'Connor, at Margate, in 1798.

"Ballentra House, Donegal,
"11th June, 1864.

"MY DEAR MR. FITZPATRICK,—I have a friend in Paris
who is on the Committee appointed to collect such correspondence of Napoleon I. as can be discovered. He
deems it probable that the Emperor was in corres-

pondence with parties in Ireland, especially with Emmet, in 1802-3, and that the letters are in the possession of parties in Ireland belonging to the families of those to whom they were addressed. Any one having such letters in his possession, and being disposed to lend them for perusal, will receive the most positive assurance of their being safely returned. I am desirous of rendering what assistance I can, and as I know of no one equally competent with yourself to direct me in the search, I venture to ask if you could kindly point out any channel through which access could be got to the documents? It seems there is good reason to believe that such documents *were* in existence.

" Believe me, sincerely yours,

"W. G. Scott".

All communication between Bonaparte and the Irish Executive Directory was maintained through Thomas Addis Emmet. As far as we have been able to ascertain, no documents of the character in question exist in Ireland ; and it would appear from the following extract of a letter addressed to us by the Hon. Robert Emmet, Judge of the Supreme Court in New York, that the archives of the Emmet family in America are equally destitute :

"At all events, it would be out of my power to furnish anything of the kind, if it existed, as I unfortunately placed my father's papers and correspondence in the hands of the late Wm. Sampson, Esq., who then desired to prepare and publish a sketch of my father's life and career. I have never been able to get them since, and I presume they could not now be found. I was with my father in France in 1803-4, and saw my uncle Robert up to the time of his leaving us to return *to* Ireland and engage in his ill-fated undertaking ; but *I* was then too young to have known anything that could be appropriate or interesting in the work you are en-

gaged on. I shall look forward eagerly to its publication, and am truly sorry that I can send you nothing
but my best wishes for its success and your own.

"I am, etc.,

"Robert Emmet.

"W. J. Fitzpatrick, Esq.".

T

JUDGE ROBERT JOHNSON.

The history of Judge Johnson, whose name occurs in
a previous page, discloses some curious features.

In "The Step-ladder" of General Cockburne, we
obtained a view of the Backstairs Cabinet, who carried
on the government of Ireland, to the almost utter ex-
clusion of the Viceroy, during the reign of terror. This
clique was succeeded by another, less sanguinary but
equally mischievous. Lord Hardwicke, who became
lord lieutenant in 1801, was a prim but pliant nonentity,
personally amiable, though easily made a tool of by
designing men. He stood a vapid cipher in the midst
of a cluster of figures. Every newspaper in the country
applauded his policy. Even the *Dublin Evening Post*,
the long recognized organ of Irish nationality, flung the
censer with unceasing energy. The fate and aim of
the United Irishmen found a sympathy in the *Post* of
'98, but when the unfortunate Emmet, five years
later, lay ironed in his cell, charged with attempting to
carry out their objects, he was denounced by the organ
of nationality with a violence which saddened his last
days, and doubtless influenced the result of the trial.
Emmet's speech—one of the most eloquent and touching on record—was suppressed, with the exception of a

few garbled passages, more calculated to damage his position than to serve as his vindication.*

To the plausibility of Lord Hardwicke's government, men hitherto considered as staunch patriots fell victims. Grattan eulogised him, Plunket accepted office. The press teemed with praise ; the people were cajoled. One man only was found to tear aside the curtain which concealed the policy and machinery of the so-called Hardwicke administration. A judge, with £3,600 a year from government, was perhaps the last man likely to take this course. And yet, we find Judge Johnson penning in his closet a series of philippics under the signature of "Juverna". He declared that Lord Hardwicke was bestrode by Mr. Justice Osborne, Messrs. Wickham and Marsden, and by "a Chancery Pleader from Lincoln's Inn", which was immediately recognized as Lord Chancellor Redesdale. Giving rein to his indignation and expression to his pity, he exhorted Ireland to awaken from its lethargy. The main drift of the letters was to prove that the government of a harmless man was not necessarily a harmless government. The printer was prosecuted, but to save himself he gave up the Judge's MS.† Great excitement greeted

* Frequent payments to "H. B. Code" appear in the Secret Service Money Book, in 1802 and 3. This individual was engaged to conduct the *Post* during the long and painful illness of John Magee, but for paltry bribes he quite compromised its politics, until John Magee, junior, rescued the paper from his hands. Mr. Code subsequently received, under Mr. Beresford, an appointment of £900 a year in the revenue. A notice of him appears in Watty Cox's *Magazine* for 1813, p. 131.

† Lord Cloncurry, in his *Personal Recollections*, says (2nd ed. p. 253): "The manuscript, although sworn by a crown witness to be in Mr. Johnson's handwriting, was actually written by his daughter. This circumstance he might have proved ; but as he could not do so without compromising his amanuensis, the *jury* were obliged to return a verdict of guilty". We have been *assured*, however, by Miss Johnson herself, that the MS. was *really in* the autograph of her father. She added that the judge having taught her to write, their hands closely assimilated.

this disclosure, and Judge Johnson descended from the bench, never again to mount it.

A public trial took place, of which the report fills two portly volumes; and the Judge was found guilty. Before receiving sentence, however, the Whigs came into power, and Johnson was allowed to retire with a pension. But he considered that he had been hardly dealt with; and the prosecution had the effect of lashing the Judge into downright treason. He became an advocate for separation, dressed *à la militaire*, and wrote essays, suggesting, among other weapons of warfare to be used in " the great struggle of national regeneration", bows, arrows, and pikes. The *Journals and Life of Tone*, the ablest organizer of the United Irish Project, was published at Washington, in 1828. Public attention was immediately called to it by a book, printed in English at Paris, entitled *A Commentary on the Life of Theobald Wolfe Tone*, which has always been confidently pronounced as the work of Judge Johnson.[*] The Memoirs of Tone, and the Commentary which succeeded it, appearing at a crisis of intense political excitement, and displaying conclusions of singular novelty and daring, produced a powerful impression. The Duke of Wellington, then premier, assured Rogers that he had read the Memoirs of Tone, from cover to cover, with unflagging interest. But it is doubtful if the Duke would ever have seen it had not " the Commentary" reached him from the British Ambassador at Paris. An interesting letter from the late Robert Cassidy, Esq., narrates the fact, previously a secret, that the material only came from Judge Johnson, and that Mr. Cassidy edited the MSS. The letter was written in reply to one from the present

[*] See *Recollections of Lord Cloncurry*, p. 253 ; Moore's *Journal*, v. vi. p. 146 ; Daunt's *Recollections of O'Connell*, v. i. p. 18 ; *Irish Quarterly Review*, v. ii. p. 10 ; *Irish Monthly Magazine*, p. 120, etc.

writer, mentioning that he had purchased, at the sale of
Mr. Conway's library, a volume of scarce pamphlets,
containing the " Commentary" with Mr. Cassidy's
autograph, and offering it to his acceptance.

" Monasterevan, July 3, 1855.

"DEAR SIR,—I have received, and have also to thank
you for, your very considerate, as usual, communication
of 30th June.

"The Commentary on the Life of Wolfe Tone was
published under very peculiar and rather strange circumstances. The papers forming it were detached, and
not arranged. In a state just out of chaos, they were
entrusted to me, to make such use of for the advance of
this country as I might deem useful.

"The dedication, written in Paris, puzzled the few
French printers able to print English.* Didot, under
guarantees supplied by my banker (D. Daly), published
the book almost *malgre lui*. I had to attend more than
one summons at the Palais de (*in-*) Justice in 1828, to
protect the printer.

"The Paper caused some sensation. Every ambassador in Paris paid for the sheets as printed—some
for ten copies, before bound. One hundred copies
were sold in sheets.

"I had to correct the press for French compositors,
and brought over fifty copies. I have made a look
through my books this day, and, to my surprise, find I
have not a copy of the original exemplaire.

"To repossess the copy most probably lent Conway,
is desirable. I shall receive it from you not as a resti-
tution, but as a gift.

" Yours faithfully,
"To W. J. Fitzpatrick, Esq.". " ROBERT CASSIDY.

* They could not, for the life of them, imagine why an Eng-
lish book, dedicated to all the Blockheads in the service of his
Britannic Majesty, should be printed in an alien country.—
Subsequent communication from Mr. Cassidy.

Judge Johnson was a fluent correspondent, and some of his letters on the capability of Ireland for effective warfare appear in the *Personal Recollections of Lord Cloncurry*. His grandson, Robert Alloway, Esq., now holds an interesting selection from the judge's papers. It may scandalize surviving politicians of the old Tory school to hear that among his chief correspondents were John Wilson Croker and the King's brother, the Duke of Sussex.

O'CONNELL "A UNITED IRISHMAN".

The uncompromising attitude of hostility maintained by O'Connell towards the advocates of physical force, specially evidenced in his censure of the men of '98 at the Repeal Association on May 21st, 1841, and which led to the resignation of some influential repealers in America, imparts additional interest to the fact, hitherto hardly known, that he himself had been a United Irishman. We are indebted to the late Mr. Peter Murray of the Registry of Deeds Office, Dublin, a man of scrupulous veracity, for the following curious reminiscence of O'Connell in 1798: "My father, a respectable cheesemonger and grocer, residing at 3 South Great George's Street, was exceedingly intimate with O'Connell, when a law student and during his earlier career at the bar. Mr. O'Connell, at the period of which I speak, lodged in Trinity Place adjacent, an almost unexplored nook, and to many of our citizens a *terra incognita*. I well remember O'Connell, one night at my father's house during the spring of 1798, so carried away by the political excitement of the day, and by the ardour of his innate patriotism, calling for a prayer-book to swear in some zealous young men as United Irishmen at a meeting of the body in a neighbouring street. Counsellor —— was there, and offered to accompany O'Connell on his perilous mission. My father, although an Irishman of advanced liberal views and strong patriotism, was not an United Irishman, and endeavoured, but without effect, to deter his young and gifted friend from the rash course in which he seemed embarked. Dublin was in an extremely disturbed state, and the outburst of a bloody insurrection seemed hourly imminent. My father resolved to exert to the uttermost the influence which it was well known he possessed over his young friend. He made him accompany him to the canal bridge at Leeson Street, and after an earnest conversation, succeeded in persuading the future Liberator to step into a turf boat which was then leaving Dublin. That night my father's house was searched by Major Sirr, accompanied by the Attorneys' Corps of Yeomanry, who pillaged it to their hearts' content. There can be no doubt that private information of O'Connell's tendencies and haunts had been communicated to the government".

Mr. O'Connell's intimacy with Mr. Murray is confirmed by Mr. John O'Connell's memoirs of his father, p. 14 ; and Sir Jonah Barrington, in the third volume of his *Personal Sketches*, p. 396, gives a very animated description of the sacking of Murray's house by the Attorneys' Corps, or "Devil's Own". The *Personal Recollections of O'Connell*, written by Mr. Daunt, and mainly devoted to a record of conversations with his great leader, describe O'Connell as in Dublin during the spring and summer of 1798, and lest some officious persons might endeavour to implicate him in their disaffection, "quitting the city in a potato boat, bound for Courtmasherry", (vol. i. p. 117). But the circumstances detailed by Mr. Murray are not given.

S.

THE REBELLION IN KILDARE.

We are indebted to the Rev. John O'Hanlon, the able Biographer of Archbishops O'Toole and O'Morghair,*for the following traditional reminiscence of his grandfather's connection with the Rebellion in Kildare:

"In 1798, soon after the general rising, a comfortable grazier named Denis Downey, who held a considerable tract of land, on which stood the Gray Abbey ruins, near the town of Kildare, had been induced by a relative to take up arms and join the insurgent ranks. Having been engaged in some of the desultory affairs previous to the Curragh massacre, and his helpless wife, with two small children, having been daily exposed to insults, and the rapacity of the military force, during his absence from home, it was at length found necessary to abandon the farm-stead. His wife and her infant charge sought a temporary place of refuge in Derryoughter, near the river Barrow. Here her aged father and mother resided. The insurgent husband found means for communicating to her his intentions of surrendering, with others at the Gibbet Rath on the 3rd of June. It is a fact, well remembered and handed down by tradition amongst the townspeople of Kildare, that on the very day before, several of Lord Roden's Foxhunters, in a riotous and drunken brawl, appeared in the streets, carrying articles of apparel on the top of their fixed bayonets, and swearing most vehemently, 'We are the boys who will slaughter the Croppies to-morrow, at the Curragh!' This announcement deterred many rebels from proceeding to the spot, and proved instrumental, no doubt, in saving their lives. Amongst the unnotified, however, Downey, in hopes of obtaining pardon, and mounted on a fine horse,

went to the fatal trysting place. Having surrendered
his arms, and an indiscriminate slaughter of the
rebels having commenced, he at once got on horseback,
and was endeavouring to escape, when he observed a
near relative running away on foot. The horseman
stopped for a moment, but when stooping for the purpose of mounting his friend behind, a bullet brought
Downey to the ground, when his horse galloped wildly
forward towards Derryoughter, where it had been previously stabled. Meantime, Mrs. Downey, whose mind
had been filled with alarm and anxiety to learn the
state of her husband, remained up nearly the whole
of that night, immediately preceding the 3rd of June.
Towards morning, wearied and careworn, she had been
induced to take a brief rest. The most strange event
of all then occurred, as afterwards frequently certified
by herself and those with whom she at that time resided. About the very hour when the massacre took
place on the Gibbet Rath, she started from a troubled
sleep, during which she had a frightful dream or vision
of her husband weltering in his blood. Her instant
screams drew all the family to her bedside. In vain
did the aged father represent to her, that such a dream
was only the result of her disordered fancies, and that
better news might soon be expected. She wept bitterly
and in utter despair of ever seeing her husband alive
The old man, taking his walking stick, turned down
retired road branching from his house towards the mo
public thoroughfare, leading from the Curragh. Alm
the first object he encountered on the way was Down
horse covered with foam and galloping furiously, with
any rider, yet bridled and saddled. This unwonted s
furnished a sad presentiment of his son-in-law's
Soon again he observed numbers of country p
running along the high road in a state of wild e
ment. The old man asked some of them what
from the Curragh. 'Bad news! bad news!'

exclaimed, 'our friends were all slaughtered on the Curragh to-day!' This heartrending intelligence was afterwards conveyed to his unhappy daughter. With all the energy of despair, Mrs. Downey insisted on having one of the common farm cars prepared. In this she proceeded to the scene of this diabolical massacre. She afterwards stated, that on the blood-stained plain, she turned over at least two hundred dead bodies before she recognized that of her husband. This latter she deposited in the car, covering the corpse with straw and a quilt. Thus placing it beside her, the forlorn widow escaped without molestation to the house of a relative of her husband, living near the old burial place, named Dunmurry, near the Red Hills of Kildare. Preparations were made for the interment. That very night, however, a rumour went abroad, that the military were searching every house throughout the district. Wherever a rebel corpse was found, it was reported that the house containing it would be consigned to the flames. Hastily acting on such information, a grave was dug in an adjoining family burial place of Dunmurry, whilst the body of Denis Downey was wrapped in a shroud and covered with sheets, for time would not allow of a coffin being made. In this manner the remains were consigned to their last resting place, and covered with earth. The poor woman soon returned to find her former comfortable home a perfect wreck. For nights in succession, with a servant maid, she was obliged to rise from bed and allow the ruffian soldiery to despoil her of almost every remnant of property. Desponding and broken-hearted in her unprotected situation, and happily wishing a retirement from the scenes of former happiness, the farm was afterwards sold to a purchaser, and the desolate widow, with her small infant charge, removed to the neighbouring town of Monasterevan. Rarely could she be induced, in after years, to recur to this earlier period of her life, without tears moistening her eyes and stealing down her cheeks; nor could she ever regard a soldier without feelings of deep aversion. The foregoing narrative furnishes a dark illustration of baneful events, connected with the Irish Rebellion of 1798. It is no isolated episode", adds Mr. O'Hanlon; " for many other family afflictions, equally deplorable and tragic in results, must have chequered the lot in life of thousands who became victims during this sad period of civil commotion and disorder".

T.

PROJECTED REBELLION IN CORK—SECRET SERVICES OF FATHER BARRY.

The appendix to the new edition of the first volume of *The Lives and Times of the United Irishmen* displays, under the head " secret service money revelations from original accounts and receipts for pensions", a curious selection from these documents, to each of which, with some few exceptions, Dr. Madden supplies interesting details regarding the circumstances under which the pension was earned. At page 395 appears a receipt from the late Rev. Thomas Barry, P.P. of Mallow, who enjoyed a secret stipend of £100 a year; and as no explanatory statement is volunteered, it perhaps becomes our duty to supply the omission, while furnishing at the same time a note to the remarks of our own which appear at page 146 of *The Sham Squire.*

The following letter, addressed to the Very Rev. Dr. Russell, Roman Catholic Dean of Cloyne, by the Rev. T. Murphy, of Mallow, containing the result of some inquiries instituted at our suggestion among the oldest inhabitants of Mallow, will be read with interest:

"Mallow, October 2nd, 1865.

"VERY REV. AND DEAR SIR,—After many inquiries about the subject matter of your kind letter of Sept. 9th, I thought it well to await the return of an old inhabitant who was absent from Mallow until yesterday.

"The following is the substance of his account of the *émeute*, which I believe to be the most authentic. Shortly after the Insurrection of '98, the Royal Meath Militia were stationed in Mallow. They had conspired with the disaffected to blow up the Protestant Church, when the yeomanry troops were at service on a certain Sunday. Abundant materials were at hand, as Mallow contained several parks of artillery at the time in a field near the Protestant Church, and hence called Cannon Field to this day.

"On the Saturday preceding, two of the wives of the militia, who lodged at one Canty's, at Ballydaheen, were noticed by Canty's wife stitching or sewing the extremities of their petticoats together, and Mrs. Canty (wife of Canty, a cooper) expressed her astonishment. The soldiers' wives were equally surprised, and asked her did she not hear of the *rising* about to occur next day. An expression of more unbounded surprise was the response. The poor Meath women expected they could fill more than their pockets. Canty (whose son still lives in Ballydaheen) communicated the news to his gossip, Lover (a convert). Lover went to confession on that Saturday, and Father Barry refused to absolve him except he disclosed the case *extra tribunal*. His wishes were complied with, and both Lover and Father Barry went forthwith to General Erskine (*sic*)? who lived on Spa Walk. As soon as the plot was revealed, Sergeant Beatty with nineteen men on guard for that night (all implicated), aware of the treachery, immediately decamped. The yeomen pursued them in their flight to the Galtees, and when one of Beatty's men could no longer continue the retreat, his wish of dying at the hands of Beatty was complied with. Beatty turned round and shot him! The body of this poor fellow was brought back to Mallow next day, and lies interred near the Protestant Church, and Sergeant Beatty himself, (God be merciful to him), was taken finally in Dublin, and hanged. Lover had four sons. They all emigrated after arriving at manhood. I am sorry to say *one* of them became a priest and died a short time since in Boston.

"The father received a pension of £50 a year for life, and Father Barry was in receipt of £100 a year until 1813, some years before his death,[*] when a dispute arose between him and the Protestant minister of Mallow, about the interment of some Protestant who became a convert on his death bed. Father Barry insisted on reading the service in the Protestant church-yard, was reported to government for not persevering in proofs of loyalty, deprived of his pension, and died and is buried in our Catholic cemetery adjoining the church. The only prayer I ever heard offered for him was " God forgive him !"

" Yours very sincerely,

"T. MURPHY.

"To the Very Rev. Dean Russell".

Dean Russell, in enclosing his correspondent's letter to us for publication, corrects an error into which the Rev. Mr. Murphy fell, in stating that Lover received £50 a year in recognition of his timely information. A previous letter from the Dean observes:

" Protestant gratitude, unfortunately for Mr. Barry's

---

[*] The pension was finally restored to him, as his receipts prove. In the Secret Service Money Book, now held by Charles Haliday, Esq , and from which Dr. Madden has quoted the salient points, we find Father Barry's name frequently figuring as a recipient of various gratuities exclusive of his pension.— W. J. F.

character, obtained for him a £100 a-year, but poor
Lover never received a farthing. Having been reduced
to great poverty, a petition was sent to government,
signed by twenty-five gentlemen, stating his services.
The answer was, they knew nothing of him; but the
rebellion was then smothered in the blood of the people".

The Dean adds, that this and other information
recently reached him from clergymen who were born
in Mallow or its vicinity. He adds:

"I do not think that Mr. Murphy's informant knew
much of the fate of Sergeant-Major Beatty and his men
after they left Mallow. I recollect, when a boy, and I
am now nearly seventy-two, to hear a highly respectable
and intelligent clergyman speak in raptures of the singularly gallant retreat of that poor Sergeant and his
men. A few worn out by fatigue were unable to per-
severe. They of course were captured by the cowardly
yeomanry, who satisfied their loyalty by looking at the
Sergeant, but dare not approach near him".

It would be difficult to find a pastor who presented a
more venerable and paternal aspect than the late Father
Thomas Barry of Mallow. His flowing white hair and
thorough benevolence of expression impressed most
favourably all who came in contact with him, and commanded their entire confidence. The late eminent and
lamented Daniel O'Connell, on being shown one of
Father Barry's receipts for "blood money", as it was
then somewhat erroneously presumed to have been,
started, and, to quote the words of our informant, who
still holds his receipts, "became as white as a sheet!"
For thirty years O'Connell had been on terms of close
intimacy with Father Barry, and reposed unbounded
confidence in his counsel. In the *Dublin Evening Post*
of the day an obituary notice appears of Father Barry,
who died January 18th, 1828. The singular fact is
mentioned, that the priest's pall was borne by six Protestants. Having directed the attention of Dean Russell

21

to this article, he writes: "The statement that Mr. Barry's coffin was borne to the grave by six Protestants, can hardly be correct, as nothing was known of the pension he received till some time after his death. He was buried in the same respectful way in which Catholic clergymen are usually buried".

Conspirators and informers will coëxist until the crack of doom. Some of the seemingly staunchest hearts in Smith O'Brien's movement of '48 were false to their chief and colleagues; and when the crisis came suggested to the police magistrates, that in order to preserve consistency and keep up the delusion, they ought to be arrested and imprisoned.* Even while we write, the ranks of the Fenians, although knotted as it seemed by the most binding oaths of secrecy, are broken and betrayed by internal spies. Nor are the informers confined to Ireland. One of the American correspondents of the *Times*, in a letter dated Philadelphia, October 24th, 1865, writes: "The Fenian Congress continues its sessions, and has so much business to attend to that they are protracted far into the night. The green-uniformed sentinels still guard its doors closely, and hope to keep the secret of the deliberations within. They have changed their weapons to loaded muskets, in order to terrify attempting intruders, but their watchfulness is of little avail, for not only are there informers inside in the interest of your Government, but I learn that others assist in the deliberations who are in the interest of our own, who send daily reports of the proceedings to Washington, that the Government may know in time the adoption of any measures tending to violate the peace between England and America".

In concluding a book which deals largely with Irish Informers, we have no desire to convey the inference that treachery or duplicity, for what Shakspeare calls "saint seducing gold", is a speciality of the Celtic cha-

* Communicated by F. T. P., Esq., ex police magistrate.

racter. The records of every age and nation furnish ample illustrations of both, even in the most aggravated form. Philip of Macedon said that he would "never despair of taking any fortress to which an ass might enter laden with gold". The physician of Pyrrhus informed the Roman general Fabricius, that he was ready to poison his royal master for pay. King Charles the Second received large douceurs from the French monarch, and shaped his foreign policy accordingly. Sydney was secretly subsidized by France, and Dalrymple's memoirs disclose many similar cases. The publication of the French Official Records shows to what a great extent the members of the English legislature were in the pay of Louis XIV. To come down to a later period, we learn from Napier's narrative of the Peninsular war, that Wellington had paid informers on Soult's staff, and Soult had similar channels of information through officers on Wellington's* staff. Again, we are assured by Barry O'Meara, the Boswell of Napoleon at St. Helena, that the wife of an English statesman was subsidized by the Emperor, to the extent of £2,000 a month, for revealing to him the secrets of the British cabinet.

---

* The Duke, in one of his conversations with Rogers, describes an informer, called Don Uran de la Rosa, and sometimes Ozèlle, who, during the progress of the Peninsular war, was wont to dine with the English and the French alternately. "When I was ambassador at Paris", added Wellington, "he came and begged me to make interest with Soult for the settlement of his accounts. 'How can I?' I said, laughing, 'when we made such use of you as we did?' They were settled, however, if we could believe him. After his death, a Frenchman came to me in London, and when he had vapoured away for some time, declaring that Ozèlle had won every battle and saved Europe, he said, 'Here are his memoirs; shall we publish them or not?' I saw his drift, and said, 'Do as you please; he was neither more nor less than a spy'. I heard no more of them or of him. For *full details, see Recollections by Samuel Rogers, pp. 198-201.*

CORRIGENDA.

At page 119, for " Dolphin's Barn" read " Portobello".

At page 160, beginning with line 15, a misprint occurs, which may be thus corrected:

" movement, it possessed no more staunch partizan. But flesh is weak; and we find Cox, during thirty-five years that he personated the character of an indomitable patriot, in the receipt of a secret stipend".

At page 271, it was intended to have inserted the following note as an additional illustration:

" In the interval which elapsed between the French expedition to Bantry Bay and their arrival at Killala, the Mayor of Drogheda hired a staff of spies, whom he dressed up in French uniforms, and despatched through the country to entrap the unwary peasantry".

J. F. FOWLER, Printer, 3 Crow Street, Dame Street, Dublin.

Printed in the United Kingdom
by Lightning Source UK Ltd.
131376UK00002B/56/A

9 781432 676209